W9-BNR-169

digital babylon

digital babylon

how
the geeks
the suits
and
the ponytails
fought
to bring
HOLLYWOOD
to the internet

by

john geirland & eva sonesh-kedar

arcade publishing @ new york

FIRST EDITION

ISBN 1-55970-483-7
Library of Congress Catalog Number 99-73646
Library of Congress Cataloging-in-Publication information is available.

Published in the United States by Arcade Publishing, Inc., New York
Distributed by Time Warner Trade Publishing

10 9 8 7 6 5 4 3 2 1

Designed by API

BP

Printed in the United States of America

Hollywood is Babylon. It's the craziest, most self-obsessed, self-congratulatory culture that has ever existed in the history of man. The culture of Silicon Valley is highly focused, it's super–goal oriented, and its style is pocket-protector. So you have the Armanis and the pocket protectors.

—Russell Collins, chairman, American Cybercast

The Web is one big, creative entanglement.

—Halsey Minor, CEO of CNET

— CONTENTS —

1997-1998: Entertainment Asylum

1999 and Beyond

digital babylon

Introduction

This night belongs to Scott Zakarin.

Two searchlights cut paths across the night sky, randomly reflecting off the metal-and-Plexiglas Asylum facade. A long row of cars snakes up to the entranceway as smartly dressed entertainment execs stroll along the Astro Turf welcome carpet toward the Asylum's door. Upon entering, the guests are immediately consumed by fog and pounding music and greeted by a mime dressed in black taking a choreographed bow under a green spotlight. Cameramen try to keep up with Nancy Sinatra as she wanders about in a green-and-black Asylum windbreaker. The usual suspects are in attendance—starlets, agents, young actors in leather pants—as well as the industry's heavier hitters, like Steve Tish and Tri-Star mogul Mike Medavoy. But this is Culver City, not Westwood, and those driving past the building this October evening in 1997 might mistake this spectacle for some kind of movie premiere or Hollywood wrap party. It is neither. This is the launch of the Entertainment Asylum, America Online's most ambitious venture into online entertainment.

The pace of activity leading to the launch has been addling, even in an industry that clocks events in Internet time. Scott Zakarin's company, Lightspeed Media, had been acquired that spring by America Online's content development shop, Greenhouse Networks. Since then he and his team had been building the Entertainment Asylum—and a "virtual company" of seventy people—at warp speed. Greenhouse executives promised that the Asylum would be an edgy new network delivering "information about entertainment packaged as entertainment."

Ted Leonsis had flown out from AOL's headquarters in Vienna, Virginia, for the launch. He was a member of the troika that ran AOL and known as a legendary marketer. He built AOL from a service with 800,000 households in 1993 to one with more than 8 million in 1996. He turned the service over to former MTV executive Bob Pittman in October of that year in order to run the newly formed AOL Studios, of which Greenhouse Networks was a part. He had pulled out the stops to ensure that the launch party would be up to snuff for the Hollywood community. Leonsis anchored himself in a corner and allowed the party to gravitate toward him.

Charlie Fink, Greenhouse Networks' chief creative officer, was also in attendance. Wearing a black leisure suit and a wrinkled tab-collar shirt with the top button undone, Fink held court, his booming voice carrying above the din. Charlie had a reputation for being irrepressible, enthusiastic, and blustery. He was a Disney animation division alumnus, where he worked under Jeffrey Katzenberg. When he joined AOL in early 1996, he had been one of the few people in the company who had genuine Hollywood credentials.

Scott and Charlie were among the Internet entertainment pioneers featured in a *USA Today* story called "New Breed of Executives" that ran earlier that year. The story also featured executive producer Bob Bejan, thirty-seven, Fink's counterpart (and rival) at the Microsoft Network (MSN). Bejan had a working relationship with two other pioneers featured in the article. He brought in Matti Leshem, thirty-four, and his Santa Monica–based Cobalt Moon to produce a satirical news show called *Second City Headline News* for the network. Leshem was the pit bull in the bunch, a stocky, cigar-smoking former actor whose aggressive hustler charm made him a publicist's dream.

Bejan also had a working relationship with David Wertheimer, twenty-nine, of Paramount Digital Entertainment (PDE), which produced *Star Trek: Continuum* and *Entertainment Tonight* for MSN. Wertheimer had been wooed from Larry Ellison's Oracle to help build an interactive-entertainment company within the huge bureaucracy of Paramount Studios—itself a part of Viacom, a vast entertainment megaglomerate.

Their photos were carefully laid out on the front page of the life section of the paper. Striking how much these pioneers resembled each other. Shiny-headed and frowning, Zakarin, Fink, Bejan, and Leshem looked like a litter of bald white males from a cloning experiment gone awry. Wertheimer stood out from the others, with his full head of hair and a sunny smile on his face.

Absent from the *USA Today* story was another pioneer, Josh Greer, twenty-nine, of Digital Planet. In some ways, Digital Planet was the Web-entertainment poster child. Greer's company had launched the

Stargate site, one of the first promotional Web sites for a major motion picture. A year after the appearance of Scott's first site, *The Spot*, Digital Planet followed up with an animated online sci-fi story called *Madeleine's Mind*. But Greer's company always seemed overwhelmed by larger players, and he never clicked with what he called the "Mr. Clean Crowd"—Scott, Matti, Charlie, and Bob.

Though singular in perspective and style, they all had something in common: they had turned away from safe and predictable careers in entertainment or technology to break ground in Internet entertainment, a gray zone where Hollywood intersected with Silicon Valley, a business with no precedents, systems, financial models, rules, masters, or success stories. They wanted to be the Warner Brothers, D. W. Griffiths, and Louis B. Mayers of a new age in entertainment.

The launch of the Entertainment Asylum was the culmination of a long, fierce war of attrition between AOL and Microsoft, one that had co-opted some of the best content-development talent in the industry and consumed hundreds of millions of dollars. Microsoft had inaugurated its own proprietary online service, the Microsoft Network, in 1995 as a direct competitive move against AOL. Like a million tiny cruise missiles, every single copy of Windows '95 shipped that August was programmed to kill AOL. A prominently displayed MSN icon appeared on the opening screen, beckoning any consumer with a modem to become an MSN member. Registration could be accomplished in a matter of seconds.

As it happened, MSN limped out of the launch gate. By the end of 1995, Bill Gates made a corporate about-face that portended a more serious and ambitious assault on AOL and the Internet. Gates reversed the company's attempts to build an online environment employing proprietary protocols and embraced the open standards of the Net. Throughout 1996 MSN was reengineered for an October relaunch. Gates was investing hundreds of millions of dollars in new content initiatives to differentiate the service from AOL and draw new subscribers. The new MSN adopted a television metaphor, with "channels" and "shows" designed to appeal to different Internet demographics. Gates also implemented a new flat-rate pricing structure—$19.95 per month for unlimited service—that posed a direct challenge to AOL's hourly-rate structure.

Mindful of the threat from Microsoft, Ted Leonsis had teamed Scott Zakarin with Brandon Tartikoff, one of the great television programmers of all time. Tartikoff brought his talent for shaping mainstream hits; Scott understood how to translate that sensibility to the Web. Their mission was to create a "category killer" in the online entertainment news space—a show or network that was so entertaining and compelling it killed off its competition.

Sadly, Tartikoff died from complications of the treatment of his Hodgkin's lymphoma two months before the launch. All involved grieved the loss of their friend and hoped that they had "front-loaded" enough of his instinct for the mainstream to give the Asylum a good send-off.

The new-media world Scott navigated had attracted some of the brightest and rawest talent from all the major entertainment and technology disciplines—television, film, software development, telecommunications, writing, design, music, finance, investment banking, and even anthropology—drawn by the possibilities of the Internet and the rare opportunity to be part of something that they believed would change the world. The denizens of new media could be divided into three distinct tribes—the geeks, the suits, and the ponytails. Often they seemed like the blind men with the elephant. More often than not, their visions for the Internet collided.

The geeks were the programmers and technologists who created the enabling technology, the Marc Andressens (co-founder of Netscape) of Silicon Valley. Geeks were motivated by the desire to create ever more powerful technology and "solutions." They were the engine powering the medium, and had created much of the Net's early content offerings. Geeks were consumed with technolust, the desire for continuous innovation of technology and "features." They lacked marketing instincts, and had trouble accepting the fact that most consumers liked their technology to be simple, if not invisible.

The suits were the entrepreneurs, chief financial officers, investment bankers, attorneys, marketers, and vice-presidents of business development, sales, business affairs. This tribe saw the Internet and digital media as a business in the making. They brought the major media brands and technology companies, Silicon Valley venture capitalists, and other cash-laden investors to the table. Suits asked tough questions, like "How are we going to make money with this stuff?" These tribal members didn't create content or hack infrastructure—they built enterprises and brands. They worried about brand awareness, financing, making the business attractive to investors, and targeting market segments. Mindful of the declining market share of network television, they saw the Internet as an opportunity to move in and build new media empires.

Finally, there were the ponytails, the writers, directors, producers, and artists who saw the Internet as a powerful tool for creating new entertainment experiences. Ponytails wanted to break through all the geeky technology that stood between the artist and the audience, to make the medium as transparent as possible. The Internet was exciting for ponytails because no one knew the rules of the new medium. They had the freedom—lacking in other media—to *invent* the rules.

The three tribes did agree that Internet and digital technology could transform the way media and entertainment content was produced. When the Internet invaded the popular consciousness, many in the technology and entertainment industries likened its arrival to the early days of television. Here was the first entirely new medium to appear on the entertainment scene in almost fifty years, a medium that was unlike all those that preceded it. For the first time in two generations, engineers, writers, artists, and producers had the opportunity to experience the same excitement as the early pioneers of television, radio, and film. Original content would attract the masses to the online world. "The biggest application of the [information] superhighways," then Silicon Graphics chairman and CEO Ed McCracken said in the early 1990s, "will be entertainment."

There followed a period of great excitement when technology companies like Microsoft and Intel, online companies like AOL, talent agencies like Creative Artists Agency (CAA), and the major Hollywood studios embraced the Internet and backed Scott Zakarin and other young pioneers who were inventing the concept of Internet entertainment. Then, in two short years, all the major players abandoned the genre. Internet entertainment was dead.

By the winter of 1998, the general consensus was that Internet Entertainment had been an exhilarating failure. For all the creativity and money that had been invested, online entertainment never attracted the "eyeballs" (audience) needed to make it a business. The collaboration between Hollywood and Silicon Valley seemed to have yielded nothing but a string of "convergence collisions." The CD-ROM business that preceded the emergence of the Net had generated great excitement, then failed in the marketplace. Interactive television had been trumpeted as the wave of the future only to become a costly embarrassment for the media companies like Time Warner or telcos like USWest, both of whom invested millions in expensive and dismal trials of the service. Now online interactive entertainment seemed a failure as well.

However, by 1999 the deployment of cable modems, set-top boxes, digital television, and other broadband technologies has sparked a renewed interest in the possibilities of interactive entertainment. Silicon Valley and Hollywood are interested. New Internet entertainment companies, like Santa Monica–based Intertainer, are launching. John Malone's Liberty Digital is preparing to launch ten to fifteen channels of interactive television content in late 1999. In summer '99, Time Warner plans to launch Entertaindom, an ambitious original content venture featuring Driveon.com. Warner Brothers executive vice president Jim Banister refers to it as the "first broadband interactive show," offering TV news magazine-style content loaded with audio and video fare. Entertaindom will also offer short films, cartoons, and other forms of pure entertainment. A new and rapidly growing company called the Digital Entertainment Network (den.net) is distributing dozens of video shows like *Fear of a Punk Planet* over the Web. Other original content ventures are in the wings. Online entertainment is set to explode.

This time, the stakes are of a higher magnitude. Major players, like AT&T, Microsoft, AOL, Time Warner, and others, are bringing billions of dollars to the table. Talk is that content will be a major driver of the digital economy in the next century.

As we enter into the broadband era of digital media and experience a realignment of the media world, many uncertainties loom. Development teams still struggle to crack the code for creating compelling interactive content. Despite all the talk about portal strategies and e-commerce, the business models that will undergird digital media in the next century remain unrefined. Complicating the search for profitability is a media world that promises to become even more fragmented than it is today.

Former Chinese premiere Chou En-Lai was once asked what he thought was the legacy of the French Revolution. His response reflected the perspective of five thousand years of Chinese civilization: "It is too soon to say." But we now live our lives in concentrated Internet years. It took radio thirty-eight years to reach 50 million listeners. It took television thirteen years, and cable TV ten. The Internet reached 50 million users in five years. It's not too soon to take a look back. It's time to reflect on the story of the first wave of pioneers, to build on their successes and avoid repeating their mistakes as we speed wildly into the next era.

1995: *The Spot*

"My Most Favorite Idea Ever"

The Fattal-Collins advertising agency was located on the ninth floor of the North Marina Tower overlooking Pier 44 in Marina Del Rey. Across the street, hundreds of sailboats were moored, their tangle of masts and lines looking like a clutter of telephone poles. The offices were much what one would expect from a hip advertising agency in the marina—the closer to the beach, the hipper the agencies. The floors were laid out in a black checkerboard pattern, and the walls were dark mauve. The reception area had a polished Italian granite table of irregular shape in soothing earth tones. The ceilings were painted dark gray, with exposed thick ventilation tubing with speakerlike ducts on the ends. The only thing that rescued the interior from morbid darkness was plenty of bay windows that let in floods of natural light.

Scott Zakarin, executive producer of Fattal-Collins's film production department, squirmed in the seat of his 1990 Toyota Camry as he sailed down the 405 Freeway on his way to work one cool winter morning in 1995. He'd slept badly, nearly waking his fiancée, Debra, his head revving at high speed with ideas, characters, and situations. In the middle of the night he'd had an epiphany, following many evenings spent cruising AOL chat rooms. As he wended his way around the southbound traffic, he was exhilarated by the notion of a Web site about the attractive Generation-X occupants of a Santa Monica beach house. It was an idea that could draw the attention of the Hollywood entertainment community. One thought dampened his enthusiasm: that someone else had already done it. If you had a good idea for a TV show or movie in Hollywood, chances were that someone else had the same idea as well. It happened all the time. (In the summer of 1998 major studios released two meteor-destroys-the-earth movies and two animated films about insects.) For the Internet, the problem was amplified. It could take many months or even years to take a TV or movie pitch through the development process and into production. But the Internet sped everything up. Building a Web site didn't require jumping through the bureaucratic and financing hoops found in traditional media. A determined team could build a site in a matter of weeks—or even days.

Striding out of the elevator, Scott gathered producer Troy Bolotnick; Rich Tackenberg, the unit's video editor; and his assistant Laurie Plaksin into a conference room. "Last night I dreamt my most favorite idea ever," Scott began excitedly.

Rich and Laurie knew that Scott and Troy were investigating the CD-ROM business in their spare time and trying to develop a product. Scott told them, with a certain dramatic flair, that he had been on the Net, and that the Net had no entertainment programming. When Scott got excited he acted like a young boy at 3:00 P.M. on the last day of the school year. He made wild gestures. His soft, guttural voice had an audible lump as he laid out the concept: a beach house in Santa Monica called *The Spot* where five young L.A. types live. The house has a long and nefarious history of "wild partying and debauchery" going back to the days of Marilyn Monroe. It was built by a notorious cross-dresser named Bobby Dooley Jr. Tara, a twenty-three-year-old female film student, and other characters Scott had created in a week of chat-room mania, would live there. Characters' stories would be told through the posting of their diary entries and photos. In order to fit into the Web milieu, *The Spot* would look like real people's lives documented online, rather than a story presented on a Web site. Scott wanted to recreate the illusion of reality he had concocted with his made-up identities in the AOL chat rooms.

The inspiration for *The Spot* was easy to trace. Back in Scott's bachelor days, he and Troy had once been roommates in a beach house on the strand in Manhattan Beach, California. With *The Spot* he wanted to bring the spirit of those days, and of *Melrose Place* and MTV's *The Real World*—the latter being a show featuring real twenty-somethings that blurred the line between fiction and reality and had a great following—to the Internet.

Scott realized that people got on the Net for more reasons than to download information or use e-mail. People wanted to be diverted and entertained. Most of the people who crowded into chat rooms were looking for interesting people to eavesdrop on and interact with—real or imaginary. *The Spot* would fill that need.

Scott was anxious to know if there was anything like *The Spot* already on the Web. Troy, the only one in the group who had a broad familiarity with the Internet—and the one who had introduced Scott to the online world in the first place—couldn't think of anything that came even close. The four began to brainstorm. Troy had the idea of using a neighbor's dog as *The Spot* house mascot and first Siberian husky in cyberspace. They'd call him Spotnik. Rich suggested that in order to give the diary entries a *Rashomon* flavor, the characters shouldn't be able to read each other's postings. Laurie, who had been the inspiration for Tara, was excited by the sense of ownership the show would give them and liked the idea that they'd be creating a story for themselves, as opposed to grinding out stories for clients as they had been doing at Fattal-Collins. The more they talked, the more Scott's bare-bones pitch began to take shape. But could they pull it off? Troy and Rich Tackenberg knew computers, but neither of them knew HTML or had ever designed a Web site. Rich had never even been on the Web. The four of them would have to work evenings and weekends to educate themselves and put the project together.

A major question was how much it would cost to produce the site. The scale would be similar to what Troy and Rich had known in their theater days in college. Troy suggested, "Well, I guess if we got a computer and a scanner and we put in about two thousand dollars in equipment from our pockets, we could probably do this." Although the equipment for the photo shoots wouldn't be too hard to come by, there was the question of talent. They'd have to hire attractive actors. Fortunately, Scott and Troy were using a lot of struggling actors in the commercials and radio spots they produced for Fattal-Collins. They could pull in some favors, tell the actors, "Hey, we'll make sure we keep using you in commercials that you're qualified for if you do us a little favor."

Scott was passionate and persuasive, and in the end no one needed to be sold—all the more remarkable when one considered how little he knew about the Net, which was almost nothing. The others believed in Scott's creative instincts and trusted his vision. Later, after what they had hatched that day generated a media buzz around the world—after Scott had almost single-handedly created the genre of online entertainment—Rich would say that "the reason everything we've done—knock on wood—has been so successful is because Scott can barely turn on the computer without help."

Geeks in the Pilot's Seat

Technology was moving so fast, I wanted to get started with a project as soon as possible. If I started early, I thought, perhaps I could be the first to do a movie on a PC.

—digital filmmaker Phil Flora

On a shivering February evening in a West Los Angeles apartment complex locally known as the "pink palace"—located next door to the Barrington branch of the U.S. Post Office and only a few blocks from the condo where Nicole Simpson had her last Ben & Jerry's—Scott Zakarin and Troy Bolotnick plotted their attack on fortress Hollywood.

The two had grown tired of continually adding to their stack of unproduced screenplays. They were looking for a way to crash the party. The entertainment industry was an exclusive club; one could work on the fringes of the business for years, slave away as a production assistant, wait tables in the Sky Bar at the Mondrian Hotel, always writing, taking directing classes, making contacts—and never get in.

Scott and Troy weren't waiting tables. Scott had his executive-producer position at Fattal-Collins, spending much of his time making industrial videos and Thrifty Payless Drug Store commercials in Spanish (a language he didn't speak). He had always expected that his break would come along—or rather, that he would create his own opportunity and seize it.

Scott was born in 1963. His father was an auto-parts salesman who wanted to be an entertainer. (Both of Zakarin senior's sons would live out that wish; Scott's older brother Mark would become executive vice-president for original programming at Showtime.) His mother worked as a caterer. A bright and imaginative child if underachieving student, Scott grew up on Long Island, where he wrote stories and books throughout his childhood. He had a lifelong passion for comic books and pictured himself as a heroic figure in the make-believe comic-book worlds. As a six-year-old, he used to wear Superman pajamas under his clothes at school so that if another child needed help, he could take off his clothes and come to the rescue.

In 1978, at the age of fifteen, he convinced his parents to allow him to use his bar-mitzvah money to buy a videocam. Wanting to be an actor, Scott wrote thirty-minute movies, which he taped and then edited with a borrowed machine. His talent with video enabled him to build a business taping weddings, bar mitzvahs, and (his favorite) sweet-sixteen parties. While attending Binghamton University in New York, he started to make industrial films. His new business made it possible to pursue more creative projects, one being a forty-eight minute high-production musical called *Creating Rem Lezar*, about two children whose imaginary friend comes to life, an ambitious effort that Scott felt had been a critical success but a commercial failure.

Scott's next project was a feature film called *The Gifted*. *The Gifted* was partly financed by the sale of his video business and partly by NBC president Paul Klein. Scott brought the film to Cannes where, emboldened by too much wine one night, he managed to talk film critic Roger Ebert into attending a screening of his film. Near Ebert's seat, he posted a friend who reported afterward that the corpulent critic seemed to laugh in all the right places. Scott never learned what Ebert thought of the movie since it was Ebert's policy never to tell the filmmaker his opinion until the review appeared. Scott's film was never released domestically, so Ebert never wrote a review.

Getting Roger Ebert to come to his film was typical of Scott's ability to persuade people to get involved in what often seemed like quixotic quests. His abiding faith in his own talent enabled him to convince others to suspend disbelief. He was aggressive, unafraid to ask people to extend themselves for him, but also vulnerable. Grandiose, he deeply believed in everything he did and opened himself up to the possibility—probability—of failure. The vulnerability softened him, made people willing to give him the benefit of the doubt. It also made him at times mercurial and impulsive.

Back in New York, Scott found himself in the bottom of a trough. *The Gifted* was ignored. He'd broken up with his girlfriend. His video business was gone. Seeing how depressed her son was, Scott's mother cut him a check for two thousand dollars. He took it and headed for the West Coast in a van. After a few months of fairly riotous living in North

Hollywood and just past his thirtieth birthday, a balding and contrite Zakarin retired his toupee. He began doing freelance promotional work for Disney and Paramount Home Video, gigs that helped pay the bills. The experience also landed him a job at Playboy On-Air Promotions—and later the position as head of production at Fattal-Collins. While Scott was picking up the pieces of his life out in California, he was joined by his best friend, Troy Bolotnick.

Scott and Troy made a striking duo. Scott was thirty-one and balding with small, animated eyes, a man whose creative energies sprayed wild and strong like a loose fire hose. He was impractical in terms of the mechanics of everyday life: he couldn't make coffee, had no sense of direction. Computers puzzled him.

Troy, on the other hand, had a dense, wolfish head of hair and large soulful eyes. Six years Scott's junior, Troy was the "grouchy old man," and with his heavy-lidded eyes, often looked it. Where Scott could be a charmer and put anyone at ease, Troy was impatient and hard on others—though no harder than he was on himself. For a man in his mid-twenties, he projected a clarity of purpose far beyond his years. Even his voice had a solid, measured quality that was commanding and reassuring—the subtext being, "It'll get done." As a kid, he loved to take things apart to discover their inner mechanisms, then try to put them back together to see if they could be made to work again. Troy obtained his first computer at age eleven, and he quickly mastered it. He was the typical computer geek. As comfortable as Troy was with technology, it was film, media, and writing that intrigued him. His idea of a relaxing day off was to watch four movies back to back. His typical conversation would be sprinkled with lines from classic movies.

As a team, Scott and Troy shared a lot of history. They met in June 1985 when Scott videotaped fifteen-year-old Troy's black-belt karate test. Troy's mother had called in a favor from her best friend's husband, who was Scott's partner in the video business. Troy later worked in Scott's business and helped with his self-produced video movies. While Troy took premed courses at Binghamton, he would call Scott in California to ask his advice on women and other diverse subjects. Two days after Troy's graduation, he was sleeping on Scott's couch in North Hollywood.

Scott lined up a job for Troy at Marquee Productions, a company that produced trailers mostly for B-movies. Marquee worked Troy around the clock. As a result, he absorbed a great deal of craft in a short time. Scott also got him freelance production work around town and eventually brought him to Fattal-Collins as a producer. He would be best man at Scott's wedding.

Neither Scott nor Troy wanted to make a career in advertising. Fattal-Collins gave them a maintenance roll to subsidize their aspiring film careers. In late 1994, the CD-ROM game business seemed like a promising shortcut. Silicon Valley geeks were in the pilot seat, but a growing community of people mainly on the fringes of the entertainment industry believed that digital technology would transform the way that content got produced in Hollywood. The emergence of CD-ROM as a platform for multimedia interactivity created great excitement among software developers, game masters, artists, and musicians. CD-ROM inspired visions of a grand convergence and collaboration between Hollywood and Silicon Valley. Here was a medium that combined the power of computing with digital art, video, sound effects and music, and new forms of storytelling.

Stories abounded of friends who created best-selling titles with a couple Macs and copies of Macromedia Director (authoring software), working out of garage shops. The masses, Marx might say, now owned the means of production. Any moonlighting actor, would-be producer, writer, or director who took the trouble to learn the technology could, in theory, develop his own CD-ROM title. The two best-selling CD-ROM games, *Myst* and *Doom*, had come from such humble beginnings.

The empowerment that the new technology out of Silicon Valley brought was coupled with a sense of urgency. The industry was changing on a weekly basis; CD-ROM companies appeared and folded, and there was no telling when small players would be shut out by the major studios and media giants. But in early 1995 opportunities still abounded. CD-ROM game companies like Rocket Science and Activision, searching for the next best seller, were open to pitches from unknowns. Hollywood executives were also excited about the CD-ROM business. They saw the platform as a way to package "pre-owned" content, such as turning a blockbuster adventure film into a computer game, or taking a successful game brand and adapting the backstory for the screen or television. The studios opened multimedia divisions, and almost anyone with a multimedia idea could snag a meeting in Hollywood.

Planet ROM

The goals of magic are the same as the goals of multimedia. To create worlds in which you can learn without being hurt, and in which you can back up and change your mind.

—Tod Foley, As If Productions

To Scott and Troy, the CD-ROM business looked like a way to get noticed. After days spent filming sexual harassment training videos and commercials in Spanish, the two would regroup in the evenings at the pink palace, where they spent hours developing entertainment concepts for the CD-ROM platform.

Troy tried to get Scott interested in *Myst*, a contemplative puzzle game that combined striking graphics of beautiful surreal worlds with a compelling backstory, labyrinthine underground tunnels, and rooms filled with strange devices. (Because of its immense popularity, many industry observers credited the game with propelling the sale of CD-ROM drives in the mid-1990s.)

When the opportunity came to submit a proposal for a game title to the people at Rocket Science, Scott forced himself to check out *Myst*, with Troy helping in the background. The Miller brothers, who had created *Myst*, were outsiders who lived, of all places, in Spokane, Washington—about as far from Hollywood (at least mentally) as one could get. They had gotten coverage in all the national magazines and major newspapers. *Myst* was a media phenomenon. Scott and Troy, with their understanding of the entertainment industry and their love of film, could surely do as well.

As the two continued their research, reviewing stacks of computer games and CD-ROM titles, they were struck by the low production values and the prevalence of niche products. Most games seemed aimed at a very narrow and geeky market, leaving an open season on the traditional genres or high-concept CD-ROM interactive adventures.

Scott also sensed that in many CD-ROM titles technology got

more attention than the quality of the content—bells and whistles were more important than the story, characters, or gameplay. In other words, storytellers took a back seat to the Silicon Valley geeks who were running the show. "Incredible as it may sound," Interval Research Media artist Michael Naimark said in 1997, "the word *content*, which is heavily flaunted in any multimedia forum you'll go to today, didn't enter the vernacular until three or four years ago. It's so amazing, at these conferences people would talk about features, not about content."

In the early days the relationship between the folks with the tools and those who created the content was about as smooth as one would expect when mating polar opposites. Putting a writer together with a programmer often caused an explosion. Writers would make suggestions that might sound trivial enough on paper but would translate into days of computer coding. Programmers sometimes seemed oblivious to the creative intent of the products they worked on. "This notion of taking some Hollywood types," said CNET chairman and CEO Halsey Minor, "and putting them in a room together with some technology people and saying, 'Have at it,' has tended to produce more divorces than happy marriages."

Cultural stresses between the game producers—many of whom came out of the computer business—and Hollywood talent became apparent early, particularly when deals were being made by the few Hollywood agents who worked the new-media space. An International Creative Management (ICM) agent named Steve Stanford was involved in a negotiation with an action star he represented and a large video-game company based in Silicon Valley. Stanford had been a product manager at Oracle in the 1980s when he caught the entertainment bug and moved to L.A. in 1990 to become a talent agent. (He would eventually represent Scott and Troy.) If the deal had gone through, it would have been unprecedented in size—$10 million in cash and stock.

Just when he was about to sign, the actor got cold feet. The computer game was brutally violent. How would his audience react to his killing scores of people? Was it really worth the potential damage to his image and film career to appear as a tiny, pixilated image on a computer screen? The action star backed out.

Stanford became involved with another game deal with yet another major action-movie star. The deal promised to be sweet—big bucks for the lead in a fast-paced, exciting CD-ROM game. The designers went to great lengths to educate the actor about the medium and explain the various branches in the story. Naturally, some of the user choices would result in the hero losing the battle to his foes. "Wait a minute," the star said. "If someone goes down this branch, my character loses? I don't want my character to lose." The game producers exchanged glances. "Well, the game won't be very interesting if your character never loses," they explained. That deal went south as well.

But as Scott and Troy brainstormed ideas for a CD-ROM title, the tide was turning in Hollywood against the multimedia business. The studios were discovering just how little they really knew about developing software. Many established Hollywood writers were also souring on multimedia. The prospect of crafting five-hundred-page scripts loaded with complex and tedious story branching seemed a waste of time when they could work in shorter, linear, more lucrative formats like film and television.

There just wasn't that much money in the CD-ROM business. The suits soon discovered that the product was at an immediate disadvantage because the route to the customer, via retail stores, was treacherous and expensive. CD-ROMs came in big packages and fought for limited shelf space. The risk was high because developers had to bake everything onto a CD-ROM, pay a lot of money to get it onto those shelves, and then hope that kids, adolescents, and adults liked it. The studios would eventually cut back or shut down their fledgling multimedia units.

By the winter of 1995, many CD-ROM producers were struggling to stay in the business. Few appreciated that in a matter of months—weeks even—their world would change completely. Few realized it at the time, but the whole multimedia business was about to be blindsided by a new, rapidly morphing technology. More and more people were referring to CD-ROM as a "dead platform." Almost overnight, multimedia producers clamored onto the Internet—Scott and Troy among them.

Inter-WHAAA?

In some ways the Internet is one long e-mail extravaganza in which a stream of consciousness is more readily obvious than real, deep concentration.

—Howard Stringer, president of Sony America

Despite the looming troubles for the CD-ROM business in early 1995, the big game producers were still receptive to speculative scripts and pitches. Developing a hit CD-ROM game still seemed like the best way for Scott and Troy to get on the Hollywood radar. Scott wasn't thinking about the Internet; he hardly knew it existed. For Troy, the Net was an awesome tool—one he wanted to bring to Scott's attention—but just a tool.

Troy began using the Internet to research the multimedia industry and figure out the commercial side of the business. When questions came up about the industry, he would tell Scott, "let's look it up on the Internet." Scott was oblivious to what Troy was saying until the umpteenth iteration, when the phrase finally registered with him. He stared at his friend. "Inter-WHAA?"

"Anything you want to know about, there's something on the Internet about it," Troy told him.

In February 1995, the Internet was just beginning to get a head of steam in the media—"a peculiar blending of the personal computer and citizen's band radio," was how *Business Week* described it—and was well on its way to becoming the story of the 1990s. Troy had been trying to get Scott on the Net for weeks. Scott was a passionate "big vision" guy and famous among his friends for being computer illiterate. What would happen when Scott finally came face to face with the bit stream? Troy didn't know, but his instincts told him that getting Scott online was the right thing to do.

Having positioned Scott in front of the computer, Troy took his friend on a brief tour of the Net and of AOL's proprietary online world. Scott wasn't interested in most of the content offered on AOL. What intrigued him were the service's chat rooms. "Let me see what people are interested in," he told Troy, "let me see what they're saying so I can figure out what to give them, what to sell them." The chat rooms were a revelation. It wasn't the technology that dazzled Scott so much as the novelty of being in an electronic cave with a group of strangers.

Troy would put the technically hapless Scott into a chat room and walk away. Scott yelled every three minutes—"Somebody is sending a message!" "How do I do this? How do I send a message?"

Scott was struck most by the banality of the chat-room experience. People wanted to talk, to interact with others, but no one seemed to know what to say—other than to talk about their penises or ask for endless rounds of "sex/age" checks. People in chat rooms seemed to digress very quickly into the lowest kinds of conversations. Scott picked up on this quality of the experience instantly; his observation occasioned a genuine and important insight. *These people were dying to be entertained.* If the CD-ROM platform had little compelling entertainment content, then the Net seemed to be a virgin continent. At age fifteen he had recognized the grass-roots entertainment potential of the videocam—demonstrated years later in shows like *America's Funniest Home Videos.* The Net was another technology that could be turned into an entertainment medium—perhaps the ultimate one.

Troy told Scott one more thing about the Internet: "Everybody in the world can see this stuff."

Scott threw his hands up and turned on Troy. "Why the hell didn't you tell me about this sooner?"

Prior to the early 1990s, the Internet had been the domain of the geekiest of geekdom's denizens. The network of networks began in 1969 as the ARPAnet, a computer network linking government-research and Department of Defense institutions around the country. The builders of the ARPAnet once conducted a research study to see what purposes the network was being put to. The researchers were shocked to discover that the network, which had been originally intended for the transfer of research documents and other scholarly content, was being used primarily for sending personal messages among its users.

The vast majority of Web users in the mid-'90s were computer literate, and most Web sites were built by geeks, making the Net an exclusive club. Using the Internet required considerable technical skill and the mastering of arcane Unix commands. The emergence of a graphical user interface for the medium—known as the World Wide Web—opened the Internet to everyone.

Many geeks were ambivalent about the Web and recoiled at anything that tended to make the technology accessible to the masses.

The simpler the user experience, the less appreciation people would have for the hard work involved in creating it. The fact that greater simplicity increased the commercial and artistic potential of the technology was less important. Transforming new technologies into commercially successful products required a different mind-set. As psychologist Mihaly Csikszentmihalyi noted, discovering new ways to bundle information, develop better machines, or create new Internet technologies "tends to be done by people who love to do it and hope to make some bucks out of it. But the money is not what drives them."

All this made the Net an alien setting for Hollywood's creative community. The Internet reflected the geek culture from which it emerged: free wheeling, democratic, anarchic, and anticommercial. John Perry Barlow, cofounder of the Electronic Frontier Foundation and former lyricist for the Grateful Dead, articulated this spirit when he said that the essence of the Net was that it liberated information from notions of property and ownership. "If I own a horse and you steal it," Barlow said, "I can't ride it anymore, and its value has been lost to me. But if I have an idea and you steal it, not only do I still have the same idea, but the fact that two people now have that idea makes it intrinsically more valuable."[1] In other words, if you put an idea out there, if you give it away, it will come back as a bigger and better solution. This perspective on sharing intellectual property did not find a happy home in Hollywood. The Walt Disney Company sued the Academy Awards one year for dressing a dancer to look like Snow White.

The Internet wasn't an entertainment medium in the sense that Hollywood thought of entertainment—as a vehicle for storytelling. Still, while Scott was discovering AOL's chat rooms, marketing groups in the major studios were already wise to the power of the Internet as a tool for marketing feature films.

The breakthrough came with a film called *Stargate*.

Stargate

With Kurt Russell and James Spader starring in the futuristic, special-effects-laden movie, Stargate *was regarded in the industry largely as a footnote on the fall release schedule.*

—Richard Natale writing in the *Los Angeles Times*

Unlike Scott, Josh Greer knew a lot about computers. He was part of the generation that began grade school around the time that personal computers entered the marketplace. The PC would replace the paper route as the preferred means of earning some bucks outside of school hours. Greer started working with computers at age thirteen, and began getting his first professional gigs at fourteen. Short and slight with dark hair, he grunted out code, pushing himself hard straight through high school, burning out at the venerable age of eighteen, when he resolved to "retire" from the computer business.

Surprisingly, Greer avoided computer science in college and enrolled in theater classes. For the next two years at Ontario's York University, he mustered for theater the same intensity he'd delivered to his coding work. Josh was very much attracted to the collaborative aspects of theater life. In his hacker days he'd found working with computers to be a very solitary experience. He recognized that he needed to develop his ability to work with people.

Computer technology began to creep back into his life. He used Autocad programs to design sets, loaded Excel to create budget spreadsheets, and built little theater-related businesses using the PC. He was able to fund some shows from the sale of T-shirts he'd designed on his computer. The one thing he found discouraging was that theater was a dead end in terms of earning a living. Josh didn't want to sell T-shirts all his life. For his own economic survival he walked away from the theater in 1990 and seized an opportunity to move to Los Angeles.

Josh landed a job at Universal Pictures, starting as an assistant to the senior vice-president of marketing. He kept a low profile for a year and a half but met many of the most prominent people in the industry.

At the time, Universal was preparing to market *Sneakers*, the 1993 film about a group of freelance electronic eavesdroppers led by Robert Redford. The film was loaded with high-tech wizardry and featured Dan Aykroyd ranting about CIA conspiracies, space aliens, and cow lips.

Greer was one of the few people in his marketing group that understood technology, who saw the PC as more than a superannuated word processor or spreadsheet. During a raucous meeting over how the studio might promote *Sneakers*, he finally broke protocol and spoke up. "We should put the movie's press kit on a CD-ROM," he said. The conversation froze.

Soon after, Josh found himself in the marketing department's "special projects" group, a kind of catchall group for odd ball projects that didn't fit anywhere else. While there, he found a kindred spirit in Thomas Lakeman, an ashen young man who was a publicist and speech writer in Universal's marketing department. Like Josh, Lakeman had a theater background (M.F.A., Carnegie-Mellon University). Unlike Josh, Lakeman didn't become acquainted with computers until he came to L.A. in 1989 after spending a year in England on a Thomas J. Watson Fellowship.

Most motion-picture press kits were attractive, glossy packages filled with graphics and a videocassette with film excerpts. The kits could cost as much as fifty dollars apiece to put together and were routinely sent out to as many as four thousand press contacts. Copies of a floppy-disk version only cost two or three dollars to produce. The studio agreed that it would be a clever trick, given the geeky premise of the film, if the *Sneakers* press kit were issued on a floppy (Universal wasn't ready for CD-ROM). Working with Lakeman, Greer loaded the floppy with the press-kit material, but also added a game. The content was given a narrative structure so that users would have the illusion that they were hacking their way into forbidden computer files—a reflection of the movie's theme.

Greer still wanted to develop CD-ROM press kits—especially for *Jurassic Park*. The studio wasn't interested, saying that no one else was handing out CD-ROM press kits, so why should they? He found the studios to be plagued by inertia, bloated entities that were unwilling to take risks with new technology. The studios didn't realize that software development was different from film production. Software development thrived on the freedom to experiment and chase technology.

If a new tool became available, one had to be able to buy a copy quickly. One had to upgrade. The process by which the studios procured software and equipment required four signatures to buy anything. In the fall of 1994, Josh was, remarkably, the only person in the building who had Windows 3.1 on his machine; everyone else was running DOS. He decided he had to get out.

He left the studio and began to do freelance work, experimenting with multimedia production on a Macintosh LCII. Eventually he got work with Paul Grand at a film and TV company called the Berkeley Group. Like Greer, Grand had a programming background. He and Paul talked for five hours at their first meeting. The two decided to start an interactive-media company immediately. Josh spent the next year learning the multimedia business, acquiring all the necessary tools, hooking up with CD-ROM projects, and making forays onto the Internet.

While everyone in new media seemed to be deeply engrossed in the development of CD-ROMs, Josh and Paul were convinced that CD-ROM was not going to happen. The two focused instead on proprietary online networks like AOL and Compuserve, competing head to head with Hollywood Online, another company that sprang from the Universal marketing department.

Two things happened that made them shift their attention from the proprietary services to the Web. Mosaic, the forerunner of Web browsers, came out. When the pair downloaded the Megadeath site, they saw the potential for creating online interactive media. (Megadeath was a heavy-metal band that pioneered the use of the Web for promoting the sale of CDs.) The site was one of the first where Josh stopped and said, "Holy shit, there's the ability to do a whole lot more with this medium than we thought."

Lakeman, who was still working at Universal, told Greer and Grand about a vendor search for a Web development company, which was being handled by Universal's corporate information-services group. The Web was emerging as the place to be, and they shifted their focus accordingly.

At one point Greer and Grand went to the Berkeley Group with their first business plan and asked for $30,000 to expand the company's interactive division. The management, thinking interactive wasn't going anywhere, said no.

"Forget Berkeley," Paul said. "We have to do this stuff." Grand put up the $30,000 himself and Josh quit his job. They would build interactive media working out of their respective apartments.

Josh and Paul were pitching interactive projects to the studios when they took a meeting with John Hegeman at MGM/UA. "We've got this movie with no audience awareness. We've got to do something," Hegeman said. The movie was a sci-fi picture called *Stargate*. An otherwise mediocre film (two thumbs down from Siskel and Ebert) with dazzling special effects, *Stargate* (1994) starred Kurt Russell and James Spader in a story whose central gimmick was a hieroglyphic-decorated-stone time portal to an ancient Egyptian world filled with space aliens.

"Let's do a Web site," Paul suggested.

"Great. Can you have the site up by next Friday?"

The two were handed a check for six thousand dollars. Josh and Paul spent Saturday and Sunday building the Web site. They received all the "assets"—the standard press kit stuff like photos, synopses, bios—on Monday, and the site was ready the following Thursday. The next day, Friday, they went to all the Internet news groups to promote what was the first official movie Web site. By Sunday morning they had already registered thirty thousand hits—big numbers in those days.

Stargate was the perfect movie for a promotional Web site. It appealed to young, male, testosterone-engorged sci-fi fans—and the Web had the perfect demographic for building buzz about the film. More important, a reporter for the entertainment section of the *Los Angeles Times* named Richard Natale wrote an article entitled "*Stargate*: The Creative Selling of a Surprise Hit." "By last Saturday morning," Natale wrote, "Sci-fi fans were digitally discussing the heretofore unheralded film almost as if it was the latest installment in the 'Star Trek' series." *Stargate* had garnered a "stratospheric" $16.7 million its opening weekend, the studio's best-performing opening weekend in ten years.

Back to Chat

Chat makes me giddy.
—Charlie Fink

By the time Scott had discovered the Internet, it was on its way to becoming a significant promotional tool for the Hollywood film industry. But building promotional sites was a far cry from creating original entertainment or shows for the Web. That nut had yet to be cracked.

For Scott and Troy, dropping their CD-ROM projects and switching to the Internet seemed like a smart tactical move. Production budgets for CD-ROM games were exceeding the million-dollar mark. Pursuing the big game companies, as Scott and Troy were, meant pitching their ideas and getting someone to fund them. There was already a glut of product in the CD-ROM pipeline. Scott and Troy didn't want to end up shoving unproduced CD-ROM scripts into the drawer with all their unproduced film scripts.

In contrast, the barriers to entry on the Internet were nonexistent. There were no production companies to pitch an idea to—one could be one's own production company. Even more exciting, one could be the *distributor* as well. No worries about getting onto store shelves, booking theaters, or squeezing into the network fall schedule. The Net had infinite shelf space.

The other exciting thing about the Internet was that it was a medium with no lineage. Every artist, movie director, or television producer had a traceable line of descendants, people who had a cumulative downstream influence on their ideas, style, production methods, and business models—except for Web producers. There were no old masters, only new ones in the making.

Scott Zakarin came up with the name for the site before they had a concept: *The Spot*. It was different than *site* and had cool connotations: *The Spot to go on the Web. That's The Spot*. It didn't sound geeky. It was pure Hollywood.

His earliest ideas focused, ironically, on an entertainment-oriented merchandising site. Specifically, the two considered creating a *Scream Queen* site, capitalizing on their connections to B-movie actresses like Rhonda Shear—the curvy blonde star of USA Network's *Up All Night.* Maybe they could get Shear and others to "brand" items like T-shirts and mugs. From the start of their creative efforts—like their movie scripts—Scott and Troy tried to maintain a strong commercial sensibility. There was no point in creating art-house content —this was mass media. While they thought the scream-queen concept had commercial potential, they began to lose interest. Scott returned to his research—which meant hanging out in chat rooms.

He found himself continually, almost obsessively, drawn to chat rooms. He quickly got tired of being ignored by chat-room habitués (no one wanted to talk to a thirty-one-year-old male), so when the next wave of "sex/age" checks rolled through, he typed "f/23." He—or she—got inundated with IMs (AOL jargon for *instant messages*). Everyone wanted to know more about her—and more important, what she looked like. Scott thought of his assistant at Fattal-Collins, Laurie Plaksin, and more or less typed a description of her: "Blonde . . . slim . . . blue eyes . . . film student." She needed a name. Zakarin hesitated, then typed "TaraHHH" ("Tara" had already been claimed as a user name).

From then on, he spent every evening in AOL chat rooms, first as Tara, then as other characters that he invented. He gave these characters quirky, neurotic personalities—anything to push people's buttons. Scott knew that many chat-room habitués were suspicious of female visitors who talked salaciously. He made an effort to peel away the masculine layers of his own personality in a way that would be provocative and credible at the same time. Once he had Tara share her hurt feelings over being expelled from a film-school class for making a movie about masturbation. The masklike quality of his creations intrigued him, as did the responses from the people in the chat rooms he visited. Tara quickly made Scott "the most popular girl on the Internet."

After a solid week of chat rooms, Scott came home one night and crawled into bed. He slept badly. An idea preyed on his mind. As the idea took form, Scott got excited, turning it over again and again. In the middle of the night, he got up and scribbled a note on a piece of paper:

> The Spot—The first serealized [sic] Virtual Reality. Real World
> meets Melrose Place (Reality Bites). Photo art—& story—Dra-
> matic past day Drama—artistic intelligent—

Scott climbed back into bed, careful not to wake his fiancée Debra.
Tomorrow he'd pitch the idea to Troy, Rich, and Laurie. He was excited about his epiphany, and troubled by the thought—surely the
near certainty—that someone else was already doing it. There was no
way he could have had such an original idea, he mused, staring up at
the ceiling. *Somebody's got to be doing this shit.*

A Fertile Environment

An advertising agency was the perfect environment for producing a
new form of entertainment like *The Spot.* Unlike the Hollywood studios, agencies were generally small, agile companies used to moving
fast. The advertising world was a portal to the worlds of television and
film, and as such was full of writers, artists, video technicians, and
hopeful actors. While ad agencies in New York tended to aggregate in
places like Madison Avenue, L.A. ad agencies could be found adjacent
to art communities like Venice, where they had the pulse on what was
edgy and new. Aside from all that, Fattal-Collins was a particularly fer-
tile environment for Scott and Troy to be developing an entertainment
Web site—even though their intention was that they would moonlight
the production.

   Scott's boss at Fattal-Collins was Russell Collins, forty-five, an ex-
seminary student and ex-writer. He had made a smooth career transition to marketing, building a successful agency in Marina Del Rey.
With his preppy-ish, boyish good looks, cropped brown hair, wire-
frame glasses, and a smile reminiscent of David Letterman's (minus
the gap tooth), Collins was the classic image of an ad man. He had
been an early proponent of interactive television (ITV). Because of
the structure of interactivity—the five-hundred-channel universe, the
branching and tiering of information—he believed ITV would require
huge amounts of content. He also believed the production of that content would of necessity be a low-budget phenomenon, creating an immense market for low-budget production houses. Certain that an
advertising firm like Fattal-Collins would be well positioned to take

advantage of the ITV wave, Collins and his colleagues had set up a division of Fattal-Collins called Prophesy to pursue ITV programming. The idea was for Prophesy to create and own content, then sell that content to distributors, as opposed to doing work for hire.

Some small-scale ITV trials were already underway in early 1995. Time Warner's interactive cable service for some four thousand homes in Orlando offered video on demand, shopping, and interactive gaming, among other things. What these trials would eventually demonstrate, to the chagrin of many investors and industry observers, was that interactive television was a very expensive, engineering-driven idea that failed at the time to plug in to any compelling consumer need.

Collins recruited Sheri Herman to head up Prophesy. Herman was an attractive, dark-haired thirty-ish former E! Entertainment Television executive who had started a company called Marketing Solutions before coming to Fattal-Collins. Prophesy's principal client was USWest, which had its own ITV trial in development. Collins enlisted Scott to produce the promotional video for USWest's GOTV. By early 1995, Prophesy had been trying to sell shows to USWest for some time—not, as it turned out, a very productive or enjoyable process.

One of the shows Herman tried to develop, *Chanimals*, was based on an idea Collins had for an interactive TV show about pets. The Prophesy group was thinking seriously about category-based content. The notion was that category-based content shows like *Chanimals* would attract advertisers who had some tie-in—in this case to pet owners. As it happened, Scott's *Spot* project would soon cause Collins to reassess his strategy.

For a while after Scott, Troy, Rich, and Laurie's brainstorming session, it looked like *The Spot* might turn into one of those legless inspirations that went nowhere. Everyone was still working full time for the agency. They started booking more Hispanic commercials. Scott threw himself into commercial work, keeping Rich busy in the editing bay.

Like Scott and Troy, Rich was from Long Island, though he grew up close enough to Queens to consider himself a city boy. Rich had been slogging his way through electrical engineering at Binghamton University when he decided to take a technical theater class in order to hang around a girl he liked. Rich, who had once dismissed theater as "fucking show tunes," found to his surprise that he loved technical theater. Arranging lights and sets involved the best elements of engineering—designing mechanisms and executing them in a meticulous manner—but also allowed for creative expression.

He eventually founded a theater company called the D.C. Players at the college and became a kind of all-round theater grunt, doing lighting design, carpentry, acting, producing, and directing. One day in 1989 he was painting a picture of a fireplace on a blank sheet of wood for a production when he met the show's assistant director, an overweight nineteen-year-old kid with long hair tumbling off his shoulders. The two began to talk. Rich could be extremely quiet (Scott thought he was a mute the first time he met him) but on this occasion he was loud and effusive. Words fired out of his mouth like bullets from an Uzi. The young assistant director, Troy Bolotnick, thought Rich was "the loudest, funniest human being I had ever met."

Rich earned a reputation for his ingenuity in theater production. Once while working on an off-Broadway production of a Stephen Sondheim musical, a sliding door that Julie Andrews used to enter the stage wouldn't budge. He nonetheless found a way to get Julie Andrews onstage in time to sing her opening number. Troy would later say that "there's nothing I can't count on Rich to do. If I said to Rich, 'We gotta figure out how to get that hedge on top of that tree,' I know that it would get done one way or another."

Rich eventually followed his friend Troy (who had followed *his* friend Scott) out West and took Troy's old job at Marquee productions after Scott recruited Troy to work at Fattal-Collins. Rich's first day at Marquee was the day of the Northridge earthquake in 1994. Marquee had just acquired an Avid digital-editing system. Being one of the few people in the company who was comfortable with computers, figuring out the Avid fell to Rich, who quickly mastered the system and added editing to his everyman skill set. Rich's editing prowess came to Troy's attention when Scott's production unit at Fattal-Collins needed a video editor. He was hired and began to work on a number of commercial and corporate video projects.

Soon after joining Fattal-Collins, Rich got a call from Laurie Plaksin, Scott's assistant. Scott was producing a management training video on sexual harassment, she told Rich, and he was wondering if Rich could play a character in the video.

Rich was taken aback. "I'm not an actor."

"It's a small part," Laurie replied. "Two lines. You play the man who delivers the buns."

That sounded reasonable. Rich certainly wanted to be helpful to his new boss. "OK, I'll do that."

When Rich showed up on the set the next morning, he discovered that instead of having two lines he had "a ton of lines," that he was in fact playing the harasser opposite a blonde woman named Debra Mostow. The script called for Rich to grab Mostow, slap her on the butt, and call her "cutie pie." The woman that Rich was going to be so offensive toward in front of thirty people was his new boss Scott's fiancée. The two had to go through take after take, while Scott yelled "Come on. Get into it. *You're holding back!*"

Convincing Rich Tackenberg to act in Scott's sexual harassment video was just one of many unusual assignments requiring a deft touch that fell to Laurie Plaksin. One's first impression of Laurie was of a vulnerable and trusting creature. Like her *Spot* character Tara, she was twenty-three years old, very blonde, and very much a student of film, though not enrolled in a film school.

Laurie grew up in Sherman Oaks, writing poems and stories that featured women protagonists, and eventually wrote a play. She wanted to become an actress and took classes in the entertainment program at nearby Valley College. She was struggling for acting jobs when a friend told her that a guy who worked at an advertising agency in the Marina was looking for an assistant. Laurie gave Scott Zakarin a call.

Working for Scott gave Laurie more than a steady paycheck; it offered an opportunity to act in some of the corporate videos Scott produced for Fattal-Collins, to write a bit, and to do some walk-ons for Spanish-language commercials. The work was fun for a while, but began to pall on her. Laurie was dying to extend herself creatively. She was interested in the writing. While the others had fairly mainstream tastes, Laurie liked off-beat movies and quirky, subversive media. Despite a certain shyness, she loved to clown around. She had a talent for cultivating good relationships with the myriad agents and talent that came their way. Scott's *Spot* pitch came at the right moment for her. The only question was, would they follow through?

High Concept

The program . . . is merely fodder for a mediated but witty conversation between friends. It is stimulus for a social event, even a Web site, and not an end in itself.

—Douglas Rushkoff on *Melrose Place*[2]

By the Spring of 1995 the Internet was a technology still searching for a business model. To develop a Web site, it seemed that developers basically had two choices—to do it themselves for nothing or to spend money hiring real talent to create the site. Most sites were homegrown affairs, built by those who did it for the challenge. The result was a glut of amateurish, typo-filled, poorly designed sites. Professionals cost real money (minimum thirty dollars per hour), though it was still possible to find talented artists, programmers, and designers who would work cheaply just to get the Web-development experience.

Scott and his friends had decided out of necessity to take the homegrown route, bartering for professional input here and there. Even if they saved money by hiring cheap labor, no one had any idea how the site would actually make money, other than the hope that the site could be spun off as a TV show, movie, or book. At this point the goal wasn't to make money; it was to get attention.

A month after their initial meeting, Scott was fleshing out the characters, building the backstory, even writing some of the diary entries on his honeymoon. Pretty soon a treatment for *The Spot* began to take shape.

The team wanted an objective opinion about their scheme. Scott and Troy were friends with Jeannine Parker, a new-media business consultant and a ubiquitous player in the L.A. new-media scene. Her consulting work often involved helping businesses to move into the multimedia or online worlds. She was also a kind of digital matchmaker who enjoyed bringing potential business partners together to make things happen. Scott and Troy brought her a copy of the treatment for *The Spot*. Parker agreed to take a look and get back to them.

The Spot wasn't high-brow, PBS material. It was what entertainment folk referred to as "high concept," meaning that it was a simple idea with great appeal to a large audience. For a Web audience in 1995—the geeky, sex-starved males Scott had encountered in the chat rooms and a smaller percentage of women—high concept was mostly cheese cake and beef cake. Scott had tried his hand at the serious, deep, and emotional—and failed. He was nothing if not pragmatic. His target audience wanted something fun and edgy that reflected its own preoccupations and problems. He knew his site had to be about one of three things: computing, sports, or sex.

Parker pinched her nose and suspended her judgment—*The Spot*'s *Melrose/90210*ish elements weren't to her taste. But she recognized what Scott was trying to do. There was a lot in *The Spot* that would appeal to the Web demographic. She had to admit that the project was quite viable, even potentially groundbreaking.

A detail in the treatment caught her eye. Scott and Troy had written that *The Spot* characters would answer viewer e-mail in character. "If you make a 100 percent commitment to being true to having *Spot* characters answer e-mail in character," she told them, "this will be successful."

Collins Signs On

There's a lot of Web stuff out there because a lot of people are producing it for fun and for free, between the hours of midnight and four o'clock in the morning.

—David Baron, Microsoft Network producer

This is the first time in history that people who make stuff own the same equipment as people who consume the stuff.

— Tod Foley

It quickly became clear that producing *The Spot* in off hours would be nearly impossible given the demands of everyone's day jobs at Fattal-Collins. Scott knew that Fattal-Collins's efforts in ITV were going nowhere and that Russell Collins was looking for interactive projects. One day Scott showed him the results of the first *Spot* photo shoot and explained the concept for the show. Collins saw in this extracurricular project the opportunity for Fattal-Collins to gain a "first mover" advantage in a whole new entertainment medium. He expressed his strong interest in being involved and put up a few thousand dollars as seed money. Scott saw the advantage of bringing production of *The Spot* into the daylight hours and being able to spend more time developing the show. The two shook hands. From that point forward, he and his small group had permission to start working on the show during business hours.

Meanwhile, Collins's own thoughts about the Web were evolving. Like others, he began to understand that the technological infrastructure undergirding interactive television was too expensive and couldn't be justified, given the cost of creating the deep programming that the medium required. What Collins took away from the ITV experience, though, was that entertainment could be a magnet for audiences. The Web at that time—having little or no audio or video to speak of—offered a less-expensive alternative. It was possible to create content far more cheaply on the Web than in an ITV environment with its television-style production values.

The limitations of the Net could even end up being an advantage of sorts. While interactive television (if it had existed) would have used broad bandwidth from the get-go, ITV was also creatively limited by the television model on which it was based. Making television interactive meant being saddled with all the baggage of fifty years of television tradition. Having instant broad bandwidth would present content developers with the same creative traps they encountered with CD-ROM—the temptation to simply, dumbly, repurpose existing video to a new architecture without working out the medium's new rules. The temptation with ITV was to approach it as another way to package television content rather than as a uniquely new medium.

On the other hand, the Net had a narrow bandwidth, so Web developers had to set aside everything they knew and build an entirely new medium. Through trial and error they would discover new formulas for online content. The Internet forced artists to make choices, to come up with clever ways of conserving bandwidth. (Writers and artists at Disney Online were struggling to come up with an animated detective character that would work in 14.4 bandwidth, an almost impossibly restrictive environment for animation. The solution was to create a character called "Detective In A Jar," a smooth-talking, noirish detective who was literally a brain in a jar of fluid with a hat and raincoat. Producing full motion animation on a human brain was a hell of a lot easier than animating a Sam Spade cartoon.)

While Scott and company were thinking about getting the attention of the Hollywood establishment, Collins was concerned about the bottom line. How would a site like *The Spot* make money? Clearly it couldn't in the short term, but big technology companies like Intel and Silicon Valley venture capitalists might be willing to invest in such an enterprise. Collins knew these companies were about to begin placing small bets on Internet start-up companies throughout the valley.

Collins saw the Internet as a place dominated by people who had libertarian views. The Web was free form, with flat venues and very flat architecture that presented users with a panoply of options and the ability to flow from place to place. The problem with that architecture was that the sheer width of navigational options left designers flummoxed. One could produce sites that millions of Web surfers would miss due to the vastness of the medium.

Collins was nothing if not a marketer. Casual conversations with him tended to morph into brainstorming sessions. For Collins the marketer, the business of mass media was to get people to visit a specific place. *The Spot*, a Web site devoted to pure entertainment, could lure people to come. Once you had your audience, you could worry about what to do with them later.

In time Collins would become a true believer in the idea of online entertainment. He didn't think that the Internet would result in the kind of socially isolating world described in E. M. Forster's Edwardian-era story "The Machine Stops," in which people lived separately in sterile cells, communicating through something similar to the Net-phone. Quite the opposite, the Net would enable the most socially rewarding experiences. The future of our social culture would be enmeshed in the Net.

Collins saw the potential in creating a new advertising model for interactive media. Television advertising involved a kind of sausage-link model of Show-Ad-Show-Ad, etcetera. That wouldn't work in a medium where people didn't have to go to your message. He hadn't mapped out a specific plan but knew it had to be a proprietary effort. Like most people in the media world—particularly in Hollywood—he believed that ownership was the secret sauce of the creative process. He wanted a model that was so distinctive that it could be copyrighted or patented. He didn't buy into the geek ethic of "giving back to the Net." He wasn't about to spend three years, or however long it took, creating a new advertising model, only to have everyone else use it without paying royalties.

Guerrilla Producers

Scott's production unit soon turned into a full-time Internet unit, dedicated to creating *The Spot*. In retrospect, it is clear that Scott and the others could not have found the time and resources to put together *The Spot* as quickly as they did if not for Collins backing the project. The company continued to pay their salaries and provide facilities during the production.

Jeannine Parker set about showing the team how to produce *The Spot* "guerrilla fashion." This meant asking favors, taking short cuts, stealing what they could. Parker pulled together her friends John Millon, Josh Sherwood, and Richard Gilligan at a company called Interverse to do the programming for a song. She also found an Internet service provider, Primenet, that would lodge the show on its servers for a relatively small fee. The team already had access to actors, some photo equipment, and Photoshop on Fattal-Collins's PCs. Development progressed through the spring with their sights set on June for the official launch.

The team brainstormed ideas for promoting *The Spot* over the Net. Kay Dangaard, a public-relations person at Fattal-Collins, spent three hundred hours building a "global buzz" prior to *The Spot*'s launch. Using the Net, she contacted editors at what she estimated at one thousand newspapers in twenty-four countries. She seeded college bookstores, seminars, and theaters with information; "started a dialogue" with electronic café denizens around the world; and touched base with computer labs at universities in Hong Kong, the U.S., and Europe. A native of New Zealand, Dangaard made sure to include knowing references to native birds in her pitch to a university there. When kibitzing with Hong Kong reporters, she "talked about downing a pint and watching *The Spot* in Lan Kwai Fong, the hip restaurant area and playground of the young turks in Hong Kong."[3]

In the days leading up to the launch on June 6, 1995, Scott and the others knew they were hitched to what would become a shooting comet. They would be able to do things, entertainment-wise, that could never be done with television, film, or radio. The night before

the launch, Scott, Troy, Rich, and Laurie traveled the chat-room circuit, telling people about the soon-to-debut site. A teaser page had already been posted at www.thespot.com that showed a photograph of
Spot characters on the beach in Santa Monica.

The Spot would instantly become available to people all around
the planet, in every country that had access to the Internet. Though
the numbers of people who had Internet access numbered around 20
million, no other show in the history of the entertainment business had
had such wide and immediate geographical distribution. They had
built it . . . now the question was, would people come? Would there be
an audience? How many hits would they get?

Scott and the gang worked the chat rooms hour after hour into the
night. Exhausted, her eyes dry and red, Laurie left Scott at the offices
of Fattal-Collins at 1:00 A.M. that evening to go home and catch a few
hours of sleep. When she returned at 8:00 A.M., Scott was still in front
of the computer, working the chat rooms. He looked like a lonely gambler on a caffeine jag in a Vegas casino, riding out the bet of his life.

More Real Than Television, Less Real Than Your Life

The Spot became an instant "phenom," with 15,000 page hits on day
one and an astounding 55,000 page hits on day two—more than
tripling the team's seemingly optimistic projections. (The stats were
collected by *The Spot*'s ISP, Primenet. The ISP's previous record
holder for page hits was porn star Brandy Alexander's site.) The message boards were filled, and the site racked up more than 300 e-mail
messages. Some cagey hackers had managed to break into the staging
server, ripping off content and posting it to the Web. One of the items
was a graph, or "score card," illustrating a character named Lon's history of success with women. The vandals also found Scott's real home
address. But the vandalism seemed only to feed the buzz.

Many of the people who found *The Spot* were geeks with time on
their hands. Harry Zink was a thirty-one-year-old computer consultant
working at a major entertainment company in the L.A. area. (Zink says
his consulting arrangement prevents him from publicly identifying the
company.) On June 8 around 9:00 P.M., while he and his coworkers were
unwinding in the multimedia lab over greasy pizza, he checked
Netscape's "Cool Sites" column and saw a posting for *The Spot*. Zink

clicked on the link and downloaded the picture of Tara Hartwick. "Hi, I'm Tara Hartwick . . . " *Hmmm, pretty girl,* he thought. He clicked his way deeper into the site until he reached Michelle in a bathing suit on a diving board by an azure pool. *Even prettier* . . . In the weeks to come, Zink would become an habitué of *The Spot,* checking in six, seven, eight times a day, often to post e-mail messages to the various characters.

One of the intriguing aspects of *The Spot,* and doubtless one of the things that accounted for its sudden popularity, was that visitors had no idea if the beach house existed and if the inhabitants were real people. For Scott, this was a filmmaker's ultimate fantasy—to fool the audience. "From the beginning we were going to present this as the real deal," Rich said some time later. The site contained nothing that indicated it was a fictional story. Scott would later tell people that *The Spot* was "more real than television and less real than your life."

Zink, for one, was a passionate defender of the view that *The Spot* was real. The idea of five twenty-somethings living in a beach house in Santa Monica with a server in the basement seemed perfectly reasonable. After all, he had a server in his own basement. He knew that Victorian-style house was out there somewhere. One weekend, Zink grabbed a friend and jumped into his car. They spent the next two days driving down what felt like "every goddamn street in Santa Monica and Venice" trying to find the house. Even after a fruitless search, Zink was convinced the house was out there and that Tara and her friends had loaded the site with misleading information to avoid intrusive fans.

Others were similarly confused by the dividing line between reality and fiction. The team posted an announcement of a fictional party being held at *The Spot* house. E! Entertainment Television reporter Greg Agnew called a friend of Scott's who worked at E!, asking where the party was going to be held.

Other fans were more skeptical. One called "Spamboy" e-mailed that he knew *The Spot* people weren't real and that the show was scripted months in advance. *If you guys are real,* challenged Spamboy, *have Michelle stand in front of a refrigerator in a bikini eating a strawberry.* The next day a photo was posted showing Kristen Herrold, who played Michelle, dressed in skimpy beach-wear, looking sultry, holding a plump strawberry between her fingers. As an added touch, the photo had a strawberry border.

Variety ran a story on June 12 describing how hackers had ransacked the Web site (BREAK-IN AT WWW HOT "SPOT"). The piece created a media tsunami. *Variety* quickly followed up with a second piece. "Tara Hartwick," the second story read, "is making the efforts of the communication giants look like Edsels on the Infopike." Stories about *The Spot* began appearing in dozens of publications:

Wired magazine: "Tired: *Melrose Place*. Wired: *The Spot*."

Entertainment Weekly: *The Spot* "gives audiences, as well as creators, something TV can't—instant response."

USA Today: "Soap Fans Hitting Net's Hot Spot."

Entertainment Tonight called. *Extra, CNN*, and *Fox News* broadcast stories as well. "Television is boring compared to *The Spot*," Russ Collins told the *Extra* reporter, "because you blaze your own trail, you create your own experience with *The Spot*." John Henson, the host of *Talk Soup* on E!, held a *Spot* T-shirt up to the camera. *The Spot*'s overnight success was an example of what happened when one traveled in Internet time. A week on the Web was the equivalent of a season in television.

Stories ran in respected mainstream publications like *The Economist*, the *Times* of London, and the *New York Times*. The *Washington Post*, of all places, ran a lengthy article on *The Spot* in the paper's style section.

A high-school intern at America Online named Pippa Gage happened to catch the *Post* article. Gage's job at AOL was to surf the Web looking for interesting sites and writing notes about what she found. She told her boss, Miguel Monteverde, about *The Spot*. Monteverde began following the exploits of *The Spot*'s residents:

Tara Hartwick was a big fan of Martin Scorsese. She had aspirations to be a director and could "see no reason to hold back just because there are no funds to produce my celluloid dreams." Tara posted *The Spot*'s manifesto of sorts. "The Net gives us all an opportunity for self-expression in the most candid and provocative way . . . with a potential audience of 20 million and counting. And a captive audience as long as we don't disappoint. So this is our story but more than that, the continuing adventures of *The Spot*. Just to make things interesting, we've agreed not to read each other's pages."

Lon Oliver had the dark good looks of a young Cary Grant and the pecs of a Venice-beach devotee. Naturally, he was an actor. While he had the usual young actor's arrogance, he also exhibited a touch of humor about his prospects. "Most of my performances consist of recitations of the nightly dinner specials at the restaurant where I work," Lon wrote. "You may have seen me before in one of my commercials. Or not. I'm not a big star yet."

Carrie Seaver was the new roommate, fresh from the East. She was (Tara wrote) "really pretty but . . . strange about her looks, like she doesn't know or doesn't really care that she's attractive. Weird." Carrie worried about the tendency in L.A. to care more about football players than the homeless population and the shrinking intellectual capacity of the city's upper middle class, which she attributed to excessive listening to Howard Stern during morning commute time.

Unlike Carrie, Jeff Benton had been living at *The Spot* since he was a kid. Maybe the house's strange aura had rubbed off on him, but others found Jeff a little scary. "He knows more about *The Spot* than any of us but unfortunately he won't share any of this juicy information," Tara writes. "He barely talks to us and I doubt we'll ever get him to be involved with our project."

Michelle Foster was the "model/receptionist extraordinaire" who spent her weekdays doing receptionist work at an advertising firm that bore a strange resemblance to Fattal-Collins. Weekends she did lingerie shoots, department store ads, and the odd commercial. Michelle was an aggregator of eyeballs.

She also had a bit of a drinking problem, which brought out the white knight in Monteverde. He got hooked, and checked in on *The Spot* almost every day for a month. There was something about the voyeuristic sense of seeing something (i.e., diary entries) he shouldn't be seeing and being able to exchange e-mail with Michelle, if he chose, that gave the site a sense of intimacy. *The Spot* also tapped into the medium's uncanny ability to confer anonymity—an anonymity that liberated users to share ideas, feelings, fantasies, and selves that would be unthinkable in other circumstances. Later, thousands of sex-oriented Web sites would capitalize on this potent combination of anonymity and intimacy. *The Spot* wasn't a sex site, but it fulfilled people's need for intimacy that was safe and at a distance. It also allowed fans who were stuck in dismal, provincial, backwater communities to feel like they were part of a hip young household on a sunny beach in L.A.

An Open Channel

Laurie Plaksin received e-mail from people—many of them men—in many of those far-flung communities. She soon found herself on the receiving end of e-mail from small midwestern towns, European capitals, Far East centers of commerce, and elsewhere on the planet. Plaksin was fast becoming (arguably) the first actress to become a star in the online medium. She played Tara in the photography sessions and began to write for Tara soon after the launch. A fan named Charlie Flynt began to write Laurie—or Tara—e-mail all the time. Flynt, who lived in Indiana, gave her advice, pep talks, shared his feelings. To Laurie's initial shock and consternation, Flynt came out to California to interview with Scott. Rather than a stalker, he turned out to be the "sweetest, coolest guy." He ended up staying in California and eventually went to work for Scott.

For Laurie, writing for Tara felt like "an open channel," a method of expressing her inner thoughts and emotions without having to face a huge audience. "I think that's one of the most interesting things about this medium," Plaksin later said. "Even if the audience grows to millions and millions of people, it can still feel completely intimate." Her parents would follow Tara's exploits as if they were hers; she'd have to remind them that they were reading about her character's debauchery, not her own.

It Takes A Community

Jeannine Parker had predicted that *The Spot* would blow out the servers on its small local Internet service provider, Primenet. She was right. She directed Scott and Troy to Silicon Reef, a company in northern California that could handle a site with *The Spot*'s amount of traffic. Silicon Reef lodged *The Spot* on, as one member of the company described it, "two Pentium 90 servers using Berkeley Software Design's BSD 2.0, and a Sun SPARCstation5 running Netscape's Netside and Secure Commerce Server. *The Spot* was connected to the Net by two T1s." There was also a RealAudio 2.0 server.[4]

Having characters post separate diary entries allowed Scott and company to invent and elaborate story lines, which drifted from the sincere to the sophomoric. The first week of the show, Lon Oliver (the actor) made a heavy-handed pass at Carrie Seaver. Carrie resisted Lon's attempt to "jam his tongue down my throat." "Not the response I expected," wrote Lon. "Or wanted. Suddenly, a little light goes on in my head. Carrie, my friends, is a LESBIAN!" Carrie, on the other hand, had a different interpretation of the facts of the supposed seduction. She thought Lon was at best impetuous, and at worst an "asshole," for assuming such liberties.

The Lon-and-Carrie encounter generated an enormous amount of viewer e-mail and provided the "first hint we were really on to something," Rich later recalled. Scott, who was answering Lon's mail at the time, was ripped to shreds by one outraged female viewer. The viewer later sent a follow-up message to apologize. "I know you're just a fictional character," she wrote to Lon/Scott, "but I still feel badly about how I spoke to you." Confusing phase shifts between reality and fiction became commonplace.

Interacting with fans on a daily and hourly basis would have been exhausting if Scott and the others weren't convinced that they'd hit on something truly awesome. *The Spot* was a labor-intensive production. New material was being posted five days a week and the site was now receiving on average about five hundred e-mail messages a day, and each message garnered a response in character. Scott and the team were slowly ascending the learning curve. They were constantly being surprised by the audience, and the excitement of this interactive chaos made each day an adrenaline rush as they tried to push the show to what Scott called the "next evolutionary level"—whatever that was.

One of the innovations was *The Spot* board. Many of the early *Spot* fans began to build connections to each other through IRC, the Web version of chat. While IRC was good for fostering friendships, it was not particularly useful for growing communities. They needed a bulletin board. *The Spot* board was one of the first examples of a bulletin board adapted for use in a fictional universe. The team at Silicon Reef took Hypermail, a threaded message board that was available as shareware, and tweaked it to be able to handle the hundreds of messages *The Spot* received each week, and to archive the thousands of messages that accumulated.

The Spot board was instrumental in the development of *The Spot* community. In the early going it was difficult for an individual viewer to gauge how large the community was, since the interactivity went through the site's characters. Once the board was put up, it became clear that hundreds of people were sending and receiving e-mail, and it became possible for fans to respond to, bounce off of, and follow discussion threads from others as well. *The Spot* board pierced the veil of isolation.

"I'll be in Los Angeles August 6–10 for Siggraph [a computer graphics conference]," wrote "Purple Tiger" in a July 30, 1995, posting. "If anyone wants to join me for some '*Spot* Hunting' send me an e-mail. I'm curious to see if I can find *The Spot* House. Note to Tyler: I'm not going to stalk anyone :), but would be happy to meet on a friendly basis with anyone involved in the project."

On Harry Zink's first day at *The Spot* board, he posted more than twenty messages.

Online communities, such as the one that formed around *The Spot*, were like concentric circles. At the center were the hardcore members who posted the most messages, kept the discussion threads going, enforced the social code, and socialized new initiates. Maybe 1 or 2 percent of visitors were in this category. The next circle contained the semiregulars. These people came to the site often, but were not as active and communicated a lot less. They might respond to a discussion thread, occasionally send an e-mail to a character or other community member, but they would disappear from the site from time to time. These semiregulars might account for 15 to 20 percent of the site's traffic. The outer circle consisted of the lurkers, people who came to the site but didn't interact with anyone, didn't post to the board.

Online communities had life cycles; they grew and shrank over time, and there was considerable churn among their members—except for the hardcore. Long after *The Spot* disappeared from cyberspace, hardcore Spot fans continued to interact with each other through their own sites, and even had annual get-togethers—much as the Trekkies continued to meet during the '70s after *Star Trek* had gone off the air and before the first movie came out. A fan community—particularly an online one—could build a brand in a way that no marketer could ever hope to do.

During *The Spot* photo shoots, Zakarin tried to draw on his skills as a director, but he soon discovered that attention to things like lighting and other directorial tricks didn't work with this medium; the photos fit the medium better when they had a serendipitous quality. More polished and staged photos ruined the illusion that this was the home page of a group of young people. Scott had to set aside most of what he had learned photographically about directing films and videos. Almost everyone who gravitated to the Internet came from some other discipline or industry, toting their own baggage of preconceived notions. In the world of Web development, being able to set aside your prejudices about the medium was referred to as "parking what you know." Those who came from a different medium and tried to apply what they knew from that medium to the Web were headed for trouble. (Television producers would eventually pour into the Internet space and mistakenly apply the rules of television production to the new medium—with horrendous consequences.) What one knew was less important than what one could learn—and how fast.

To save money, Scott shot many of *The Spot*'s interiors in his own home in Santa Monica (an apartment, not a beach house). His wife, Debra, would come home exhausted from her job at Universal Studios to find their apartment filled with photographic equipment and twenty-somethings with jaw-dropping figures traipsing up to her in bikinis. "Hi, Mrs. Zakarin! How are you?" It felt like the set of a trashy soap opera.

Though the Net was a unique medium, producing *The Spot* was in many ways like producing a television soap opera. Story lines were developed running weeks into the future. The characters were fully fleshed out, their motivations and goals outlined. Content was carefully crafted, edited, revised. Unlike television writers, Scott and his team could follow audience feedback on an hourly basis and use audience input and news events to give the show a sense of immediacy and emotional resonance—or spin the plot off in a whole new direction. Scott and the others quickly realized that audience interactivity was every bit as important as the writing that went into the show, maybe more so. They were beginning to understand that some of the best material came from the audience, and they became adept at pushing the right buttons to spur a flood of e-mail from their fans.

This improvisational quality of *The Spot* was never more evident than in the chat rooms. "I need to communicate, people," Carrie Seaver had written in her first post. "It's just that sometimes I get tongue-tied. I am pretty open, but I'm not an actor. I'm a reactor. I've been known to spill my guts if the right buttons get pushed. Please, push away. Please talk to me."

During one of the first large chat sessions, the four hung out in character (including Carrie) with over eighty frenetic *Spot* fans. As the dialog scrolled on and the fans' questions stacked up, the four sat in the same open space at Fattal-Collins, frantically screaming to each other. "Set me up! Argue with me," Rich yelled, setting up a joke involving Laurie's character. Often the details and nuances of the characters were invented in these sessions through interactions with the fans. "Scott, I'm making Carrie from Ohio!" said Rich. "Carrie has a brother now!"

For Scott, the success of *The Spot*, after the crash and burn of his film career, had an element of vindication. He also felt like "a big fish in an empty pond." Even as he enjoyed the first blush of success, the habitat was changing.

"That's the World I Should Be In"

One October morning on the commute from his home in Glendale to the offices of Virtual World Entertainment (VW) in downtown L.A., Charlie Fink decided it was time to resign from the company. VW operated a chain of 3-D gaming centers in storefronts around the country and overseas. But rapid improvements in the home PC gaming platform had forced the company to focus its research-and-development efforts on improving its 3-D hardware, which slowed the development of new game software. Without new games to play, store revenues declined. The company was having trouble raising private equity to cover its expensive R&D and retail operations. For its own survival, Virtual World would have to move away from its original vision of location-based entertainment and begin to morph into a more traditional video-game company.

That is probably the right business for VW but the wrong business for me, Fink thought. He and Tim Disney had envisioned VW as a kind of networked social/digital theme park. But just as movie people needed to have a passion for cinema, game people needed to have a passion for games. Games weren't Charlie's passion.

Something on the radio broke his drive-time reverie. A reporter was interviewing Scott Zakarin, the creator of the latest sensation on the Internet, a show called *The Spot*. The show had just won the "Webbie," Infoseek's cool-site-of-the-year award, in a ceremony held in a small upstairs conference room at the Roosevelt Hotel in Hollywood. The award had grown out of Glen Davis's popular Cool Site of the Day Web page.

Fink had been a big fan of the site and knew all the characters. The more he listened, the more Fink thought that what Zakarin was doing sounded like fun—a lot more fun than developing computer games.

Charlie Fink was the "happy warrior" of new media. He liked to say that the reason he became a new-media executive was because of his penchant for "making it up as I go along"—the "it" being business strategy, models, tactical decisions, and besting the competition. His handle among coworkers was "Taz," short for Tasmanian Devil, the swirling, hyperactive creature in the Warner Brothers cartoons. Fink had wanted to make movies since he was eighteen. Like his erstwhile look-alike, Matti Leshem, Charlie attended Sarah Lawrence ("a girl's school") and later went on to the Art Institute of Chicago, where he met his wife, Jane. Rather than Charlie going immediately to Hollywood, Hollywood came to Charlie. After graduating from the Art Institute, he landed a job on a big Hollywood movie that was shooting in Chicago, *Nothing In Common*, which was directed by Garry Marshall and produced by Alex Rose. Rose offered the young Fink a job in her production company in Los Angeles, reading scripts and running for lunch.

Fink's opportunity to elevate out of assistantdom came more quickly than for most. A friend of Charlie's, who had also come out from Chicago, introduced him to Peter Schneider. At that time Schneider was a production vice-president in Disney animation (later he would rise to president of the division). The mid-1980s marked a renaissance for Disney's animation division, which had suffered through years of decline. Led by Jeffrey Katzenberg and Michael Eisner, Disney animation was about to receive an infusion of fresh young blood. Fink spent five years at Disney, where he worked on projects like the hit animated films *Aladdin* and *Beauty and the Beast*.

In some ways, working in animated features was the best possible preparation for a career in the Internet-content business. The production of animated features in the late '80s involved the management and integration of legions of graphic artists, computer programmers, and musicians in a technically evolving medium. As Fink tells it, he approached Peter Schneider, Roy Disney, and Jeffrey Katzenberg in 1988 with the idea of doing an animated "Bambi in Africa" film with lions. Katzenberg balked at the idea at first, making fun of Fink in staff meetings. "You know about Fink's movie, where the King of the Beasts eats all the other animals?" Nonetheless, Katzenberg encouraged Fink and his colleagues in their efforts to invent a mythos to explain how the lions actually did a service to the other animals by eating them. Out of that dynamic, creative mix came *Lion King*, the most successful animated feature of all time.

Charlie later moved over to Disney's live-action division, a switch he regretted almost instantly. He felt out of his element. Fortunately, he was soon to be rescued by his good friend Tim Disney (nephew of Roy) who had a role in Shamrock Holdings, the investment company for the Roy Disney family. Tim was interested in investing in something called multimedia.

In 1992 Charlie and Tim were looking at what impact emerging technologies might have on entertainment. For someone with Fink's inordinate energy and desire for maximum leg room, multimedia, or new media, was the perfect playing field—level and wide open. They spotted something they thought was promising in virtual reality (VR). Coming out of Disney, where intense fictional universes were the order of the day, the two young men instantly saw the possibilities of using VR to create such worlds for storytelling purposes. At the time, military and medical applications for VR existed, but no one had attempted to apply the technology to entertainment. A full eighteen months before VR came into the public eye, Charlie and Tim were talking to scientists at NASA and to VR pioneers like Jaron Lanier. Eventually they heard about a Chicago-based company called Virtual World Entertainment and decided to investigate.

Virtual World had opened up a storefront entertainment operation called the Battle Tech Center in 1990. The Battle Tech simulation center used a low-cost network of modified flight simulators to network players into a fictional landscape where participants piloted thirty-foot-tall attack robots. Though the robot's windshield one saw other robots that were being operated by people in other simulators. The fact that those robots had human intelligence was incredibly compelling and fit Charlie and Tim's growing conviction that the next big thing would be networked multiplayer interactivity. Playing against machine intelligence could never be as much fun, they felt, as being pitted against other emotional and cunning human creatures. In 1992 Charlie had caught a glimpse of America Online and had his first exposure to chat. Chat made Charlie feel silly, but he also saw that it could be a powerful and entertaining role-playing technology. He filed the thought.

Jordan Weisman was the chief creative officer at VW. He and his partner Ross Babcock III had had the idea of using computer-generated imagery for gameplay while the two attended the maritime academy in 1978. Recruiting ex-military engineers from Russia and Poland, and ex-aerospace software engineers, Weisman and Babcock built the real-time 3-D simulation technology, funding the R&D from the profits of their video-game business. The huge investment in the Battle Tech Center paid off. At six dollars for ten minutes of gameplay, the store generated a ton of revenue.

Charlie and Tim recruited Andrew Messing, then twenty-eight and head of retail investments for Shamrock Holdings, to help them see how they could make a big business out of the Virtual World model. To grow, Virtual World needed capital for R&D and a big roll-out of retail stores. Tim, Andrew, and Charlie formed a company and bought majority interest in VW with Tim's money. Tim assumed the post of chairman, Messing became the CEO, and Jordan became the chief creative officer. Charlie was named senior vice-president and stayed in L.A., where he could use his Hollywood connections to do licensing deals, spin off books, videos and shows, and otherwise nurture the brand.

Two years later the partners had built a chain of twenty-five simulation centers and linked all the remote locations—some as distant as Japan—together so players could battle their foes in different cities in real time. The partners knew that despite all the dazzling effects that VR made possible, people still needed the kind of social interaction—the bragging rights, if you will—afforded when people got together to play games. Remembering AOL chat, Charlie and his partners set up Internet kiosks so that customers could use IRC chat to talk to other people at sites all over the world.

They began to notice something strange and powerful. As they hoped, customers began to gather around the kiosks and communicate with each other via IRC chat—a little bit at first, then more and more. After a while, customers became so absorbed in chat that they didn't want to play the games anymore. Eventually, the kiosks had to be removed. People were coming only to talk to each other, not to play the game. The phenomenon made a big impression on Charlie. The ability to socialize with strangers over long distances could be more compelling than battling thirty-foot robots. What was play, after all, but "social lubrication," as Sony's Rob Tercek would later put it. A strong argument could be made that people played games in order to be with people, not the other way around. "We need the desperately fundamental quality of interpersonal celebration-conversation," said psychologist Karl Weick. "I don't think the mind is located inside a single head." People could bond powerfully with each other through content.

As Fink drove south on the 110 Freeway in his Chrysler Eagle Vision, approaching the Chinatown exit and listening to the interview with Scott and company, a strange and exhilarating sensation of *déjà vu* overcame him. He would later look back at this moment as a punctuation mark in his life. *That's what I should be doing*, Fink couldn't help but think. *That's the world I should be in.*

"What's So Compelling About Text and Pictures?"

"People like that? What's so compelling about text and pictures?" said Kerry McCluggage, the chairman of the Paramount Pictures Television Group. He seemed underwhelmed by the photos of Tara, Carrie, Lon, and the accompanying text on the tiny laptop that sat on the conference table in his capacious office. A handsome, silver-haired man in his forties, McCluggage was a quiet, analytical executive.

McCluggage had never been on the Internet before. In the summer of 1995, there wasn't even Internet access on the Paramount lot. David Wertheimer, who was walking McCluggage through *The Spot* and other sites, had had to bring his own laptop to the chairman's office in the studio's administrative building with downloaded Web pages saved on the hard drive.

Wertheimer had to admit that McCluggage had a point. Compared to television, *The Spot* seemed pretty static. The images took time to download. It was heavy with text. Hard to imagine Mom, Dad, and the kids gathering around the computer for an evening with *The Spot*. All the site seemed to do was make one want to watch television. (Scott Zakarin and Troy Bolotnick would later visit McCluggage's television division to pitch *The Spot* as a television show. The studio passed.)

"Don't look at it for what it is now," Wertheimer said. "See in it what it can become." He reminded McCluggage that television itself had not seemed very impressive when the experience consisted of snowy images on a three-inch screen. Early television was exciting because of the implications of the developing technology, and the same was true for the Net.

Wertheimer was doing more this afternoon than trying to sell the Chairman of the Paramount television group on the opportunities presented by the Internet; this was also a job interview. Wertheimer was being courted to head up a new business unit at Paramount, one that would establish an Internet foothold for the studio. The new company would be called Paramount Digital Entertainment. Wertheimer was twenty-seven years old.

This wasn't his first visit to Paramount Studios. He had been there before as an executive in Oracle's content group, where he regularly made the rounds of the Hollywood studios. Paramount was nonetheless an evocative place, unlike any office or corporate campus he had ever visited. Silicon Valley was filled with countless office parks that were characterless shelters for workaholic technologists. The atmosphere on his first visit to Paramount was entirely different; the walls oozed with history. He remembered arriving at Paramount's Bronson gate—the same gate that Gloria Swanson and Erich Von Stroheim had driven through in the movie *Sunset Boulevard*. He'd walked around the lot, half expecting Marlene Dietrich to appear around a corner.

McCluggage's eyes began to glaze, signaling the end of the Internet demonstration. Wertheimer quickly moved on to his strategic analysis of where the business was going. He believed that the major media brands—shows like *Friends, Seinfeld,* and *60 Minutes,* to name a few—would eventually establish their own independent Web presence and that the Net would embrace (like television) a syndication model. That was in the long term. For the immediate future, major brands would be introduced to Web surfers by the proprietary online services like AOL and MSN, who would battle for the right to pick them up. AOL had relatively recently offered Web access to its users. The first version of the Microsoft Network had launched that August. Compuserve was doing well with the corporate market, and Prodigy was the consumer online service of choice. Eventually, Paramount would also want to go directly to the Web, but for now the proprietary services held the greatest business potential. Those companies were spending a lot of money trying to lure brands to their respective services and were looking for ways to differentiate themselves. Paramount's major brands, like *Star Trek* and *Entertainment Tonight,* looked like attractive properties for the likes of AOL and MSN.

If the pioneers of online entertainment had been the Marx Brothers, Wertheimer would have been Zeppo. In fact, Wertheimer vaguely *resembled* Zeppo, with his good looks and dark brown hair. And both he and Zeppo, quiet and straight looking in public, could be very funny in private. Wertheimer was born and raised in Dallas, Texas. His mother was a successful attorney who had a number of important clients. Born in the same year as Josh Greer, Wertheimer was also a child of the PC revolution. His school acquired one of the first Apple computers in 1977, which he quickly commandeered. He worked after school and saved enough money to buy his own computer a year later.

Wertheimer became a programming whiz, but was not destined for geekhood. He wanted to build businesses, and the PC was simply a tool to that end. In 1983, at the age of fifteen, he started his own company, a regional online service called The Chalk Board. He ran it for two years, then left it in 1985 when he headed off to Duke University to get a joint degree in computer science and business. His first job out of college was working for Steve Jobs at NeXT Computer, where he held positions in sales, marketing, and business development. At NeXT Wertheimer blossomed into the rarest of technology executives—a straight player who returned calls and made sure he delivered everything he had promised. After five years, he moved over to Oracle's content group, exchanging the egomaniacal Steve Jobs for the egomaniacal Larry Ellison. His career up to that point had been a white-knuckle ride through Silicon Valley.

Wertheimer was in fact something of an adrenaline junkie. An *Upside* magazine profile would include pictures of him sky diving and herding horses and mules on horseback in the Nevada desert. He was also a golf fanatic. Before their trip to Scotland, Wertheimer sent his wife to San Diego for an intense weekend of golf lessons. He returned from the Scottish trip with a Saint Andrews golf vest. He had played on five of the best golf courses in the world and owned the best clubs money could buy. Wertheimer was not one to measure life with coffee spoons.

He enjoyed working at Oracle and became fascinated with his clients in the entertainment business. While he now knew technology and entertainment, he was neither a geek nor a ponytail. David Wertheimer was a member of the third tribe, a suit.

Suits were creative in how they married people and resources in deals or opportunities. Ponytails judged their success by audience feedback, and geeks by the efficiency and effectiveness of technology solutions. For suits the key measures were even more tangible: revenue, market capitalization, marketshare. They were burdened with finding a way to bring together the component pieces of the new-media enterprise in such a way as to support the creative and technical processes while worrying about downstream implications of the choices made by the geeks and ponytails. Suits saw control, system, and process as virtues because these were the kinds of things that investors worried about. They wanted to move fast, to get to market, to give people what they wanted—and above all to maintain control. In the parlance of Hollywood, they were the producers: curbing the flights and fancies of the film directors, worrying about schedule overruns and technology costs. Bottom line: suits saw the Net as a tool of business. "The Internet is about one-to-one interaction with the customer," the Walt Disney Company's Jake Winebaum would say. "What does it take to make that individual a Disney customer? Brand identity. The Disney brand draws them back time and time again."

With Richard Lindheim, an executive vice-president in Paramount Pictures' television group, Wertheimer sat down and began to map the broad outlines of Paramount Digital Entertainment's strategy. In the short term, PDE would pursue deals with the proprietary services, which would pay licensing fees for using Paramount's major brands, and also share revenues from transactions associated with those properties. That would establish a presence at least, but not generate much income.

In 1995 the Microsoft Network, which planned to launch that August, was the proprietary online service that everyone feared. Bill Gates had put an MSN icon onto every single copy of Windows '95, which would eventually ship 30 million copies by the end of 1995. AOL, with about 4 million households, was the distribution leader, but many felt that MSN would quickly assume that role. Paramount began discussions with both right away.

Though he had not started at Paramount yet, Wertheimer helped get discussions rolling with the major online services. By the time he came on board, the decision in principle had been made to partner with MSN, and the two companies had a two-page deal memo outlining the terms. The final agreement would take an incredible eight months to negotiate, was the biggest content deal in the industry, and—over the course of the two-year relationship—would become the source of a lot of grumbling at Microsoft.

The business unit Wertheimer was going to lead consisted of staff members cobbled from around the company and what was left of Paramount's technology group up North. With regard to a business plan, he and Lindheim came to the understanding that in the new-media world, things had to be written in sand, not carved in stone. His goal was to come on board, assess the plan more closely, and reshape the strategy.

Wertheimer's preconceptions were shattered when he got a call in mid-September informing him that on his start date, October 2, he would be expected to present his *three-year* operating budget and business plan to John Dolgen, chairman of the Viacom entertainment group. Wertheimer couldn't believe what he was hearing. They weren't expecting the kind of business plan you put together in Silicon Valley—a fairy tale to placate the investment community. Business plans in the valley were commonly regarded as point-in-time guestimates with numbers that were plucked from the ether. He was being asked to *lock in* the head count for what was in effect a start up company in an industry where nobody knew what would be happening three months hence, let alone three years. What's more, some elements in the business plan were already fixed. His head count and budget were in stone after all, and he had a little over two weeks to prepare.

Wertheimer sat at a board-room table with twelve people, including John Dolgen, Kerry McCluggage, and Sherry Lansing, chairman of Paramount Pictures' motion pictures group (McCluggage and Lansing reported to Dolgen). He felt grossly unprepared.

Since being told about the meeting, Wertheimer had worked nights and weekends to pull it all together. Part of the job was justifying budget numbers that presented a string of revenue and profit figures in which he had little confidence. He had told Dick Lindheim they weren't ready, that they'd need more time to rewrite the whole plan.

No time to be had, Lindheim explained. October was when the company made plans for the coming year. Every business unit had to submit a three-year budget. That was the way the company ran. "You have to come in and do the pitch," Lindheim told Wertheimer. "They've already bought off on the business plan, so it won't be a problem." Wertheimer wasn't so confident. He was a suit, definitely in favor of building a profitable entity for the long term. He reminded Lindheim repeatedly that they were building a business, and that would require investment. If they could break even in the next few years, they ought to be happy, but any potential profits should be reinvested in the business. Focusing too much on profit in the short term at the expense of a solid long-term market position was not the best thing for Paramount to do. But Viacom was no Microsoft. Viacom was a much larger company, but Microsoft had $9 billion to dip into—more than the combined assets of the entire venture-capital industry—compared to Viacom, which carried $10 billion in debt as freight. PDE would have to be profitable.

At the big meeting Dolgen sat impassively watching Wertheimer's presentation. Dolgen had slick black hair streaked with gray, opaque eyes, and chain smoked like the "Cancer Man" in the *X-Files*. His piercing stare could shoot straight through your body, as if you were as transparent as tempered glass. He was a numbers guy and Viacom chief Sumner Redstone's main protector of the bottom line. He could pick apart a budget better than anyone Wertheimer had seen since his days with Steve Jobs. Dolgen was as inquisitional regarding one of Wertheimer's $30,000 budget items as he was with one of Sherry Lansing's $30 million movies. Somehow, Wertheimer emerged from the meeting with his skin—and Paramount Digital Entertainment—intact.

He later came to the realization that the numbers in the business plan that he'd kvetched so much about—that showed seemingly imaginary profits over the three-year budget period—were the numbers needed to get upper management to buy off on establishing the company in the first place. If the profits had been more realistic—i.e., small or break-even—PDE wouldn't have gotten off the ground. The corporate decision makers would have said, "Why bother?"

Digital Planet Courts CAA and Intel

A few miles to the east of Fattal-Collins, in Culver City, Josh Greer and the staff of Digital Planet were watching *The Spot*'s success with great excitement and deep depression: happy that someone had actually created original content (pure entertainment) on the Web and generated a buzz about it, depressed because Josh and his team felt like they'd lost a battle in the cyberspace wars. They'd been thinking about creating pure entertainment for the Web, but had never had the wherewithal or time to do it. Someone ahead of them had grabbed the brass ring.

The Spot was not the kind of show that Josh, Thomas Lakeman, or the others would ever want to do themselves. (Lakeman had been working behind the scenes before leaving Universal to join Digital Planet in January.) But having broken new ground, *The Spot* would be successful enough to "put the blood in the water for all the sharks in Hollywood," making it easier for Digital Planet to get their big shot.

Digital Planet had outgrown Josh's two-bedroom apartment in Toluca Lake. In December 1994, Josh had moved the business into their present digs, an old warehouse in Culver City that had just been vacated by Uncle Milton's Ant Farm factory, where they leased space for eighty cents a square foot. All their furniture came from a family friend of Paul Grand's; most of it looked as if it had been looted from a war zone. The building had one semifunctional toilet, no heating, air-conditioning, or hot water. What it did have was plenty of ants. By spring, the company suffered through what seemed to be a plague of them.

Digital Planet had grown rapidly, following the success of *Stargate* by securing contracts to do promotional Web sites for other motion pictures that had a technological or sci-fi edge to them, like *Twelve Monkeys*. For the film *Casper* in early 1995, they recreated the film's haunted mansion. The first "cookies"—software that allowed a Web site to recognize distinct visitors—were coming out at this time, enabling Josh and his team to create a site that would save a visitor's previous visit and offer a different experience every time. The site had full-screen graphics—unusual at the time—and puzzles and games. These were the days when there weren't many Web tools and most of the HTML had to be hand built. The site was incredibly complex. The staff worked such long hours that hardly anyone left the building in the days before the launch.

Josh wanted to get Digital Planet out of the work-for-hire business of building Web sites and into the business of creating and owning content. He initiated discussions with CAA, which was deeply interested in moving into the Interactive space. In the course of researching Digital Planet, CAA agents discovered that a hot writer they'd been pursuing, Scott Sturgeon, had written the *Casper* site for the company. Josh soon got a call from Hasan Miah, the head of CAA's Interactive practice.

Miah and Sandy Climan came down to meet with Josh. CAA could represent the company in the Hollywood community to help them get more clients and better deals. Josh told Miah that what Digital Planet really needed was investors, the equivalent of a venture capitalist. The company had no capital and was constantly plagued by cash-flow problems. At the time CAA had been working with Intel on plans for the development of a multimedia lab at CAA's headquarters in Beverly Hills. Miah introduced them to Digital Planet.

Silicon Valley companies like Intel were anxious to work with entertainment companies in Hollywood—particularly Internet-content companies like Digital Planet. Digital entertainment content fit nicely with Intel's broad corporate strategy. "We need to grow the market for personal computers," said Avram Miller, Intel's vice-president for business development. "We're making huge financial commitments by building factories . . . for products we haven't designed for markets that don't exist."[5] Online entertainment fit that description perfectly. Entertainment had loads of graphics, sound, movement, and complexity—the kind of content that required a lot of processing power. Compared to text and informational content, entertainment was a resource hog. If an audience for online entertainment could be nurtured and grown, it would be good for the chip business. CAA was Intel's Hollywood partner and guide.

Josh began negotiating with Matthew Cowan, a hotshot Intel executive in his twenties who had the demeanor of a Mike Ovitz. Cowan's intensity "scared the shit" out of Josh and his partners. He offered Digital Planet bridge financing if they used the money to build original content for the Web, holding out a larger investment further down the road. Josh took the bridge financing in October, but made it clear that if they retooled the organization to create original content, it would mean stealing resources from the company's Web-development business. If the rest of the investment money wasn't forthcoming by the end of the year, the company would have a serious cash-flow problem. In other words, they'd be screwed.

Digital Planet now had the resources to take a gamble on creating original entertainment content for the Web. Josh formed a small group under Lakeman, who ran creative services, with Daniel DeFabio, Michael Lenahan, Robert Turner, and Robin Gurney. The small team began brainstorming concepts for original online entertainment. In deference to their building's previous occupant, they decided to call the group the "Ant Farm."

Thomas and Josh had a complex and sometimes difficult working relationship. Thomas was quirky and brilliant, while Josh was high strung and often stressed. On several occasions, the two sat in front of the staff, screaming at each other at the top of their lungs. Eventually, Josh would say: "Thomas, let's go talk for a few minutes in my office."

"Yeah. Good idea, Josh."

The staff could still hear faint screaming noises wafting from under Josh's office door. Josh was usually the one offering the olive branch while Thomas was the one with the bag of arrows.

Lakeman understood Web design like few others in the nascent industry. "Design for the online medium is both like and unlike design for any other medium," Lakeman wrote. "It combines the functionality of software interface, the real-time interaction of live TV, the symbolic vocabulary of graphic design and the representational vocabulary of photography."[6]

Unlike many new-media groups, Lakeman and his development team had never produced CD-ROMs—which had its advantages and disadvantages. A disadvantage was that they were approaching the development of interactive entertainment with no clear idea of how to do it. An advantage was that they would be unfettered by the mistakes of the past.

Lakeman did have a distinct vision of the Web. He saw the technology as a malleable medium for a developer. While the CD-ROM was a finished piece of work, the Web could be wiped clean and changed daily based on audience input.

Initially the Ant Farm team spent a lot of time brainstorming what kind of experiences they wanted to create. They explored various genres that might appeal to a Web audience and worked out the conceptual basis for the project. In doing so, they opened themselves to a wide range of influences.

Comics were an important inspiration for the Ant Farm. Lakeman and the others had read and been deeply influenced by Scott McCloud's seminal 1993 book, *Understanding Comics*. McCloud argued against the narrow definition of comics that consigned the medium to the ghetto of the morning newspaper and Marvel Comics. He began his analysis of the medium by looking back at ancient sources like the Egyptian hieroglyphics, the Mayan glyphs, and the Bayeux tapestry—artifacts that, like comics, used space to convey time and the sequence of actions. McCloud's widely praised and surprisingly accessible analysis explored comics' iconography and use of closure, among other elements of the medium.

Though McCloud's book was written before the appearance of Web browsers, the medium he described shared many characteristics with the Web. Like the Internet, comics were a medium that required active participation on the part of the audience because of the limited amount of information (limited bandwidth) the medium could convey. Consider the following action: a character walks out of his house, steps into his car and drives across town to visit his girlfriend. It might take a dozen frames to capture all the nuances of this action sequence. A comic book that laid out a story in this much detail could easily run to two hundred pages. The cartoonist would quickly use up all the book's bandwidth—and the reader's patience.

For the Web, the limitations also stemmed from the narrow bandwidth that plagued the medium in its early years. Loading too many rich graphics on a Web page inevitably exhausted bandwidth and resulted in interminable downloads. The solution to both problems, Lakeman suggested, was the same: "From a design perspective, the best solution to the bandwidth problem is to pack the most information into the smallest container. To accomplish this, the messenger needs a willing partner: the end-user has to provide some of that meaning by him- or herself." The cartoonist/designer needs to provide enough information to enable the reader/user to fill in the gaps. The conceptual term for this gap-filling was *closure*—the leap of intuition that enables one to see more than is actually on the page. "Closure is a dynamic act of cooperation between storyteller and his or her audience, using images more or less as a set of hand props."

In comics, closure came from the actions that readers interpolated between the panels. In Lakeman's example, panel one showed a man pointing a gun. Panel two showed another man lying dead on the ground. The reader interpolates the action of murder and brings closure to the sequence. End-users, Lakeman argued, performed similar acts of closure with Web pages. "Because the Web's protocol divides each site into discrete documents or 'pages'—and because there's a time lag every time the user links to a new page—closure is not simply a choice, but an absolute necessity."

Lakeman's theory about closure was also shaped by Digital Planet's contract to develop a Web site for Terry Gilliam's film *12 Monkeys*. In researching the project, Lakeman discovered that *12 Monkeys* had been inspired by the French movie *La Jette*, a film done in a series of still photos. The film had "closure all over the place," requiring the viewer to connect the dots between the successive still images. Lakeman also learned that Gilliam had earlier in his career done work in photo comics and was obsessed with the art form.

With the *12 Monkeys* Web site, "we created a virtual tour through the world of Terry Gilliam's film," Lakeman remembered. "Within each image are various visual cues that add information as to where the user 'is,' where he or she came from, and where it's possible to go next. The trick was to convey this effect with as few 'in-betweens' as possible—which the user, given the minimum information necessary, is generally happy to supply."

The great power of the Web, Lakeman decided, was that like comics, no single element predominated. Visual and textual information were equally important. The weakness of *The Spot*, in Lakeman's view, was that it was too text-driven. They could do better.

Not surprisingly, the Ant Farm would gravitate toward an animated storytelling format for the Web site they were to develop. The Net was a particularly unforgiving environment for technically challenging content. Lakeman lamented the limitations of the medium, its poor reliability and lack of tactility and clarity compared with other media. "Under current conditions," Lakeman later wrote, "developing good content for the Web is often like trying to print Picasso's *Guernica* on the back of a *Bazooka Joe* wrapper."

Eventually, the Ant Farm generated about fifty concepts. Five pitches were selected out of the pile for closer scrutiny. The five concepts effectively cut up the "Internet pie" into five markets. One idea was a show called "Super Sexy Secret Agents of the '80s," a campy *Charlie's Angels* meets *Spinal Tap* for a young male audience. "Oinsin" (pronounced "O'Sheen") was narrative storytelling aimed at an older audience. Another was an educational program similar to James Burke's popular *Connections* on PBS.

The winner was an idea that came from Michael Lenahan, one of Digital Planet's in-house creative people. Lenahan had an idea for an animated science-fiction story involving the daughter of an American scientist. The idea that would become *Madeleine's Mind* had been chosen mainly for its high-concept appeal. Lakeman and Lenahan began to work out the arc of the story and flesh out the characters. They got inspiration from a variety of sources, like Anime/Manga and various American and British comics. The evolving story line also drew from other cult media, like *X-Files*, *The Prisoner*, and MTV's *Liquid Television*. Young, male geek Web developers gravitated to this kind of cultish, sci-fi content naturally—much like their audience, who also tended to be young, male, and technically adept.

Josh, Thomas, and the Ant Farm team tried to get CAA on board for the show, hoping that Miah's people would be helpful with sponsorship. As they described *Madeleine* to the folks at CAA, Josh could see that they weren't getting it. CAA couldn't figure out how to package and sell the project. If Josh, Tom and the Digital Planet team wanted to produce *Madeleine*, they'd have to do what Scott and his team did: roll up their sleeves, start working, and take a leap of faith.

CAA had gone lukewarm on Josh and Digital Planet, in part because they saw a much bigger opportunity developing elsewhere. Josh had been right about *The Spot* bringing out the sharks in Hollywood. CAA and Intel were in deep discussions with Russ Collins and Sheri Herman regarding the building of a company with Scott's site as the nucleus. At the same time, Scott's show also drew the attention of one of the entertainment industry's most legendary and best-loved players.

Prince of the Mainstream

Brandon Tartikoff had seen it all before. On a December morning in the pseudogentrified district below Market Street in San Francisco known as SOMA—home turf of *Wired* magazine—Tartikoff felt surprisingly underwhelmed.

During the year, the Internet had become the biggest story in the media—bigger than the trial of O. J. Simpson. *The Spot*'s launch and subsequent publicity was only one of innumerable developments in the Internet story. That fall Sun Microsystems' Java was hot software technology that promised to bring multimedia razzle-dazzle to a static World Wide Web. Many in the industry hoped it would dislodge Microsoft from its hegemonic desktop dominance. CNET was pioneering the yoking of the Internet and cable TV, offering cable shows on technology and computers with (in Robert Reid's apt phrasing) a "throw to online" that created powerful synergies.[7]

It was in the wake of CNET in particular that publisher Louis Rossetto and his team at *Wired* magazine contemplated creating a cable show based on their *Netizen* brand, a section of the magazine devoted to political, social, and public policy reporting with a technological slant. Rossetto and his staff had resisted the notion of a TV show for the first three years while building the magazine. Now with *Wired* well established, an online company kicking in, and an election year about to start, it seemed the right time to think about television. Rossetto had invited Brandon Tartikoff to *Wired*'s offices in San Francisco to discuss the concept for a show.

Tartikoff was a logical choice for such a discussion. He had one of the most impressive CVs in Hollywood. In 1980, at the age of thirty-one, he was the first member of the television generation to become the head programmer for a television network. During his tenure at NBC, Tartikoff had midwifed the production of blockbuster shows like *Cosby*, *Cheers*, and *Seinfeld*. Later he left NBC to become the head of Paramount Studios. After a short and disappointing year, he moved over to New World, a production company, as head programmer. As a programmer and producer, Tartikoff was always looking for ideas and stories.

That month *Wired* published two articles that likely caught his eye: "The New Hollywood: Silicon Stars" by Paula Parisi and "The *Toy Story* Story" by Burr Snider. Both stories trumpeted Hollywood's interest in (and anxiety about) the digital revolution. Tartikoff's trip to San Francisco was to get a firsthand glimpse of the new-media phenomenon. He knew very little about the Internet. There was obviously a lot of heat, but was there any fire? Was there a piece of the story he could wrap his mind around and package?

After greetings all around, Rossetto, his lieutenants, and Tartikoff settled into a beat-up light-brown imitation leather couch in Rossetto's office to talk. The *Wired* team began pitching Tartikoff the *Netizen* TV show. Rossetto was fully aware of what Tartikoff could bring to the table. There was something about the presentation of information—regardless of content—that required a little showmanship, a little savvy about what people wanted to see, what fascinated them. The technology industry could learn from the Hollywood and New York media worlds.

Rossetto was surprised by Tartikoff's quiet and attentive demeanor, the polar opposite of what he imagined someone from Hollywood and television to be. Tartikoff's response to Rossetto's *Netizen* pitch was thoughtful and measured. "You're thinking with too much spin on the ball," he said at one point. "I don't know if a mainstream television audience is going to get what you're talking about." *Wired* had a reputation for publishing content that was geared to an audience intimately familiar with the language and references of digital culture. The magazine could be off-putting to the uninitiated. If there was one thing that Tartikoff prided himself on (not a modest man, he was definitely proud of more than one thing), it was the ability to get the greatest number of people "under the tent." Tartikoff was prince of the mainstream.

The meeting broke off, and Rossetto, being a proper host, said, "Come on. I'll show you our operations." He led Tartikoff out of his office and into the bowels of *Wired* magazine. *Wired* occupied a floor in a light-industrial building that for years had been filled with Chinese seamstresses making garments for the local trade. It was one of the first tenants, taking the entire fourth floor and displacing some of the workers. Eventually, most of the building would be overgrown with high-tech and media companies. ("This building is like NAFTA in operation," Rossetto said.) One-half of the floor, 16,000 square feet, had been purpose built for the magazine with an intelligently designed open office plan.

Tartikoff had worked for magazines and dealt with magazine publishers before. What he saw now was a very recognizable operation. He told Rossetto, "It's like *Esquire*." Tartikoff could see a conference room with pages posted on the walls where people were arranging the contents for the next month's issue. "I know what that's all about," he told Rossetto. Sales people tramped about in suits and ties, on their way to sell *Wired* ads to the world. "I know who they are." A graphic artist labored in front of a computer, laying out text and graphics. "I know what this is." This was the vital center of the digital revolution?

"Come on," Rossetto gestured. "Let's go through the air lock. There's another building that's connected. It's this warehouse." Rossetto led Tartikoff out of the seemingly familiar turf of *Wired* through the "air lock"—a hole punched through the dividing wall—to the magazine's online alter ego, *Hotwired*.

What Tartikoff saw now was anything but familiar. Unlike the purpose-built Wired offices, this second half of the floor—another 16,000 square feet—was entirely improvised. No walls, no offices. The space was crammed with people—120 of them. (One manager, Carl Steadman, somehow managed to squeeze a couch into his work area. Eventually the staff would move into a 40,000-square-foot space— three times larger than the one Tartikoff saw.) Huge desktop computers with bright color screens connected by black and pink wiring running along the ceiling were everywhere. Everyone at *Wired* seemed to be in their thirties. Here at the cramped, chaotic operations of *Hotwired*, nobody seemed older than twenty-five. At *Wired*, world beat jazz and classical music wafted from cubicles and offices; here, grunge rock and hard-pounding industrial music reverberated off the cluttered desks. Dogs wandered freely through the spaces between desks as people were either typing frantically and moving blocks of text around on their screens or having impromptu discussions. Whereas the division of labor and hierarchy were clear on the *Wired* side, here there was no sense of hierarchy, no clue as to the division of labor. Like the Internet itself, there seemed to be no center. The physical sensation was that of a huge, pulsating hive.

Tartikoff had no clue what anyone was doing.

* * *

Hotwired's improvisational appearance was typical of new-media operations. "You can't underestimate what it means to be involved in a new industry without any ground rules," Rossetto said. "You just did the Louisiana Purchase and you have no idea what's west of the Mississippi." Rossetto had learned from *Wired*'s various digital enterprises how undefined the whole business could be. There was great excitement and drama in that, but also a lack of security. New media wasn't like other established industries—like the cellular-phone business, for instance. In other industries one could develop a solid business plan. One could envision how the infrastructure would roll out, how the market would likely develop, where the cash flows would come from. One could lead from the plan—and feel like there was solid ground underfoot. That wasn't the case for *Hotwired*, or for any new-media company. No successful business models existed. No one knew what the industry was all about because the Web (to speak of one platform) was still inventing itself and had several transformations to go. For Rossetto, it was more like collecting a guerrilla army to accomplish a big objective. Between the recruiting and the objective there was a whole period of improvisation, refining, shifting course.

The organization—a generous description—tended to blur at the edges. The "army" was young; for many this was a first job out of school. They all had a key and could come and go as they pleased. Many slept at the office, wore pretty much whatever they wanted, and *said* pretty much whatever they wanted. These HTML programmers and engineers seemed all of a type—much like members of a tribe. Sometimes Rossetto wondered if things were too decentralized, if the sense of center was less strong than it ought to be for an organization to function well. This kind of operation could be inefficient. Like many Internet companies, *Hotwired* burned through mounds of money.

After exiting *Hotwired* and returning to the *Wired* offices, Tartikoff had to leave, and the discussion ended. Rossetto and his team temporarily shelved plans for a *Netizen* cable show. (The idea of doing television was derailed by *Wired*'s two disastrous attempts at an initial public offering on Wall Street, which occupied a great deal of management and thought. Eventually, Rossetto would talk to Andy Lack at the World

Economic Forum about doing a *Netizen* show for MSNBC, which Lack was in the process of forming. Four broadcasts of *The Netizen* were produced before the show folded.) Rossetto and Tartikoff would never meet again. Rossetto would later rue the missed opportunity to do a project with the television giant.

Visiting a new-media production shop, Tartikoff once said, was like "being behind the scenes at Disneyland's Pirates of the Caribbean." For Tartikoff, though, the visit was a precursor for the last great adventure in his career. A few months later Rupert Murdoch would acquire New World, a move that would triple the value of Tartikoff's stock options in the company. Tartikoff would exercise those options and leave New World a wealthy man (well . . . wealthier). An independent producer again, Tartikoff would be looking for his next opportunity and he would remember his visit to *Hotwired* and the throbbing energy in that room. He had been born a generation too late to be part of the pioneering days of television and had been too invested in network television to become involved in the early days of cable. He had always wanted to be a player at the creation of a new medium.

Original Concepts

Will we recognize it when we see it?

—Richard Lindheim on the search for an original
entertainment concept on the Web

As 1995 came to an end, Scott Zakarin, Troy Bolotnick and the others marveled at how much their world had changed. Scott and Troy had begun the year struggling to find an idea for a CD-ROM project and making little headway. Now, ten months later, they were cyberstars. *The Spot* was an international sensation, and the team had been written about in nearly every major newspaper and magazine and interviewed on radio and television all over the world.

Scott's show created a new genre—"web episodic entertainment," or, simply, the "webisodic"—and provided a point of reference and self-definition for other pioneers in the online space. Josh Greer was alternately inspired and goaded to break free from the drudgery of Web work for hire and to bet the Ant Farm on his own brand of original content. David Wertheimer was able to use *The Spot* to convince Paramount executives that however feeble the medium might appear, the Web was destined to be a powerful new entertainment medium. Charlie Fink's drive-time musings on *The Spot* would give him the resolve to resign from Virtual World and take him one step closer to AOL Greenhouse. Others would use *The Spot* as a point of departure in their own efforts to develop new forms of online entertainment.

Online interactive entertainment differed from preceding entertainment forms like television and film in several important ways—ways that were discovered or elaborated upon each day at *The Spot*. First, it was an active medium. It required viewers to *do* something, to make choices, navigate, communicate. In fact, the term *viewer* was a misnomer because it implied a passive role that was more appropriate for television or film. (The industry continues to struggle to find the correct terminology to describe the consumers of Web content.)

Related to the active element was the illusion of control. The key task facing the creators of linear entertainment, such as television sit-coms, movies of the week, and feature films, is to get the audience to suspend disbelief—to pretend for thirty minutes or two hours that what is happening on the screen is real. Online-content creators have an additional burden—to create the illusion that the viewer has control over what s/he sees, where s/he goes, and even (as was the case with *The Spot*) the outcome of the story. The key word is *illusion*, because all those choices have been orchestrated by the content creator.

This new form of entertainment was also social in nature. Television and movies were communal media, in the sense that people shared a common media experience in the same physical space—usually with minimal interaction. (Even the communal aspect of television and film is diminishing. Movie theaters have gotten smaller. Most homes have multiple television sets. It is not unusual to find husband, wife, and child watching different programs in far-flung corners of the home.) Web content like *The Spot* provided a context and opportunity for genuine social interaction—not only with fictional characters but with each other.

By 1995 many observers were both decrying and trying to ignore the proliferation of sexually oriented sites on the Web—many of which were homegrown (e.g., Floyd's Polaroids of his nude wife). Few stopped to ask why the medium was so well suited for sexual material and what that meant for other kinds of content. *The Spot* in particular brought out the voyeuristic and exhibitionistic elements of the online medium but in a (usually) nonsexual way. Visitors could read the personal diary postings of the characters and view photos of the goings-on at *The Spot* house. Television also showed the intimate side of people's lives, but what made the Web site voyeuristic was the illusion of control. Visitors to the site actively invaded the private moments of the characters by opening up their diary postings and rummaging through their stuff.

The Spot and similar content sites also offered unparalleled opportunities for exhibitionism—again, in the broader sense of attracting attention to oneself. *The Spot* board was replete with ranters and hell raisers. The interactive aspect of the medium enabled visitors in effect to insert themselves into the story through their e-mail to the characters.

As groundbreaking as *The Spot* was, it did not represent the ultimate evolution of the medium (its creators never claimed it did). The webisodic was an important first step, just as *The Great Train Robbery* (1903) demonstrated an early recognition of the power of film.

The search began for original concepts. Interactivity remained a little-understood phenomenon. Content developers struggled to find new forms that leveraged the power of the Net. Few could describe what those new forms would be. "We'll know it when we see it," they said.

Every day Scott and company were learning more about the power of the medium and breaking new ground. CAA and Intel were coming to court Fattal-Collins, their partner and benefactor. Scott finally had the attention of the Hollywood establishment. As the new year approached, he made the decision to walk away from it all.

1996: Lightspeed Media

Leaving *The Spot*

Hollywood is a place where money gets spent like water, but the amount of money that these big cash-register technology firms like Intel and Microsoft can bring to the process of growing this new industry dwarfs what Hollywood can bring. . . . It's MSNBC, not NBCMS.

—Russell Collins, American Cybercast (1996)

The Spot had fulfilled the main goal of any media property: aggregating an audience. Now it was time to think about what to do with it. Scott wanted to develop the show into a television series. Russ Collins believed in the concept and the show, but it had placed Fattal-Collins in a precarious position financially. Despite its success as a Web phenomenon, the show was costing Fattal-Collins an enormous amount of money—by some accounts almost half a million dollars by the end of 1995—and Collins no longer owned the agency (it had been acquired by Grey Advertising). *The Spot* couldn't operate indefinitely without a business model, Collins felt. The show needed investors, and investors wanted to see a real business with genuine infrastructure: the ability to make deals (i.e., business affairs), sales people, a development and acquisition group. To Collins's thinking, it didn't make sense to put all that infrastructure in place for just one show.

An Internet company needed money to get it through the first uncertain years as it grew. The Internet was too immature as a medium to expect to generate enough revenue from advertising, so the money would have to come from big companies and investors like Intel, who would soon start seeding Internet-content companies with investment cash. The dilemma was that with the exception of search engines like Yahoo, the Internet's architecture did not encourage the concentration of traffic and transactions. Unlike television and radio, which had limited spectrum (and consumer choice), cyberspace was endless. Consumers had thousands—potentially millions—of sites to choose from. As long as the Net remained an endless plain without landmarks, big companies wouldn't know where to put their investment or advertising dollars, and might decide to stay out of the medium altogether. Collins wanted to build a company that could grow an audience. He wanted to erect a monument that would stand out on the darkling cyberplain, one with big, blazing neon call letters. *The Spot* was the cornerstone of that strategy.

Collins planned to build a major online entertainment network. Sheri Herman and another Fattal-Collins associate named Erika Verfaillie cranked through several revisions of a business plan. Herman worked with Collins and Buzz Kaplan to line up investors for the new start-up. With initial backing from Intel and CAA—the same folks who were investing in Digital Planet—American Cybercast (which would later adopt the call letters AMCY) launched in January, 1996. Based in the offices of Fattal-Collins, American Cybercast would eventually take office space one floor below in the North Marina tower. Russ Collins became the chairman of the new company, with Sheri Herman taking the position of president and Buzz Kaplan signing on as vice-chairman. American Cybercast would launch with one hit show already in its stable. Collins and Herman envisioned launching as many as a dozen more shows by the year 2000.

"The idea of this company [American Cybercast] is to be the ABC of the Internet," Collins told a reporter. "No one knows how to do Web shows but us."[8] Like most start-ups, things got very hectic very quickly. In one day Sheri Herman had a presentation to give to Andy Grove, chairman of Intel, who was roaming the building meeting various people. She also had a board meeting to prepare for, further fine tuning of the business plan, and a presentation to the president of Gallo Wines.

The first company meeting was held that January in the large conference room at Fattal-Collins. About a dozen people sat around the table, including Russ, Sheri, Buzz, Kay Dangaard, Gretchen McFarland (just hired as senior vice-president of marketing), Jeff Gouda, and Dennis Dortch. Scott Nourse and Eric Bernard, who were developing a new sci-fi show called *EON-4*, were also at the meeting. (Scott Zakarin, Troy Bolotnick, Rich Tachenberg, and Laurie Plaskin were in the midst of negotiating their exit from the company and did not attend the meeting.)

Small bottles of champagne with American Cybercast labels were passed around, and the group toasted each other, excited by the idea that the enterprise they were launching had a good chance of becoming an entertainment powerhouse: the first major online entertainment company. After business was concluded everyone repaired to the Ritz-Carlton for drinks. Herman told the group that the company would likely double in size by the time they held their second meeting. She was wrong. American Cybercast would triple in size by the next all-hands meeting.

The company's portal to the Hollywood community was its investment partner CAA, who furnished the new entertainment company with writing, music, and acting talent. Talent agencies like CAA were prohibited from taking ownership of film or television studios. One of the attractions that companies like American Cybercast and Digital Planet held for CAA was that a loophole in the regulatory law allowed talent agencies to have an equity stake in the production of online content.

Meanwhile, Zakarin and company were feeling the effects of the deal. The tag line on *The Spot* was that "no box is big enough to contain our imaginations." Up to that point they had produced the show with little interference. Once American Cybercast began to take form, the show became nested in a whole new corporate infrastructure, captive to the new company's plans and inevitably shaped by them. Scott clashed with Sheri Herman over the production of the show and the direction of the company. He had worked with Herman before and told Collins that he would become involved with American Cybercast only if Herman was not part of the effort. For his part, Collins felt he needed Herman's talents to help raise money in the investment community, and brought her on board anyway.

Scott saw American Cybercast as an attempt to put him and his team into a box, an effort they immediately resisted. He felt creative controls were being imposed on *The Spot* while shows more in line with the new company's vision were being developed. American Cybercast began to act, in Scott's view, like an advertising agency—slavishly kowtowing to the wishes of its clients and investors. The pressure to make the show more low-brow was getting to him.

The conflict between Scott and American Cybercast management was fierce, and some wondered if one or the other would pull the plug on *The Spot*. Scott threatened to walk out on the show several times. He stayed and got his revenge by incorporating what was happening at Fattal-Collins in allegorical terms into the show. The story line began to take a bizarre twist that January. Professor Alex Dooley (Scott played Dooley in the photos that accompanied the text)—the son of the late Bobby Dooley Jr., the original owner of *The Spot* house—seized control of the online *Spot* and imposed his own guidelines on *The Spot*mates: the rule about not reading each other's postings was rescinded in order to avoid "sensationalizing" the diary entries. Dooley attempted to remove Spotnik from the home page. Then there was the matter of getting approvals for postings. *Spot* house occupants now had to have their postings okayed. One new *Spot*mate, Tomeiko, was barred from posting at all.

Predictably, the new rules grated on the "fictional" *Spot*mates. "What a wonderful relief not to have to get across my own distinct point of view" Carrie wrote in one sarcastic entry. No one was more bitter than Tara, the conscience of the house and the online project. "Hostile takeover in progress," she wrote early in the crisis, "assimilation nearly complete." Tara defiantly resisted the limits Dooley imposed on the group's artistic freedom:

> Alex is going to tamper with whatever I put down on this page, so why not distort, contort, exorcise and play along within this flaming hoop of jargon[?] . . . Have I not been good to you? It is I who have brought you this Spot, I who have offered a forum for your voice. And now you're selling out to the highest bidder? I cannot feign understanding nor compassion in such a situation. I only hope to be the Piper who might lead you to less petulant pastures.

Audrey and Wulf (also new characters in the expanding household) schemed to thwart the takeover. Audrey was a sensual brunette Brit who had caught the good professor's eye. She lured Dooley, a married man, into a compromising position, whilst Wulf, a maverick film-school student (written and played by Rich Tackenberg), took pictures through the window. These racy and incriminating pictures, of course, got posted to *The Spot* for the whole world (and presumably Mrs. Dooley) to see.

End of takeover.

By incorporating the conflicts he and his partners were having with American Cybercast into the story line of *The Spot*, Scott accomplished several tangible objectives. First, he was able to vent his anger and frustration. Second, Scott used the takeover to mobilize his fan audience, some of whom knew about the problems behind the scenes. The fans gave Scott leverage in his dealings with AMCY management. Finally, the takeover story line was entertaining. Even as Scott struggled for creative control of his show, he found a way to bump up the site's hits and enhance the property.

A triumphant Tara later wrote that:

> trying to control *The Spot*mates is like trying to put his [Dooley's] thumb over mercury. He might squash us a little, but if he presses too hard, we're going to spread. Like the silver surfer cop in T2, we will again become whole and reform [sic] together. Even if we part ways, we will always have the properties necessary to band together again.

Nothing Is Going to Happen
in Vienna, Virginia

By the winter of 1996, Charlie Fink had resigned from Virtual World Entertainment and was busy looking for his next gig. Fink took on consulting work to keep the wolf from the door. He gave serious consideration to returning to the animation business, where he had gotten his start. After four years in the wilds of new media, working for an animation company had a certain appeal; the money would be good and he could be a Hollywood player again. Then he got a call from Danny Krifcher, who headed AOL's Greenhouse Networks.

The Greenhouse was Ted Leonsis's idea. Back in 1994 Leonsis believed that all new media would be driven by entrepreneurs. He assigned Danny Krifcher to form an in-house venture-capital operation—with a lower case *vc* (AOL didn't have the resources that a traditional venture-capital company could command). The best way to find entrepreneurs was to put out the word that "we've got money," step aside, and watch the pitches and proposals pile up. The Greenhouse didn't buy shows—as MSN would later do. It bought interests in production companies. If there was no company, Krifcher prodded the entrepreneur to set one up.

The Greenhouse developed some successful properties, which was remarkable considering that the unit was filled with MBAs who had little or no media experience. By April 1995, Greenhouse staff had waded through ten thousand inquiries and seventeen hundred proposals before selecting six entrepreneurial teams to create content—*The Motley Fool* and *The Hecklers* among them. *The Motley Fool* was a sassy and highly successful site the Gardner brothers created for dispensing financial advice and chat in an engaging and amusing format. *The Hecklers* consisted of two "wiseguys from Tuscaloosa" who produced a comedy site. The site's top-ten lists were audience generated and ran to subjects like "least favorite Snapple flavors," or "sites that sound like porno and aren't." People at the Greenhouse were big believers in user-generated humor. The entire staff of the Harvard Lampoon couldn't crank out a Letterman-style top-ten list as funny as what two thousand AOL members—suitably filtered—could.

Miguel Monteverde was Danny Krifcher's first Greenhouse hire in 1994. One night while suffering through one of his periodic bouts with insomnia, Monteverde got up at 2:00 A.M. and wrote a one-page concept paper for a matchmaking site called Love@AOL. Later, Bill Schreiner, a seasoned producer of film and TV, took Monteverde's page, redesigned it, and developed it into a hit.

Other Greenhouse projects were less successful, such as *Lost In America*. The idea was for a bunch of young people to hop in a van and drive around the country, posting messages and pictures along the way. AOL members could vote on where they wanted the latter-day Merry Pranksters to go next. After a few weeks, the show grew boring. Monteverde had to invent ways to liven up the show, like planting drugs in the van and tipping off the cops (an impish impulse he didn't act on).

When Monteverde discovered *The Spot* in the summer of 1995 he tried to contact the creators of the webisodic, but had a difficult time reaching them. Someone at AOL managed to contact a CAA agent who represented Fattal-Collins. Word came back that Fattal-Collins had already created a start-up company around the show and had lined up $6 million from investors. The Greenhouse backed off. While there was no interest in acquiring American Cybercast, they did keep an eye on *The Spot* team. The first direct contact with *The Spot* team came when Miguel met Laurie Plaksin at a trade show, gave her his card, and encouraged her and Scott to call him.

Charlie Fink had had dealings with Greenhouse executives during his Virtual World days and had impressed several staff members as someone who could do real Hollywood deals and bring a true entertainment sensibility to the company. He was on his way to a meeting at Sony Studios when he got a call on his cell phone from Danny Krifcher, who was home with a bout of the flu. People had been telling Krifcher that Charlie was someone he ought to get to know. The two arranged to meet at an AOL partners' conference in Phoenix that December. Fink later flew out to AOL's headquarters in Vienna, Virginia.

The East Coast was mired in record blizzards that winter, and Vienna gave Fink a healthy dose of culture shock. He was an easterner by birth but had thoroughly acculturated to L.A. Charlie was now someone you'd expect to find on the patio of the Shutters Hotel in Santa Monica, kibitzing with independent producers and drinking double decaf espressos. Dressed in a Boston Harbor raincoat with a zip-in liner, he looked a little forlorn in the snowy fields of Virginia. Fink told Krifcher that he couldn't believe "anything is going to be happening in Vienna, Virginia." Privately, Fink didn't like the "amateur hour" quality of Greenhouse's approach to finding content developers.

"What if I put you creatively in charge of Greenhouse's major original content initiatives," Krifcher asked, "and backed it with unlimited funds?"

Hmmm. Maybe that would do it.

The thing that intrigued Fink about AOL was its energy and sense of momentum. People were literally running down the halls to keep up with the pace of activity. He studied the content on the Web and concluded that "the bar is really low. It's a really blank canvas." Krifcher assured him that the Greenhouse would move away from operating like a shoestring venture-capital company and would become a real studio. That was all Charlie needed to hear. He flew back to L.A. to discuss the move with his wife, Jane.

"Honey, I know very little about this online thing we're moving our family across the country for," she said. Charlie immediately fired up the PC, got online and started surfing the Web. The two sat staring at the screen, waiting for *The Motley Fool* to load. They waited some more. Then more. "So where is it?!," Jane muttered, hands raised. The page still hadn't finished loading when she turned to her chagrined husband. "This is like a big magazine with all the pages stuck together. Do you think people are going to want to do this all the time?"

Summit at Jerry's Deli

Greenhouse executives began to focus their efforts on *The Spot* team. Scott Zakarin and his crew had buzz. In January 1996, Scott and Troy Bolotnick had flown out to the Consumer Electronics Show (CES) in Las Vegas to do some guerrilla marketing in anticipation of their departure from Fattal-Collins. Miguel Monteverde arranged for Scott and the others to sit in the AOL booth signing autographs. As it happened, Danny Krifcher was also at CES. Scott, Troy, Danny, and Miguel met for an hour-long get-acquainted meeting in an empty conference room at the hotel. Afterward, Danny decided to dispatch a Greenhouse team to L.A.

The meeting was orchestrated by Steve Stanford, Scott and Troy's ICM agent. The Greenhouse execs picked up Scott, Troy, Rich, and Laurie at Fattal-Collins and proceeded to Jerry's Deli in Marina Del Rey, where they were joined by Stanford. Jerry's Deli is a big, noisy delicatessen that—like the Net—has a 24 X 7 schedule (i.e., it never closes). Charlie Fink, still living in Los Angeles, was also at the lunch. It was his first day on the job.

The group gathered around a large table in the crowded deli. Scott had his usual Reuben sandwich and Jerry's famous matzo-ball soup. He introduced the rest of *The Spot* team to Charlie and the Greenhouse executives, then—in an example of Zakarin *schadenfreude*—turned to Rich: "This is Rich Tackenberg. Rich is funny. Rich, *say something funny.*" Tackenberg froze and seemed to shrink in his chair. He muttered something unfunny, but it was lost among the general banter at the table.

Everyone had to speak up to be heard over the chatter from other diners, the clacking of dishes and silverware, and the general din that wafted through the red-wallpapered interior. Discussions centered around various ways that Scott and his group could work with the Greenhouse. The possible arrangements included a work-for-hire project, a coproduction, or capital investment in *The Spot* team itself. The upshot seemed to be, "why don't you work with us?" At that time, *The Spot* team had been approached by NBC about the possibility of developing a television series or Web properties for the network. Charlie and the others were acutely aware of NBC's interest in Scott and company. NBC had recently yanked its own site on AOL, a move that didn't sit well in Vienna. The impression was that the Greenhouse executives would have loved to stiff NBC by snatching *The Spot* team away from them.

Fink, in particular, made an indelible impression on the four partners. Everyone commented on how much he and Scott looked alike. If you subtracted five inches of height and added twenty pounds of girth,

Scott could be Charlie's twin. Charlie shook Laurie's hand, told her what a fan he was of *The Spot*, and asked her for her autograph—a small and kind touch that didn't escape Scott's attention.

Charlie was a suit—but one who got his hands dirty in the creative side of production. He smiled a lot. His facial features danced. His head bobbed and weaved. He made wisecracks and exchanged witticisms. Charlie was fun. Charlie was blustery. And Scott liked him instantly. How shrewd of AOL, he thought, to hire someone with a Hollywood sensibility, a member of the tribe, so to speak. Halfway through the meeting Scott was trying to talk him into shaving his sparsely covered head, the first of many attempts.

Stanford led off the meeting, then turned things over to Scott and Troy, who proceeded to pitch nine or ten different ideas. One pitch involved a mystery show called *Mr. E.com*. Another was an idea that would later evolve into their next webisodic, *GrapeJam*. Charlie and his team asked a lot of tough questions regarding the latter. What would they do if they got six thousand fan e-mails a day instead of a hundred? How do you do an improv with streaming media? *The Spot* team hadn't considered some of these questions before, and made up their answers as they went along. The more tough questions the Greenhouse execs asked, the more Scott and company seemed to gain confidence in the feasibility of *GrapeJam*. Later the team members discussed the possibility of producing the show themselves if AOL passed. *This is it. This makes sense. We can do this.* Later, Charlie, who well knew how much it could cost to produce a webisodic, would express astonishment on hearing that Scott and the others would attempt to produce *GrapeJam* on their own.

The conversation came around to money. Scott offered a number. Charlie, Miguel, and the others exchanged glances. "Would you mind if we walk away for a second?" Charlie asked. The Greenhouse team got up and wandered off to the reception area for five to ten minutes, kibitzing en masse as waitresses sailed right and left with plates of lox and pastrami. They returned without making a firm commitment but left the door wide open. A positive impression had been made. When a project came along that seemed like a good fit, Scott and Troy would be at the top of Charlie's Rolodex.

The Spot team were impressed with Charlie and company because they played a straight hand with them. No bullshit. *These were genuinely nice people*, Zakarin thought. *When are we going to find out there's something wrong with them?*

NBC Deal

Television executives who have grown up in the analogue medium [like television] don't see the Web as a threat yet. They don't understand it and haven't been paying much attention to it. It's not significant to them—like any new medium.

—Richard Lindheim

Scott Zakarin and his partners left American Cybercast to form Lightspeed Media a few weeks after the Jerry's Deli summit. A deal was reached where the team received $200,000 for relinquishing *The Spot* rights. After all the discord and in-fighting with American Cybercast, Scott had finally cut loose from *The Spot*. A condition of the deal was that he stay on as a consultant to the show. American Cybercast executives were concerned that fans might abandon the show if it became known he had left.

Scott felt torn. On the one hand he wanted to get his new company off the ground, but he also felt that his reputation and fate were inextricably linked to *The Spot*. He wanted the show to continue, to remain popular and to be good, even if he had no ownership stake in it. But once Scott and his partners launched a home page for their new company, he received a letter from American Cybercast notifying him that his services were no longer required. (Since it had been a pay-or-play deal, he got to pocket the $90,000 consulting fee.) His name on the masthead as the show's creator was now his only link to the project. Before leaving, Scott and the others had to figure out what to do about Tara. Laurie's leaving made it impossible for the character to continue, so they decided to have Tara killed off by Professor Samuels (the son of Bobby Dooley Jr., the original owner of the house), since it would have been out of character for her to leave any other way. The team extracted a measure of revenge when Samuels himself was later found dead, wearing a dress and clown makeup.

Despite the differences and tensions that ended their business relationship, Zakarin and Collins maintained a grudging respect for each other. Scott would tell people that Russ had been "the bravest man in the world" for seeing an opportunity in an unknown team's idea and backing it. Collins would tell people that Scott's idea for creating episodic entertainment on the Web had been a "flash of genius."

American Cybercast executives knew that Troy would remain loyal to Scott, so they offered the now-available producer position to Rich. He listened to the proposal to see what AMCY had in mind for *The Spot*, though he was never serious about taking the position, feeling that whoever ran the site would have limited creative freedom in shaping the show.

Scott and his team walked away from *The Spot* with considerable fame and notoriety in the Web and Hollywood communities. They were free to pursue television work, to develop new Web shows, and to self-fund their activities by doing Web-development work for others. Now was the time to cash in on the fame they'd garnered.

The Spot was a great calling card. ICM agent Steve Stanford had begun talking with NBC back in November. Network executives were interested in a deal to develop a television series based on *The Spot*, plus Web sites for NBC.com and MSNBC. Scott quickly signaled his interest, but when he approached Collins about the opportunity, it quickly became apparent that American Cybercast would not make the rights to the webisodic available. Scott had to report back to NBC executives that he couldn't deliver a *Spot* television show. NBC countered by offering to pay Scott and Troy for developing a "blind script" for a prime-time television series.

By January the elements of a deal with NBC began to come together. NBC sent over a bottle of Dom Perignon and a congratulatory note. Then the deal leaked to the trade magazines before it had been finalized. Neither Scott nor NBC executives were pleased about the story that appeared in *Variety* with the headline: NBC LOOKS TO WEB, SIGNS "SPOT" TEAM.

Despite the buzz, Hollywood wasn't ready to embrace the pair just yet. Some in the business were skeptical that a group of Web developers could make the transition to television. The Web was seen by many insiders as a niche audience of technology-loving geeks who little resembled the great mainstream. How could a team like Zakarin and Bolotnick, whose only real credit was writing for the wacky Web, "port to the real world of hour-long dramas?" (as one industry wag put it).

Things moved slowly over the next three months at NBC business affairs—at least it seemed so to Scott and Troy. "They didn't have the infrastructure to deal with what we were going to create," Troy said. Three months in the television world was nothing; the Web was another matter. Things were moving so rapidly on the Internet that after three months the terms of the deal no longer made any sense, production-wise or financially. NBC was demanding too much exclusivity—again, the issue of creative freedom—for too little money for the Web work. The deal fell apart. Shortly after, Scott and Troy dumped ICM.

Though the NBC deal went south, there was plenty of work-for-hire Web business. Activision, the computer-game company, came after the pair to create "Web stuff" for them. *Playboy* had work for them as well, as did several other companies. Scott and Troy never had to look for Web work—the work came to them.

With all that work for hire queued up, Scott, Troy, Rich, and Laurie were in a perfect position to make a go at the Web-design business. The sensible thing would have been to make a lot of money developing corporate and entertainment sites for others. But they had unfinished business from *The Spot*; their hearts were set on producing a webisodic, even though the economics made little sense. Without a benefactor like Fattal-Collins, or a group of investors such as that gathering around American Cybercast, they had to split their time between building Web sites for others and producing their own show. They hoped that a combination of innovative online advertising and attempts at e-commerce could fund the production. But they faced great uncertainty regarding the viability of these business models, and producing webisodics was akin to shoveling money into a hole, dousing it with lighter fluid, and striking a match. Production costs could easily run to $50,000 per month or more. But Scott and company weren't in a mood to play it safe. Everyone wanted to make another show. They'd worry about business models, investors, and finding extra work when they were farther downstream. For now, the good news was that they'd be beholden to no one. The bad news was that there was no safety net.

The four met regularly at Scott's place in Santa Monica to develop ideas for a show. *GrapeJam* owed its existence to a number of disparate ideas coming together. Rich offered the idea of a reunion of college friends à la *The Big Chill*—or *Webchill*. Scott's wife, Debra—a writer of children's books—talked about a friendly neighborhood bar on the

Upper West side in New York called The Grapes where she used to meet friends. Scott thought "The Grapes" was an evocative name, and he liked "Webchill" as a backstory. But they needed more of a plot to hang the show on.

Again Scott demonstrated his intuitive feel for the interactive medium in the idea he brought to the next meeting. One of the scripts in his fabled drawer was a screenplay about improvisational artists. Improv made a lot of sense in an interactive medium, in that it was based on the model of "accept and build"—accepting an idea or challenge from an audience and building a comedy skit around that idea in real time. Improv meant live events, a whole new level of interactivity—and the danger of failing in a spectacular way.

Madeleine Launches

The afternoon of April 19, 1996, Josh Greer felt less frantic than usual. He checked his watch less frequently and seemed more at peace with himself. It may have been because *Madeleine's Mind* was at last ready for its press launch. The six months it took to develop and produce the project had been grueling and stressful. Among other things, Josh had fired the CAA agent representing Digital Planet's interests, which created a schizophrenic situation, since CAA continued to be an investor in the company.

A writer for *Wideguide* summed up the plot of *Madeleine's Mind* this way: "You are Madeleine Leonard, the only child of a widowed scientist who's murdered on the eve of making his life's work public. You are currently being held against your will by an evil band of renegade scientists who seek access to your father's years of groundbreaking psychological research. Your problem, his research is being stored in a secure remote location that only YOU can access. A Swiss bank account? No. A safe-deposit box? No. This location is YOUR MIND. Your mission . . . is to escape your captors with no currently identifiable sources of help, gain control of the scientific secrets that your father has hidden away in the subconscious of your mind, and harness these secrets for the betterment of mankind before the renegade scientists catch up with you."[9]

Madeleine's Mind was one of the most ambitious efforts to appear in the growing arena of webisodic entertainment. It was an animated story that incorporated interactive features as complex as any found on a CD-ROM. That meant that the technical requirements for most users were daunting, including plug-ins like Shockwave to make the animation work. As a consequence, the downloads were excruciatingly long—if it didn't crash a user's system altogether. A reviewer at *Web.com* wrote: "Waiting for the scenes to load can feel like waiting for the plot to advance on General Hospital."

Like Scott, Josh had an ulterior motive behind the production of *Madeleine's Mind*. He too wanted to grab the attention of the Hollywood entertainment community. Digital Planet was mainly known—if it was known at all—as a Web development house that created promotional Web sites for motion pictures. Launching *Madeleine's Mind* was a way of becoming branded as a creator of original content. Josh was careful to say that he and his associates were developing interactive, network-based entertainment. He wanted to avoid being pigeonholed as a developer of Web content, since he was certain that in the years to come the Web would evolve into a new kind of beast—a multiplatform network with broadband connections capable of delivering quality video.

The press surrounding the launch of *Madeleine* had been good—including articles in the *Wall Street Journal* and *USA Today*, and a thirty-minute mini PBS documentary—though nowhere near as extensive as that of *The Spot*. *Madeleine* also got relatively good reviews in the trades and a rave notice from Web Magazine:

> The folks at Digital Planet have taken [the] 'leap of faith' necessary to promote the use of the World Wide Web beyond its 'information Database' paradigm. . . . In contrast to television, the viewer on the World Wide Web isn't relegated to a passive role of experiencing story lines that were originally envisioned by the creators. But [sic] instead provides the capacity for the viewer to now proactively engage in the storytelling process as it evolves, and determine a character's thoughts and resultant course of action within the story's framework. . . . The pent-up multimedia demand that has been prophesized to be forthcoming for so long, has truly started to become reality as an autonomous vehicle for content delivery.

For all that, *Madeleine* was still a niche product, a serial designed by techies for techies. It had all the elements to appeal to that demographic—the latest bells and whistles, a sci-fi theme, and, as Thomas Lakeman put it, a "babe in distress." The show demanded a high level of involvement, not just in terms of the interactivity, but also in the complexity of the story line. (One criticism was that *Madeleine* had the structure—branching in this case—and look of a CD-ROM title placed on the Internet.) Lakeman and his team went to great lengths to give *Madeleine* an *X-Files*–type sensibility. Unfortunately, many who visited the site found that *Madeleine*'s pages took a long time to download, or that their computers simply didn't meet the rigorous technical specifications necessary to run the show. Others were put off by the hassle of downloading and installing the Shockwave plug-in and went surfing elsewhere.

Josh also faced the same problem that plagued Scott with *The Spot*. How do you make money from a webisodic? The business model for online entertainment remained elusive. Josh had deficit financed the first three-month volume of *Madeleine's Mind*—to the tune of $230,000.

With that kind of debt staring at him, Josh faced a tough decision: give up trying to do episode two of *Madeleine* and go back to doing corporate Web sites full time, or begin development of the second volume and hope they could find someone to sponsor the thing before the company cratered. The alternatives were equally gut-wrenching. The first choice meant abandoning what they loved and all their dreams. The second choice was akin to leaping off a bridge and not knowing if you will land in water or splatter on concrete.

The Duplex

Business was good enough for Scott and his team to consider looking for office space. Everyone loved the idea of relocating the business in a house; then they talked themselves out of it. The team scouted office space, which proved to be expensive. Then Laurie saw an ad for a residential duplex on Madison Avenue in Culver City. The nondescript 1960s-style house was a far cry from the (imaginary) Victorian *Spot* house, but the rent was cheap, the landlord and neighbors were amenable, and the place suited their style—all four had been raised in middle-class suburban neighborhoods, after all. The Sony lot was right up the street to the north. Baldwin Hills to the south, sprouting old wooden oil derricks, was the scene of action in *The Big Sleep*, starring Humphrey Bogart and Lauren Bacall. Being juxtaposed between Hollywood totems was propitious.

Activity at the house centered around the kitchen. When the team got tired of fast food, Rich would cook up pasta. For the first month or so there was no kitchen furniture and everyone had to eat sitting on the kitchen counters. The house lacked air-conditioning as well. As spring turned into summer and the staff grew from the original four to sixteen, the place took on what Scott called a "smell-the-sweat" (or "smell-the-bytes") ambiance. Finally, one day everyone threw up their hands, piled into cars, and went out to buy air conditioners. As the weather turned warmer, the elements of the show came together.

GrapeJam was the story of a group of college friends who had been part of an improv group at Binghamton University called The Grapes. Five years after graduation, the dispersed band, splintered by interpersonal conflicts, various careers, and geography, would attempt to reunite on the Web. There was Tim "Pascal" Freed, who made a fortune in Silicon Valley. Joanne Sheldon and Erik Paxon came out to Hollywood to make careers as writers and performers. The other characters varied from Smitty, the complacent seventh-grade social-studies teacher, to Robbie Babylon, a chain-smoking "tough-and-tumble kind of chick" who did occasional work as a make-up artist for funeral homes. Like *The Spot*, *GrapeJam* also had its mystery figure, Rocco Denopoly, who joined the Peace Corp and promptly disappeared. This time, they explicitly referred to the show as a sitcom to avoid the "soap opera" label—they had, in fact, considered naming the show *Sit.com*.

GrapeJam for Scott would be a major career gamble. "I'm risking everything," he would say, "for something that doesn't have a business model, when I could be taking the little success that I've already achieved and parlay it into something I've always wanted—which is a film career." He had decided to produce another webisodic because he had not been able to take *The Spot* all the way to television, to see his vision straight through to the end. Scott had never wanted to be just a producer of cyberspace shows.

He was now in the same straits as Josh. The six-figure sum he'd gotten for *The Spot* rights gave the team some breathing room, and the influx of Web-development work ensured a steady stream of revenue. They also assumed that they could cover most or all of their production costs through advertising. But they still needed to line up investors or other sources of revenue to make a go of it. The financial uncertainties were tremendous. Scott was never one to worry about his financial situation. The money would come later, he'd tell his supportive wife. He was comfortable with the financial risks, but he wanted to make sure that his partners felt the same way.

One day in June he gathered the three on the lawn in front of the house. "Look, I'm not making this decision on my own," he began. "This has to be our decision. If we go forward with *GrapeJam* now, it is the biggest risk we will ever take. We will probably have to cut our salaries one or more times. We will be giving up our nights and weekends." (Nobody bothered to stop Scott at this point to observe that the four were already doing that.) "We either believe we can make a profitable business out of *GrapeJam* and turn it into a success—into a TV show and books and all that stuff—or we should continue getting work-for-hire clients and look for somebody to cosupport it."

Scott finished his lawn speech. Nobody wanted to pull out—again a tribute to his ability to inspire his friends to follow him on quixotic adventures.

The four got up and went back to work.

Meanwhile, Scott and company kept the dialogue going with the

Greenhouse. They thought Charlie might come through with some other project, or even buy Lightspeed at some point.

Then Microsoft emerged on the radar as another possible buyer of webisodics. MSN was in the process of reengineering itself for an October relaunch. Scott and Troy had flown up to Redmond, Washington, to pitch *GrapeJam* to MSN's producers in the summer of 1996. MSN's executive producer, Bob Bejan, was supposed to be at the meeting but, much to Scott and Troy's disappointment, ended up not attending. The MSN producers and executives took the pitch and expressed interest but didn't follow up.

Bejan in fact had little interest in the Lightspeed team. *The Spot* buzz had died down. Just the same, the snub stung Scott. He couldn't believe that Bejan wouldn't want to talk to or at least hear out one of the genuine pioneers of online entertainment.

Just as AOL had sought out and hired Charlie Fink, a Hollywood insider, to bring an entertainment sensibility and skill base to its content-development efforts, Microsoft had also reached deep into the same milieu to hire Bob Bejan to lead MSN's new content initiatives. He was almost exactly Charlie's age and had also been an executive at Virtual World, leaving the company just before Fink got there. Bob Bejan fired up every competitive cell in Charlie Fink's body.

MSN

When the Microsoft Network first launched on August 24, 1995, many feared that Bill Gates would leverage his overwhelming monopoly on the world's desktop operating systems to blitzkrieg the online industry. Each of the millions of copies of Windows '95 being shipped that summer and fall had an MSN icon that would enable PC owners with modems to easily register on the new network in a matter of seconds. The *New York Times* predicted that MSN could have at least 9 million temporary members by year's end. MSN was a proprietary service and as such reflected both Bill Gates's disdain for the open world of the Internet and his goal of creating an alternative online universe controlled by Microsoft.

But Gates had badly misjudged the lure of the Web. MSN's membership did not grow at the inflated rates that many had feared. By late November, MSN had registered 525,000 subscribers—hardly the several million the pundits had predicted. In their hastily written book, *Barbarians Led by Bill Gates*, Jennifer Edstrom and Marlin Eller wrote that "after two and a half years of development, MSN lacked content and any clear-cut advantage to show why providers should rent space from MSN rather then set up their own storefronts on the Internet's World Wide Web."[10]

By December, Bill Gates and Microsoft would announce a fundamental change in the company's stance toward the Internet, in effect discrediting their past anti-Web strategy. The subsequent corporate about-face involved an embracing of the Net's open standards. The Microsoft Network would still have a "firewall," i.e., require a membership fee to gain access to its sites, but when it relaunched later in 1996 it would use nonproprietary HTML. Along with the turn-around in strategy came a housecleaning at MSN and a new regime.

MSN's main competition was America Online, and the company needed a plan that would allow it to catch up to AOL quickly. The heart of that strategy was to reengineer the Microsoft Network into a platform for interactive entertainment that would be so cutting edge and fresh that it would do more than just differentiate the service—it would bury AOL and its often less-than-compelling content offerings. That was a tall order for what was, one had to remember, a software company. Software engineers weren't the kind of people who spent much time thinking about mass media.

MSN needed an executive producer with an extraordinary mix of qualifications. He or she would have to come from the media world, but also be comfortable with the latest technology. Web development experience was a given, but the candidate would also have to be an *agent provocateur*, a human virus capable of importing into the company what was best about Hollywood's production methodologies without contaminating Microsoft with the industry's excesses and inefficiencies. Laura Jennings, a vice-president at MSN, thought she had found just the person in Bob Bejan.

Laura Jennings didn't call Bejan, as it happened. Bejan had been working at Warner Brothers Online as a vice-president of creative development, developing shows and content for the fledgling studio unit. While at WBO, he became interested in acquiring an unreleased MSN program called *NetWits*. He called Jennings and the two began to talk. Bejan never succeeded in getting the rights to the show, but he did make an impression on Jennings, who later called him back and offered him the head creative job at the network.

Bejan brought with him the flamboyance of the entertainment business. Fifteen hundred miles from the studios of Hollywood and three thousand miles from Broadway, Bejan seemed like a lone and curious figure among the Microsoft executives. He shaved his head, wore funny clothes and funky glasses. When he talked, he kept slipping his glasses on top of his head, only to have them slip down again.

When Bejan joined MSN in March of 1996, he found a rudderless operation still recovering from the consequences of Gates's about-face embrace of Internet standards. Microsoft was also still struggling to understand how to manage creative people. The staff had been left to fend for itself, with no production methodology or structure. Production of the site was often chaotic, with important decisions being made in a rushed manner at the last minute. One evening Jennings packed her briefcase and headed out to the parking lot, only to be suddenly pulled into a production meeting. The producers were closing in on the deadline for the next day's MSN home page, and they still hadn't decided what it should look like.

Bejan knew what he was facing when he took the job. "The technology industry as a whole are not great embracers of media," he noted. Speaking of Microsoft executives, he would later observe that "in a world where you've spent your life largely shunning media, it's an interesting challenge to discover it fairly late in life." When Bejan moved into Redmond West, one of the hardest adjustments for him was the bright white walls in his office. For years he had painted his office walls black; it was part of his creative style and gave the illusion of limitlessness. There would be no black walls at Microsoft.

Bejan's position was similar to that of Charlie Fink's at the Greenhouse—a digital equivalent of a Hollywood studio boss. A *Wall Street Journal* profile described his job as "acting as cheerleader and critic for production teams, listening to pitches for new programs and deciding which ones should live and which should die."[11] Bejan had been given carte blanche by Microsoft executives to build a program of content that would blow AOL out of the water.

The task of rebuilding MSN called for inhuman measures of energy and discipline. Bejan had both in spades. When he was thirteen years old he conceived the idea of swimming the channel between Los Angeles harbor and Catalina island. For a year he submitted to a regimen of intense training and slept without sheets or blankets and shivered through cold showers to toughen himself for the cold Pacific waters. He swam the channel at age fourteen—the youngest person to do so.

After college, his discipline and animalistic vitality found expression in dance. Bejan moved to New York and performed in *A Chorus Line* on Broadway. The theater experience provided him with a rich vein of metaphorical material for talking about the emerging online medium. In his own mind, a real-time event-programming engine was a kind of "production manager," while the HTML code that controlled the presentation of media was "written" through a sixteen-or-twenty-week rehearsal schedule. The music cues in dance came twenty seconds ahead of time, just as in HTML, where one cued the music before downloading the page.

In some ways, producing a show on the Internet was much more like producing a play than a television show or a movie. You made a film once, then sent it out into the world. A TV series had more of a flavor of an ongoing production, but was still set in stone once completed. The theater, on the other hand, was a living medium. Like the Web, theater was something you did every day—eight performances a week—and that changed from performance to performance, shaped by audience reactions. Theater was an endurance event like swimming the Catalina channel. So was the Web.

The boom-and-bust cycles of the theater world forced Bejan to supplement his income with odd jobs, including a stint as a singing-telegram guy dressed in a "stupid little western tuxedo." He wrote jingles and pursued other advertising work in New York and Chicago. Bejan's bottom line improved when he launched a business putting on theatrical productions for major corporations in the late '80s. His money worries vanished when he turned the Teenage Mutant Ninja Turtles into a rock band and wrote and produced a stage show. The show toured for two and a half years and resulted in an album that sold four million copies in seven languages. Bejan could retire his western tuxedo.

Interestingly, Bejan ran Virtual World for a short time in the early '90s, guiding the company through it's prototype phase, getting it ready for sale to Tim Disney. Virtual World's network-based gameplay in a retail environment may have been the inspiration for Bejan's next entrepreneurial adventure, one that was his greatest passion and ultimately his deepest disappointment. Bejan and his Turtles partner, Bill Franzblau, launched a company called Interfilm in 1992 with backing from Sony Corporation. Bejan produced the company's first interactive film during the Christmas Season of 1992 and took the company public the following year. Eventually, Interfilm reengineered fifty theaters with control devices on each seat and computer-controlled projection systems. Viewers voted on different directions the plot could take (almost two hours of footage were required to make a twenty-minute film when all the branches were tallied).

In the late '60s, Bejan had been greatly influenced by the work of Lanterna Magica, the Czech interactive film pioneers, and the Czech exhibit at the Montreal world's fair, in which theatergoers could take a tour of Prague and use little buzzers in their seats to vote on where to go next. Projectionists on skates operated nine projectors, covering and uncovering lenses to create a seamless interactive experience.

Bejan believed that the major creative role in staging interactive films was in the voting architecture one employed as part of the experience. He experimented with consensus voting, majority rule, and setting criteria that allowed the best voters to gain control. This "choreography" became "a whole other set of language" for turning audience members "into collaborators instead of spectators."

Interfilm eventually tanked. *Ride for Your Life*, the final film the company produced, followed the adventures of two bike messengers as they sped around Manhattan in pursuit of space aliens. Bejan blamed Sony for not providing promised financing (he and Franzblau litigated the matter; it would take years for the two to untangle the mess). Despite the company's failure, Bejan thought Interfilm provided a rare opportunity to see "what it meant to put a group of people in a room interacting with some programming," and felt that the concept was "incredibly valid." In his view, Interfilm combined the best elements of live theater and interactivity—the dynamic of a live audience and the illusion of control.

During his first weeks at Microsoft, Bejan spent a lot of time outlining his vision for MSN. He recognized that the company badly needed sound production processes. Without more structure, they'd never meet their launch deadline. He also wanted to port entertainment culture into Microsoft's software-development environment. To do so, he borrowed every metaphor he could from film and television—especially from television. They were creating "shows," not sites. MSN would be thought of as a "stage," and shows would be aggregated into themed "channels."

One thing he had to do was come to grips with how the ponytails' seeming lack of structure grated on the geeks. Microsoft had gone through a similar geek–ponytail clash with DreamWorks Interactive, Microsoft's joint venture with DreamWorks SKG. To those used to the discipline of software development, the operation seemed chaotic. No one had a title. Nobody was in charge. The concept of putting a chart on the wall and following a schedule seemed beyond the pale for the creative team. In software, the product-development process was mapped out. People knew the schedule would slip, but at least there was a road map of sorts. The engineers didn't appreciate how storytelling differed from churning out code. Developing characters and story arcs was an organic and nonlinear process that had to unfold at its own pace.

Bejan now faced a similar situation at MSN. Like musical theater, online involved a lot of disparate talents coming together. There was a tension in any medium between the people who "technically enabled the medium" and those who were "creating in it." Grips hated actors, engineers hated recording artists, stage hands hated dancers. Why should it be any different in the world of the Internet? What they all had in common was the desire to always "push the envelope of the medium they were working in." He decided to use that motivation as a leverage point.

Bejan began to corner people in the halls in Redmond West so that he could draw a simple diagram illustrating his thinking about "mastery and the medium."

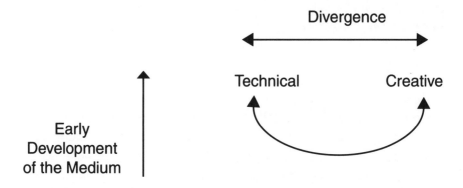

Bejan asked his listeners to assume that two individuals of more-or-less equal talent began pursuing two different aspects of the new media enterprise; one followed a "left-brain," technical path; the other a "right-brain," creative path. One becomes a programmer, the other a writer, artist, designer, or creative producer. New media was still a young field; technical and creative professionals were still struggling to understand the tools, palettes, and principles of their respective domains. It was in this early, pioneering period that the two disciplines diverged the most.

As the industry matured—as these respective professionals gained ever greater mastery of their domains—one could begin to see the distance between the technical and creative start to close.

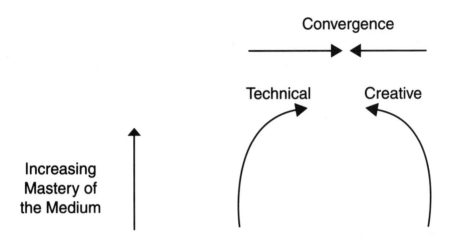

"In your pursuit of mastery," Bejan told his staff, "you actually become more empathetic and attuned to the needs and requirements of the very thing that's opposite of what you're pursuing—a kind of classic yin and yang." In other words, the gap in understanding between the geeks and the ponytails at Microsoft might seem miles wide right now, but if we work hard enough and get to understand what we are all doing, the distance between us will close.

Regardless of whether Bejan's yin-yang theory of convergence won converts or snickers, the gap between the geeks and ponytails at Microsoft was more than psychological—it was physical as well. Redmond West, where the content people were located, was its own facility, separate from the rest of the company. Constructing a separate facility for the ponytails represented a monetary commitment to what they were doing, but it also served to ghettoize their efforts. Some couldn't help but feel that the company's primary goal in creating content was to show off Microsoft's technology.

Philosophizing aside, Bejan gave his team two weeks to submit proposals. He asked them to frame their concepts in eight-page memos that described the visitor's experience and outlined the show's technical requirements.

Bejan wondered what kind of material his producers would submit. He almost felt like he was a generation removed from them. "I learned the seven basic stories of dramatic structure in six-minute increments Saturday mornings watching the Bugs Bunny Road Runner Hour," he said. "I've spent the rest of my life in the relentless pursuit of a more sophisticated version of those seven stories in terms of entertainment." But the young punks around him had grown up in a largely interactive world, playing *Sonic* and *Mario Brothers*. They were learning the next seven stories that would be the dramatic backbone of "mosaic narrative."

To Bejan's chagrin, his young producers inundated him with pitches—sixty-four in all. Out of that slush pile, he gave the thumbs-up to about a dozen shows initially, then added several more later. Bejan and his staff now faced the unfathomable task of ramping up to develop twenty shows in twenty-two weeks.

In some quarters Bejan was seen as an arrogant figure—especially since coming to Microsoft. Steven Koltai, who brought Bejan to Warner Brothers Online and later started his own Internet production company, said that Bejan was now "a little bit different than the Bob I hired. He's been Microsofted. . . . There is a kind of arrogance that I have noticed that seems to exist among people at Microsoft—sort of, 'We have figured it out, and nobody else has.'"

Bejan was aware of the criticism but felt he'd found a work culture as intense and demanding as he was. "For me," Bejan said, "it's been like finding home."[12]

The Brandon Tartikoff of Cyberspace

Across town from the Lightspeed house, in Hollywood's analogue-media jungle, Brandon Tartikoff sat in his office at New World Entertainment, gazing out the window at the members of the west L.A. little league practicing in the field across the street below. Tartikoff loved television with the same pure affection that those young boys loved baseball. The legendary TV programmer Fred Silverman, his mentor, referred to Tartikoff as "the definitive student of television." Like Scott Zakarin, Tartikoff came from Long Island (three towns away). He often told the story of his early fascination with "the box" as a child. He was famous for being able to recite entire network programming lineups going back to the '50s. The seemingly endless list of hit shows that Tartikoff either introduced or presided over during his days at NBC attested to his instincts for the mainstream—*The Cosby Show*, *Family Ties*, and *LA Law*—all classics in their way, woven into the culture of their time. He could (and did) at times misfire, as with the shows *Manimal* (a man who morphs into different animals) and *Misfits of Science*. Being the first member of the television generation to run an entertainment network, he understood the medium in a way that the older generation of television executives, who had grown up on radio, did not.

When Tartikoff graduated from Yale in 1970, he took a job as an advertising copywriter. Then in the spring of 1971, a job opened up at a small TV station in New Haven, Connecticut. He landed the job, which paid six hundred dollars a month, and began what he called a glorious period of his life. The station was small, so he could involve himself in every aspect—news, sports, sales presentations, programming. The station was like a "candy store" for a lover of television. (Later he would tellingly refer back to this experience, saying, "in a way, that's how I look at AOL.")

The young Tartikoff was reading a copy of *Broadcasting* magazine when he came across a notice for a two-day meeting of the Connecticut Cable Association. While at Yale, Tartikoff had read a lot of books and articles on cable, which was in the early days of its development.

Few households had cable. He thought it was fascinating, that cable was where TV was going to go. The conference fee was one hundred dollars.

Tartikoff approached the station's general manager and made a pitch to attend the conference—and being a member of the station's executive staff, could he get reimbursed for the one-hundred-dollar fee? He would drive out and back the same day and not stay overnight. Maybe he would learn something valuable, bring back insights that could benefit the station.

The station manager was less than impressed with the idea and launched into a rant about the idiocy of the cable concept. "There are about seven people who have cable. Nobody is going to pay for what they can get for free." Tartikoff's heart sank. The manager stopped short and leveled his gaze at the slender and earnest young man before him. "I'll give you a hundred bucks *not* to go."

Tartikoff stayed in network television, but it forever irked him that he had missed out on a chance to experience the frontier-town quality of the early cable business. He got a job as an assistant promotions manager at WLS, the ABC station in Chicago, where he made a name for himself by packaging the station's library of B-movies into campy promos. Tartikoff once compiled all the station's monkey movies—*King Kong, Planet of the Apes,* etcetera—and put together a thirty-second "Gorilla Thrillas" promo featuring a guy in a gorilla suit holding a ten-foot banana crooning "Gorilla My Dreams." The ratings shot up. These campy campaigns drew the attention of the legendary Fred Silverman, who headed up programming at the network. Silverman had used a similar strategy himself fifteen years earlier. "You know . . . you remind me of me," Silverman told him. (Years later Tartikoff would say the same thing about Scott Zakarin.) Tartikoff apprenticed with Silverman at ABC for a year, then followed his mentor to NBC, where he worked for another three years. In 1980, at the age of thirty-one, he ascended to the head of programming for the network.

Tartikoff was an intensely driven man, as one would expect from someone who would become the youngest head of programming in network history while struggling with a life-threatening disease. Tartikoff had first been stricken with Hodgkin's disease while in his early twenties, beating it back into remission. The disease surfaced again in 1982. Though there were rumors around the industry about his health, only his family and his boss, Grant Tinker, knew about the Hodgkin's flare-up. For a whole year Tartikoff took chemotherapy, losing his hair and donning a wig, throwing up on the weekends. Eventually the disease went back into remission, and Tartikoff continued what became a brilliant and successful tenure at NBC. Sensing that he had crested and that network television in general would begin losing market share, he left the job on a high note.

Shortly before leaving NBC, Tartikoff and his daughter Calla were in a near-fatal car accident during a family vacation in Lake Tahoe. Tartikoff was hospitalized for over a month and his daughter suffered a serious head injury. He moved his family to New Orleans so his daughter could receive rehabilitative therapy there.

Tartikoff's next job came in 1991, when he did a stint as studio chief at Paramount. He was responsible for several major hits, including *Wayne's World*, *The Firm* and *Indecent Proposal*, but the strain of shuttling back and forth between Los Angeles and New Orleans, and his reportedly difficult relationship with then–studio chief Stanley Jaffe, probably contributed to his short tenure (fifteen months) at the studio. Tartikoff then set up his own production company, which was later bought by New World Entertainment when he was recruited as its chief programmer. In July 1996 Rupert Murdoch would buy New World, causing the company's stock to go through the roof. Tartikoff, who held a good deal of New World stock as part of his deal, found himself free from financial anxieties.

In the '90s Tartikoff had become something of an outsider to the network-television business. His time away had allowed the tables to turn—he was the one doing the pitching. Producers were always in search of ideas or stories that could be crafted into a pitch. His talk with Louis Rosetto at *Wired* was the kind of scouting expedition that a smart producer would engage in, looking for a story to wrap a movie or television show around.

As Tartikoff watched the little leaguers kicking up dust clouds, the phone rang. It was Eddie Clontz, editor of the *Weekly World News*, the would-be tabloid that broke "stories" about Batboy and about five U.S. senators who happen to be space aliens. Tartikoff was producing a TV series for the USA Network based on the tabloid. Clontz asked Tartikoff if he'd like to get on the phone with a guy named Ted Leonsis—a "big mucky-muck at America Online"—and told him that this same Leonsis character had told a reporter from the *New York Times Magazine* that he wanted to be the "Brandon Tartikoff of cyberspace."

"Flattery will get you everywhere in Hollywood," Tartikoff later wrote of the encounter, "and I was curious to chat with this titan of the new media."[13]

The "mucky-muck" was a burly Greek American with a large nose, brilliant gray-blue eyes, and black beard who had once been the mayor of Vero Beach, Florida. If Brandon Tartikoff had an obsessive love of television, Ted Leonsis had a similar passion for the online world. Leonsis was part of the troika that ran AOL in the mid-'90s—the other two being Bob Pittman and CEO Steve Case. If Case was quiet and nondescript, Leonsis was the opposite—a colorful, swashbuckler who liked to muse out loud how he would make his "next 15 million dollars" and was willing to take risks necessary to make it happen. He loved making dramatic gestures, such as handing out twenty-dollar bills to homeless people. He bragged to fellow AOLers that when MSN got into AOL's business, it would be "Microsoft's Vietnam. We'll fight a war of attrition." After hearing about Microsoft's about-face on Internet standards he tweaked his competitor again. "Bill Gates is like Nixon in Vietnam," Leonsis smiled. "Retreat and declare victory."

Leonsis had a Mediterranean sense of fatalism mixed with healthy doses of entrepreneurial cunning, marketing panache, and testosterone. He had been an English major at Georgetown University, where he got involved with computers. After college he worked at Wang laboratories in advertising and marketing and later published computer-oriented magazines. He said he could smell the coming digital revolution.

Leonsis's association with AOL began shortly after a breakfast meeting in Boston with Steve Case in October 1993. Leonsis's company, Redgate, which he founded in 1988, was a new-media marketing company that did business in interactive shopping, database management, and private networks. Case recognized even at that early date that Leonsis had the mind of a media programmer. He acquired Leonsis's company in a deal reportedly valued at $40 million. At the time Leonsis joined the company, AOL had 800,000 households. By the time Leonsis turned the Network over to Bob Pittman in the latter half of 1996 to head up AOL Studios, AOL had 8 million households and was the undisputed distribution giant.

In his book, *The Last Great Ride*, Tartikoff had showed himself to be quite the philosopher of television programming. Leonsis similarly prided himself as being a theorist of cyberspace and felt that he "kind of invented" the category of online content. The online service, in his view, started out as an information-telecommunications business, which had wrongly migrated to a publishing model. Publishing rested on three stool legs—circulation, editorial, and ad sales. Here was AOL, with no editorial and no ad sales. This was no publishing model. Just as well, he thought. "We don't want to be in the publishing business—it's too small." The real opportunity, to Leonsis's thinking, was to be like cable—to be a conduit for content and to own channels.

Leonsis was a media suit who loved to sit back and strategize on a grand scale. Four *C*s formed the foundation of his thinking about the online medium. The first *C* was *content* programmed for a demographic. Whether it was moms or people who were interested in the stock market or young adults into body piercing, the Net gave one the unique ability, in theory at least, to identify specific audiences and hook them with the kind of content they'd find compelling.

Content served to activate a *community*, the second *C*. The Web was a people-to-content phenomenon at that time. It sometimes felt like a world that had been bombarded with neutron bombs—a world of abandoned structures and no people. Leonsis attributed AOL's success to its people-to-content-to-people equation. (Sex in chat rooms, some critics felt, was at the heart of the equation.) Online was that third place after home and work where people could meet. "We are the bartenders," Leonsis often said. "I'm the Sam Malone of this generation," using content to bring people together.[14]

When communities began bonding around content, then the third *C* kicked in—*commerce*. Commerce—advertising, transaction, and licensing crossmedia extensions (AOL did $1 million a day in licensing fees)—only happened when the community was there.

The fourth *C* was *companion web sites*. These were the independent show producers that could be paid or given distribution and threaded into an online network. If the site was good, he kept it; if not, he dropped it.

Leonsis believed that AOL would grow fast but faced a formidable challenge from the "evil empire." Microsoft was entering the market, and AOL was vulnerable. The geeks hated the company for its mom-and-pop simplicity. "There is really an opportunity to come in and bring some innovation that will help this market grow," Gates told an audience at a November 1994 Comdex computer show in Las Vegas. Few thought that Gates's motives were anything other than to dominate the online space. *Wired* had called AOL a dinosaur. Leonsis rallied the AOL staff with an infamous "dinosaur pep rally" at AOL headquarters. "It's Microsoft that is the real dinosaur," he said.[15]

If AOL was to put distance between itself and Bill Gates's Microsoft Network, it would have to develop its own content as a differentiation—just as HBO bought the big movies that other cable networks bought, but also developed shows like *Larry Sanders* and produced its own movies to differentiate itself from the other cable companies. Once AOL's "distribution footprint" got big enough—say, 10 million households—it could launch whole networks of content and own them.

Leonsis was mesmerized by the cable industry. Time and again he returned to the cable model. Ted Turner was a kind of totem mogul, the crazy guy who in 1980 looked at cable and said, "Of course it's going to work. How can I get enough money to get in there early and shut the other guys out?" People had laughed and been skeptical. CNN was called the Chicken Noodle Network until it gradually took over the space, propelled by events like the Gulf War. Years later NBC would spend hundreds of millions of dollars just to get to second place in the cable world. Leonsis wanted AOL to shut out the other guys the same way Ted Turner had with CNN.

Though he broadcast his analyses of the media space in tones of utter certainty, Leonsis was in fact a very adaptable and flexible strategic thinker who regularly revised his thinking when reality became too cold and cruel to ignore. "I used to be a Moslem, now I'm a Jew," he would say when changing direction.

Leonsis admired Tartikoff's talent for developing the kind of content that built mass audiences. He had famously said that AOL's biggest competitor on Thursday evenings was not MSN or Compuserve but *Seinfeld*. Now he was assiduously courting the man who had brought *Seinfeld* to television.

Tartikoff and Leonsis arranged to have a meal in New York at the Post House. "You should get involved with us," Leonsis told Tartikoff over the meal. "We want to become broadcasters, and there's no bigger broadcaster than you." Tartikoff was too busy with television production at the time to take the bait, but said, "Life's long. Let's keep talking." Later that year Leonsis invited him to speak to a gathering of AOL programmers.

Leonsis asked Tartikoff to build his talk around the idea that "where AOL is right now is right where NBC was before color." Tartikoff came and found a room full of AOL programmers (content developers, not coders)—175 altogether. This surprised Tartikoff; NBC had just 30 programmers. Leonsis had corralled the programmers, famous for showing up late and talking during meetings, in the auditorium in time for the event. AOLers were very smart, Leonsis later said, "bordering on being more arrogant than they should be. I always maintain we're pathetic. We just happen to be less pathetic than everybody else. We're not even good yet. But that's why I'm encouraged. Just imagine how good we'll be when we're older, smarter, and better executors."

Tartikoff knew next to nothing about the Internet, his visit to *Wired* last December notwithstanding. A chapter of his autobiography had been devoted to television in the year 2000. Published in 1992, the chapter was a concise summary of a lot of thinking in circulation at the time. What was surprising was how well it held up years later. Tartikoff foresaw the fragmentation of the television audience, which was already a fact by the early '90s, and the inevitable downward spiral of the networks. A consequence of that fragmentation, he worried, was that the nation might lose its sense of shared experience.

The good news was that interactive network technologies, coupled with the rise of niches, would increase the quality of television content. The future of television, he wrote, would come down to a "great power shift—away from the networks and toward the viewers. Instead of someone like me deciding what goes on the air—and when—you'll be making the decision for yourself. You, too, can be your own television programmer, your own Ed Sullivan. You'll be able to turn on whatever acts and wonders turn you on."[16]

One of the things that Tartikoff picked up on right away about the Internet was the low barriers of entry—people anywhere could create content for all to see. A consequence of Tartikoff's move to New Orleans was that he saw how insular Los Angeles and New York could be. If people could create TV series in New Orleans and other places around the country, TV content would have a range, depth, and diversity that it currently lacked. The Net could function the same way.

Tartikoff scanned the huge audience of AOL programmers and began to talk. He spoke off the cuff without notes for two and a half hours to a hushed audience. Tartikoff and the AOL programmers seemed to make an immediate connection. The programmers could see the commonalties between what Tartikoff said about television and their own fledgling experiences. He took hundreds of questions from the audience. *What have I stumbled on?* Tartikoff thought. Later, he took five of the top programmers to a local steak house to talk further. "I was a sponge on them, and they a sponge on me," he later said.

Leonsis's strategic thinking had been moving in a direction that would create an opportunity to lure Tartikoff to the AOL Greenhouse. Leonsis had come to the conclusion that funding small content developers and focusing on shows was not the right direction. Shows came and went. Shows "didn't scale"—couldn't accommodate large audiences. Better to create large content networks, or *destinations*.

He had been thinking about content channels on the Net since 1994, his thinking inspired, as always, by the cable-television industry. When a sports show got low ratings on ESPN, it was the show that got canceled, not ESPN. Programming might come and go, but ESPN was an enduring brand. You needed big destinations—big networks—to justify the marketing dollars needed to drive traffic to your site. *Destinations*. Leonsis and the Greenhouse executives began to think about creating "category killers"—must-stop destinations so compelling that they killed the competition—centered on women, sports, romance, and especially entertainment. Big content networks to battle Microsoft. Big content networks to claim a major portion of "mind share" in the growing Internet audience. Big content networks to build successful Internet businesses. They needed a real Brandon Tartikoff who knew how to get big audiences under the tent. Who better to be the Brandon Tartikoff of cyberspace than Brandon Tartikoff himself?

GrapeJam Launches

Scott Zakarin and Troy Bolotnick made *GrapeJam* a catchall for every idea they had for online entertainment. If there was an emergent tool for the Web—RealAudio, live cam, The Palace platform—Scott and his team bent it to their purpose and experimented shamelessly with it. Chat and live parties could be found at the "Improv theater." The team reinvented an old advertising notion from the early days of television by having characters face the camera and make sales pitches that were fully integrated into the story line. They set up a modified form of IRC (chat for the Web). *GrapeJam* used its Palace site to provide an environment of 2-D chat and improv, where visitors could create their own avatars.[17] (Mindful of how daunting these new features could be, they tried to simplify the technology to make it palatable for the masses.) Scott wanted to completely eclipse *The Spot*. He also had ambitions, once again, of spinning off a television show.

All that wouldn't be easy to pull off, as it happened. The launch of *GrapeJam* was a different affair from that of *The Spot*. The Web itself was a different, greatly expanded universe now. *The Spot* had garnered world attention because it was the first of its kind. In the fifteen months since *The Spot*'s launch, dozens of webisodics had appeared—seventy-six were indexed at Yahoo—as well as other experiments in online entertainment. Unlike *The Spot*, *GrapeJam* wouldn't benefit from the novelty factor.

GrapeJam's dilemma was an example of what happened when a novel idea, design concept, or technology was introduced on the Net: it quickly got copied and propagated throughout the far reaches of cyberspace. The Net had an insatiable appetite for innovation—new applications like RealVideo, novel tools like dynamic HTML, a new form of chat, or webisodics. This rapid burn-through of innovative ideas was helped along by the dense interconnectedness of the Net itself. New design ideas, formats, and metaphors spread rapidly through richly interweaved networks, just as tugging on a tiny corner of a spider's web distorted the whole creation.

"Today's success is tomorrow's history lesson," Kyle Shannon of Agency.com once noted. "You have a three-month window on innovation" before your new idea, design feature, breakthrough concept, or niche is invaded by what Forrester Research's Russ Manley called the "fast followers." Fast followers were those groups, companies, and syndicates that sat back and watched others make the mistakes and figure out the technology, then rapidly moved in with their deep pockets to capture the market. First movers beware. Someone was sure to eat your lunch if you didn't eat theirs first.

Word of mouth over the Net had been sufficient to get the ball rolling for *The Spot* launch; *GrapeJam* called for a different strategy to break through the thicket of webisodics and other sites. The team hired Rogers & Cowan, a major publicity firm, and targeted the television and print media in a big way. The launch would cost them nearly $100,000.

GrapeJam went live on August 27, 1996. The show was the perfect test bed for experimenting with the rapidly evolving medium of the Web. That experimentation involved the intersection of the technical with the artistic. Improvisation was a major part of the production, and Scott enlisted the help of the Groundlings, an L.A. improv group. At first, no one knew how to translate improv for the new medium. The first improvs, Rich Tackenberg remembered, were clunky. "People knew they were beta tests." The Groundlings taught the others. Over time the Lightspeed team got better at doing improv, while the Groundlings got savvy to the Web.

For Scott, the great thrill of online was the unpredictable, real-time quality of the audience interaction. Lightspeed had put together the first "Webstock" event as an expenses-only job for Do Something, a charity that empowered young people in their communities. The team took the lessons learned from that live event—among others, "if you have an event, people will come"—and applied them to a live event of their own making—the "Grape Jamathon." For two days straight, Zakarin kept the microphones open and brought in celebrities like Bruce Campbell, Dean Kane, and Stan Lee (creator of Spiderman). At one point Stan Lee was interviewed by the *GrapeJam* characters. The audience members were also allowed to submit questions to Lee. Scott and the team edited, condensed, and filtered the incoming e-mail. The team used feedback to influence the direction of the interview segments. "If this person [a particular viewer] hadn't sent in this e-mail," Rich Tackenberg later observed, "the show wouldn't have happened." In a sense they were duplicating talk radio—with a twist. Hundreds of fans could participate instead of a handful.

We'll Fix It in Photoshop

In ten years the whole movie will probably be done in postproduction.
—digital filmmaker Phil Flora

Producing *GrapeJam* wasn't the same kind of endeavor as producing a television show or a film; Web productions were much more improvisational, the production roles much more fluid. Everything about the production seemed to be bootstrapped.

One day at lunch, over a huge low-fat chicken burrito, a sick and exhausted Troy Bolotnick attempted to map the steps for producing *GrapeJam*. He sat at a varnished wooden table of the Sage Brush Cantina, a short distance from the Lightspeed house, making notes on a scrap of paper.

(1) Develop a story line,
(2) Make sure specific story notes get done,
(3) Production—the live shoot.

At the same time that production is under way, the:

(4) Design and writing gets done by two separate groups.
(5) The programming [contracted out] gets done (hopefully), and
(6) Tested.

Sniffling between spicy bites of burrito, Troy tried to capture the fluid quality of work roles in the production process, struggling to get the elements clear in his congested head:

(a) Scott and Laurie share director/head writer functions.
(b) Troy and Scott share director/producer functions.
(c) They are all writers.

    (d) Troy works directly with the programmers a lot, but . . .
    (e) Some of Troy's guys also work directly with the programmers.
    (f) Troy works with the designers sometimes, but . . .
    (g) Sometimes the writers work directly with the designers as
       well . . .

As Bolotnick continued, any semblance of a linear process deteriorated. Sometimes the photo shoot (3) would inspire an idea that would get into the story outline (2). Sometimes the design (4) would make them rethink the story outline (2). Sometimes the preparation for a story six weeks in advance would cause them to rework a story that was scheduled for three weeks ahead. And of course, viewer input shaped and molded everything. If traditional film production could be neatly divided into three phases—preproduction, production, and postproduction (the last being when the film was edited)—then Web development was mainly a postproduction affair. At the end of the day, if Troy noticed that a picture was too bright, he could go into Photoshop and change it at the last minute. There was an old joke in the film business: if you had a problem on the set, or the lighting was wrong, the standard riposte was "Fuck it, we'll fix it in post." On a Web production shoot, Troy might say, "Scott, if I shoot this, you'll have that telephone pole in the background." "Fuck it," Scott would answer, "we'll fix it in Photoshop."

But unlike a motion-picture, television, or radio production, the fixes and changes were continuous in Web production. Scott, Troy, and the others monitored feedback from their audience on a daily—even hourly—basis. Troy told their work-for-hire clients that he didn't put much stock in focus groups; the whole Internet audience was a "fucking focus group." "It's not about what you think is the right approach," he would tell a client. "It's not what we think is the right approach— it's what the audience thinks, and they will let you know instantly." Audience feedback sculpted and shaped a Web production, like a fierce desert sandstorm wearing away the rough edges of a block of sandstone.

They got very good at developing preplanned story elements that would take advantage of audience interactivity. In one episode, characters Robbie and Eric were planning to go out on a friendly date. Another character, Joanne, was in love with Eric and fiercely jealous. She conspired with her friend Meredith to eavesdrop on the date by planning to secretly tape the pair. Naturally, members of the online audience sent e-mail to Robbie and Eric warning them that their date would be bugged. The two decided to teach Joanne a lesson by playing along and enlivening their date with sexually provocative banter, knowing that it would enrage her.

Scott and the writing team sometimes went far afield from *GrapeJam*'s original premise, such as having characters cover the presidential campaigns of Bill Clinton and Bob Dole. In another example of how Scott loved to play with reality, the characters reported that Bob Dole won the election—a fiction they maintained for the next six weeks.

Writing for *GrapeJam* was like producing a newspaper every day—and just as deadline driven. The Web could bleed a writer—or team of writers—dry. Television shows like *The Larry Sanders Show* kept the quality level high by limiting the number of episodes produced in a season to ten or so. But to hold an audience on the Web, content had to be refreshed on a daily basis. Even if the writing team didn't burn out, the audience eventually would. "Show me a columnist who hasn't worn you out after a year," Sony of America's Howard Stringer once observed, "and I'll show you a miracle."

In many ways, *GrapeJam* suffered from the team's ambitions and enthusiasm. The site's excesses—like the Jamathon—reflected its creators' frantic efforts to push the medium as far as it could go. There were too many live events, too many features that distracted from the main story. Scott and his partners were bent on creating a network rather than a show—and fell short. The wild experimentation gave the site an unfocused quality. The show's premise—a disparate group of friends coming together—was similar enough to its predecessor to strike some as being derivative. While the webisodic developed new fans, *GrapeJam* was always overshadowed by its predecessor. The team would be forced to rein in their excesses when the show hit a financial wall.

Rosetta Stones

There's a schism between programmers and writers—vast psychological differences. They speak completely different languages, have intuitive senses about completely different things, and truly don't understand—sometimes to a degree of contempt—the needs, dynamics and rhythms of the other camp. But the people who have it hardest are the ones who try to bridge that gap.

—Tod Foley

New media wasn't an industry so much as a Tower of Babel. The business was a mosaic of disciplines with no center, history, solid business models, plans, or compass to guide it. In addition to the coders, graphic artists, writers, and financiers that were attracted to the business, one also found architects, anthropologists, physicists, journalists—a whole United Nations of the professional world. All that held these disparate players together was the desire to change the world . . . and maybe get rich in the process. Managing these disparate teams was like trying to steer a balloon with a fire extinguisher.

Day-to-day navigation at Lightspeed fell to Troy Bolotnick. When asked, Troy would describe Lightspeed's management paradigm—like its production processes—as being figure it out as you go. He had supervised small numbers of people before, but now the company had sixteen full-time employees and anywhere from two to five freelancers. Then there were the relationships with companies to which Lightspeed farmed out their technical chores, like programming, and their technical partner Silicon Reef, on whose servers *Grape-Jam* resided. (Silicon Reef was an equity partner in *GrapeJam*.) All the loose ends ultimately ended in Troy's hands.

As a manager, Troy often felt the urge to scream and yell, or dance for joy. The business had its share of screamers, and Troy didn't want to join their numbers. He tried hard to be a good manager. One challenge was mastering the trick of directing ponytails. You couldn't approach a writer or designer and say "here's your assignment, you have two hours. Be creative." That didn't work. Bolotnick learned the value of giving ponytails the illusion of ample time combined with "a sense of the deadline." "Sometimes," Bolotnick noted (somewhat convolutedly), "it's better to say, 'you've got two days on it,' even though we only have one, because they'll get it done in one, though they think they have two."

Geeks were a different matter. Writers might freak if you gave them a short deadline, but at least they knew what a deadline was. Deadlines were taken seriously in the entertainment business. Geeks, on the other hand, were notorious for deadline slips. "When you say 'deadline,'" Troy noted, "in their heads they must be doing some sort of internal calculation that says, 'OK, that's the day when I'm supposed to be half-ready.'" This caused no end of frustration, schedule padding, and a little forceful direction. "We grabbed our programmers by the lapels and said 'OK. You're *done* here,'" pointing at a calendar date.

Like a lot of their peers, Troy and Scott did their best to avoid the business curriculum while in college. Ann Winblad, a leading Silicon Valley venture capitalist, once said that "you don't get a chance to practice [being a leader] in this industry." Like most people trying to build an Internet media business, they were learning Management 101 on the job—only the textbook for running an Internet company hadn't been written yet. They were all writing it.

The Internet business seemed to violate a lot of the basic rules of management theory. The young people who flocked to Internet companies often had ambiguous attitudes toward the notion of authority—ambivalence about leading, and mortification at being led. *Management* was a word that got caught in their throats.

Most of the people who gravitated to Internet start-ups wanted to create cool technology and content. Some even admitted they'd like to make a lot of money. Almost nobody dreamt of becoming a manager. ("I don't want to tell you what to do," said Blur Studio's cofounder Tim Miller, "I just want you to go out and do cool stuff.") Many seemed surprised to find themselves in a position to direct the activities of others. "The first thing I had to get used to was people actually care what I think or say," Lisa Goldman, CEO of Construct (a Web design company), remembered. "When we were first starting out I noticed that if I lost my temper or made a joke at somebody's expense, it affected them in a big way." Even a couple of years later, Goldman seemed in awe at the power transformation. "I realized if I said something, suddenly it was 'Well, Lisa said. . . .'"

This ambivalence ran throughout many Internet enterprises. In too many cases the antimanagement attitude led to the propagation of collective delusions that everyone in the start-up was an equal partner in the business. In some Internet companies, the lack of discussion or consensus about roles and responsibilities inevitably resulted in energies being dissipated in too many different directions. Eventually, hard deadlines would loom and someone would have to step forward and, as *Industry Standard* columnist Carl Steadman once put it, "be the asshole" who made sure that the product shipped.

Wired publisher Louis Rosetto had got it right when he likened a new-media CEO to a guerrilla leader armed with vague tactics and a grandiose long-term goal. The CEO somehow had to unite all the different tribal groups under his or her command and keep the operation together under incredible time and money pressures.

Everyone saw the Net from his own perspective. TV people, if left to their own devices, would manage the Web as if it were a television operation. Editorial professionals would run it like a big magazine. Programmers would act as if the company were building software instead of media. If the head of a start-up ran the business like any of those things, disaster was sure to follow. The Web turned things upside-down for people who had experience in other industries. In the traditional publishing world, writers and editors were at the top of the heap, while the technology folks were the ones who made sure that payroll checks were printed every Friday. Giving the geeks a seat at the table—which they deserved because of the cool stuff they could do—overturned the industry's traditional power structures.

What the new-media business needed, *Lawnmower Man* director Brett Leonard once said, was more "Rosetta Stones," people who had a depth of experience in creative, technical, and business areas, people who could translate and mediate between geeks, ponytails, and suits.

The actual Rosetta Stone was a black, irregularly shaped stone slab found by Napoleon's troops near the settlement of Rosetta in the Egyptian Nile delta in the waning days of the eighteenth century. The stone contained three languages—Greek, Demotic, and Egyptian hieroglyphics. The ability to read hieroglyphics had long passed from modern memory by Napoleon's time. Once the three writings were discovered to be parallel texts, it became possible to decipher the once-unreadable Egyptian hieroglyphics. The Rosetta Stone provided the key to unlocking the hieroglyphs, and made the world of the Pharaohs comprehensible. If the three texts had appeared on separate and dispersed stone surfaces, the connection might never have been made.

The industry needed the human counterpart to the Rosetta

Stone. "Part of being successful on the Internet," Halsey Minor once said, "is you have to understand technology. You can't be successful if you don't understand technology. You have to understand media. You have to have relatively good aesthetic instincts. You don't have to be deep in any one of them, but you have to be somewhat of a dilettante." Internet companies needed people who had vacillated in their careers between two or more industries. The very people who had once been thought flaky because they studied computer programming, music, and business theory were highly sought in an industry that required people with multiple skill sets. "We look at them," Minor added, "and we say, 'hire this guy, hire this guy!' He understands media, he understands production, he understands technology. *He will do incredibly well.*"

"The teams that coalesce around" Rosetta Stones, Jeannine Parker once said, "are happy to be there and happy to be working together. Rosetta Stones know how to bring people together"—and perhaps more important, also knew how to "keep people apart."

Another challenge that faced Bolotnick was coping with the rate at which things changed in the chaotic Internet business. Producing a Web show meant not just accepting change, but building an exit strategy into everything designed. "I have a certain confidence," he would say, "in the fact that everything I plan, I plan for change." If *GrapeJam* were done entirely in frames, and the audience hated it, "I know what it would take to redesign it without frames and I know that's doable. No matter what I do now, it's going to be different in two months anyway."

In many ways the Lightspeed team managed *GrapeJam* the way Picasso painted a picture. Picasso treated each canvas as an experiment, painting a portrait or a scene in a particular style or perspective, scraping off the paint if he didn't think the details worked, painting them in a different way, scraping off the paint again. At one point the team introduced a feature called "Question of the Day." When the feature launched, they knew it would change and evolve when the audience became involved, even if they liked it. Within a couple months, the feature morphed into "The List of the Day."

The discipline of following viewer feedback daily was also reflected in the constant monitoring of what other Internet companies were doing, what was successful and what wasn't, following the buyers (e.g., AOL and Microsoft), and observing what they were buying and from whom. As it happened, what they observed in the fall of 1996 caused them great unease.

The Web had morphed again.

AOL Studios

In October 1996, AOL underwent a massive reorganization that provided Ted Leonsis with the opportunity to pursue his vision of launching big content networks. The reorganization split AOL into three businesses. There was AOL Networks, which was the main online business; ANS Communications, which provided network-access services; and AOL Studios. AOL Networks was headed up by a gifted former MTV and Century 21 executive named Bob Pittman, someone Ted Leonsis had wooed during a comical Mediterranean cruise that summer on Leonsis's personal yacht.

Leonsis became the president of AOL Studios, which itself consisted of three separate businesses: Greenhouse Networks, WorldPlay (the game company), and Digital Cities—the last being AOL's city-directory service. AOL Studios was about to create what the *Wall Street Journal* called a "slew of new 'programming' from scratch."[18] Leonsis, Danny Krifcher, Charlie Fink, and others also began to do the planning for the content networks they sought to launch.

"You have to get mind share," Fink said in describing the strategy for large content networks, "you have to have scale to build successful Web-based businesses. To do that, you need a big enough play to command the distribution and marketing needed to tightly target the 10 percent or so of the U.S. population that is online. The strategy for Greenhouse Networks is to do channel-sized, large-scale brands, like ESPN SportsZone or CNET." The big channels' approach was the opposite of "niche sites" that proliferated everywhere on the Net and AOL. Targeting niche audiences didn't make sense. "Assume you do the Fly Fishing Network," Fink said. "Assume 10 percent of the population is online. If 1 percent of those are interested in fly fishing, you've only got 0.1 percent going to your network. What's going to succeed are things that have 100 percent penetration," like women, sports, romance, and entertainment.[19]

Leonsis and his team had done an analysis of all the main content categories in the online space. He believed that each category had room for two players, not five or fifty. If a category already had two major players, then it probably wasn't a good place to try to build a new content brand. In Sports, SportsZone had one of those slots. In computing, CNET had one of those slots. But looking at entertainment, the field seemed wide open. Starwave's *MrShowBiz* was struggling and didn't have distribution. E! Online, in Leonsis's view, looked like E!'s home page, not the home page for the entertainment industry. Entertainment looked like a big category, one with lots of advertising dollars. It was the right medium. They decided to go for it.

Greenhouse Networks had moved away from the rest of AOL, occupying offices in the AT&T building across the street. Whereas their previous lodgings had been cramped and chaotic, the new address had plenty of private office space for the staff. The building was previously occupied by the Air Force and had a circular hallway that made the suite feel like a rabbit's warren. The Air Force had built a secure room in the center of the floor, with locks and soundproofing and an elevated floor designed to foil electronic attempts at espionage. The Greenhouse staff picked the locks, propped the doors open and brought in a ping-pong table and a basketball hoop. People now used the "secure room" to hang out and blow off steam. Charlie Fink, for one, hated the building. A massive air-conditioning unit was located above his office. It felt like he was working inside a jet plane in flight.

That fall Leonsis and Fink began to put together the team that they hoped would produce the entertainment network they intended as the first of Greenhouse's four major content initiatives. Meanwhile, their counterparts in Redmond West were months ahead of the game and ready to roll. Thousands of Waggener Edstrom–produced press kits were being mailed out to newspapers, magazines, and news outlets around the world. The Microsoft Network was about to relaunch with a new persona—television.

Ponytails at the Gate: MSN Relaunches

When asked if he worried about Microsoft's planned investment of over $400 million in interactive-media development, Charlie Fink had a clever retort. "Having the most money is not going to determine who wins," Fink said. "Great teams win; it's great programming that's going to win." Tweeking his rival Bob Bejan, he added, "As opposed to our colleagues in Redmond, we're building businesses to make money."[20] Despite the bravura show of confidence on the part of Fink and his boss Leonsis, the relaunch of the Microsoft Network was a direct and major threat to their plans. In fact, MSN's moves would indirectly threaten the existence of AOL itself.

The new Web-based Microsoft Network launched on October 10, 1996, from the Redmond West building, half a mile from the Microsoft campus. (People in the industry referred to the event in shorthand as the "relaunch," since the new service was replacing the older network.) Microsoft also announced an unlimited-usage pricing plan ($19.95 per month), a pricing feature intended to mortally wound AOL, which still charged members $2.95 per hour for connect time. MSN's new pricing scheme would prompt AOL to institute its own flat-rate pricing in January 1997.

In the press release that accompanied the MSN launch, Pete Higgins, group vice-president, laid out the new network's objectives. "People tell us two things about going on the Internet: that there is nothing there, and that there's so much there, they can't find anything," Higgins was quoted as saying. "Our goal with the new Microsoft Network is to address both issues, combining a lot of essential services, original entertainment and new information in one place and making the rest of the Internet easier to approach and enjoy." He told a *Business Week* reporter that MSN and related Microsoft content could grow into a $1 to 2 billion business in five years, and might even be profitable in three.[21]

"Our goal with the new Microsoft Network is to bridge the gap between what users expect from the Internet and what has so far been delivered," the press release quoted Laura Jennings as saying. "You have to compete on content and programming rather than technology," added Madeline Kirbach, business development manager for M³P, the content-development arm for MSN.[22]

MSN was organized into four main areas—Communicate, Find, Essentials, and OnStage. Communicate bundled services like e-mail, chat rooms, discussion forums, and Internet newsgroups. Find offered a guide for searching the Web, including access to the Net's most popular search engines. Essentials offered various online services, such as Expedia online travel service, Microsoft Investor for people who played the stock market, an Internet car-buying guide called CarPoint, and the Encarta encyclopedia. But the sweet spot, the part of the site that got the most attention, was OnStage, MSN's news and entertainment area.

Analysts and journalists who previewed the new MSN were entranced by how much OnStage looked like and attempted to mimic television. OnStage was divided into six "channels" of content and more than twenty "shows." The channels were designed to appeal to different audiences or tastes. MSNBC news could be found on MSN 1. MSN 2 was for the mainstream audience, with entertainment offerings like Paramount Digital Entertainment's *Star Trek: Continuum* and *Entertainment Tonight*. There were also a pair of webisodics: *475 Madison Avenue* was a "biting, darkly comic series about life at a New York advertising agency" while *914* was an "interactive comedy-drama set in New York's Westchester County." (Both shows were lineal descendants of *The Spot* and further crowded the field for *GrapeJam*.) MSN 3 offered edutainment content, like the online travel magazines *Mungo Park* and *Slate*. Separate channels targeted women, young adults, and teens.

"World-changing inventions," PC visionary Alan Kay once said, "are so different that they initially have to masquerade as 'better old things' rather than 'completely new things.'" MSN was trying hard to masquerade as television in order to woo viewers with something familiar looking. Bejan had pushed the television metaphor hard.

The danger was that viewers would come expecting a television-like experience and be disappointed. Why would consumers go to all the trouble of getting online for a pseudotelevision experience when they could get the real thing with the flick of a switch? MSN's embrace of the TV metaphor was nonetheless total. Nick Rothenberg, whose company W3 Design had done Web-site-development work for MSN, kept a post-it near the phone whenever he or his people were talking to the folks in Redmond West: "SHOWS! SHOWS!" the post-it read, "not Web sites!"

For Bejan, the relaunch of MSN was the culmination of a months-long adrenaline rush. It had been six months of coming to work before 6:00 A.M. every day and seldom leaving for home before 8:00 at night. The massive media tour leading up to the launch had generated a stream of generally positive reviews. These were the glory days before the network's technical warts began to show.

The press tour took Bejan back to New York, where he had struggled as a dancer and writer. Bejan, Pete Higgins, and Laura Jennings went out for a drink in midtown Manhattan to a bar that had been a dancers' hangout in Bejan's *Chorus Line* days. Coming back as a returning hero, being greeted by the maitre d' who still knew him, was like taking a victory lap.

Microsoft's research showed that the average online session was about twenty-seven minutes in length. Much of that time was used for useful activities—e-mail, search, news, and various other services. Bejan knew that the little time remaining for entertainment, combined with the enormous production requirements for online interactivity, limited them to short forms. Online users, like cokeheads, would prefer to consume their entertainment in short snorts. *Second City Headline News* fit that model perfectly; and in some ways, Matti Leshem—whose company Cobalt Moon supplied the show—was the kind of independent producer that Bob Bejan loved and needed to recruit.

Second City Headline News

Second City Headline News offered satirical and irreverent news broadcasts in the spirit of "the inimitable Second City, the world's premier improvisational theater" (as the press release read). The show was delivered via text, graphics, and RealAudio, and was inspired by real news items like the birth of Madonna's new baby, CIA spy cases, and the Texaco racial-discrimination scandal. "The humor goes from incredibly stupid to incredibly hard-hitting," Leshem told *Broadcasting & Cable's Telemedia Week*.[23] The on-air talent included the likes of Sappho Machismo, a female sports reporter, and Ivan Milkem, who posted his business reports from a minimum-security prison in Connecticut.

Second City was the product of Cobalt Moon, Matti Leshem's interactive entertainment production company in Santa Monica, California. "Why is the digital medium perfect for a guy like me?" asked Leshem. "Because on top of the content that I'm creating, I'm also creating how *you* interface with the content. It's the *ultimate* control!" Unlike some of his competitors, he did not want to be sidetracked by other kinds of work for hire. "I don't want to make corporate Web sites," he ranted. "Any asshole with a Mac can make a corporate Web site."

While Charlie Fink and Scott Zakarin vaguely resembled each other, Zakarin and Leshem really could have been twins. But compared to Scott, Leshem was something of a pit bull in temperament. Constantly in motion, Leshem was a quote machine, a self-mocking *Macher* who always reached for the outrageous remark. "You have to be either bald or Jewish to be in this business," Leshem said. He had a talent for self-promotion that irked others. It wasn't unusual for him to steal most of the sound bites at the Internet panels on which he sat.

Leshem was born in Israel but spent much of his childhood in America when his father served as the Israeli ambassador to the UN. He emigrated to the United States in 1978, settling in the New York area. He received his first computer (an Epson) in 1983 by convincing his writer father that every author should own one. Like so many of his colleagues, Leshem began his career in the theater—in his case as a starving actor. He performed in off-Broadway—and off-off-Broadway—productions, playing James Joyce in *Exiles* at the Asphalt Green in New York. He might have gone on making the circuit if he hadn't discovered interactive theater. The opportunity came when his theater teacher at Sarah Lawrence College, Megan McCombs, invited him to come to Hilton Head, South Carolina.

By the mid-'80s there had been a couple of interactive murder mysteries in which the play's action unfolded in multiple rooms that audience members could wander among. He and McCombs decided to do their own interactive murder mystery, which they called *Hilton Head Homicides.*

Leshem and his partner staged the interactive pieces on three decks of a sixty-foot yacht. The mysteries were tricky to put together; the productions had to be constructed in such a way that if guests missed some of the scenes, they'd still have enough information to solve the murder—without the solution being too obvious.

After a profitable first year with the production, Leshem made the pilgrimage out to Hollywood, where he played Dr. Dan Shae in 169 episodes of the soap opera Family Medical Center. (*If he didn't become a doctor, at least he got to play one*, his mother thought.) That experience cured him of the desire to act. He got a master's degree in directing from the American Film Institute and landed work doing music videos at Propaganda Films, Starving Artists, and other companies. The "Jew King of the black rap video" (his words) directed videos with groups like The Highland Place Mobsters and Big Mountain.

Leshem got a desperate call from a friend at MCA while on a trip to Toronto. Would he like to get involved in the production of a CD-ROM on the life of B. B. King? He caught the next flight back to L.A., setting up a green-screen shoot for King and taking charge of the production. During the green-screen shoot, Leshem got what he later called his "digital epiphany." Suddenly all the disparate elements of his wayward career fell into a recognizable pattern. Consciously or not, everything he had done up to then—*Hilton Head Homicides*, the rock videos, the project with King—had laid the foundation for his understanding of interactive media. Now the question was, what to do about it?

Several opportunities presented themselves. Leshem had attended AFI with Diane Alexander, whose husband Andrew was the owner of Toronto's famed Second City. Many of the best-known comedians in the U.S. had gotten their start at the company, such as John Candy and Mike Myers, and the SC brand carried a lot of weight. He began to pursue the digital rights.

Leshem was hired by Second City to open a development house in Los Angeles. He worked hard to develop SC projects, but after a year didn't have much to show for it. He had been thinking for some time of creating an interactive entertainment production company and offered to build one for Second City. Alexander turned him down; the idea seemed too risky. Leshem persisted in looking for a backer for his idea, but got nowhere until he met up with Joe Orr. Orr owned a company called the Image Foundry that produced high-end editorial work for a string of clients like Mazda, Sizzler, and Taco Bell. Leshem, Orr, and a third partner, Will Hobbs, set up shop in a back office of Orr's company and began to look for clients. The name of the company came to Leshem in a dream. *Cobalt Moon.*

Patient Zero

The Internet is not a fad, it's the human crossroads. The eight-track was a fad.

—comedian Dennis Miller

Like everyone else in the new-media business, Leshem abhorred the term "Siliwood." A contraction of Silicon Valley and Hollywood, the word came into vogue in the mid-'90s as a description of the collaboration between the technology and entertainment industries. Leshem didn't believe you could build hybrid companies of the sort the term implied. It would never work. Cobalt Moon was not a Siliwood company. His company was pure Hollywood, employing comedy writers, producers, and many others who had no Web experience. The exception was Will Hobbs. Hobbs had been involved with the Web and online music distribution from the very beginning, "when the Internet was a drop-down menu," as he liked to put it. (Leshem did in fact have other geeks on the payroll.)

Leshem's peers and competitors would later marvel at the "fabulous relationship" that he had with the Microsoft Network. How had Leshem managed to worm his way into the good graces of Bob Bejan and the M³P organization when so many of his peers—Zakarin, Greer, and others—had failed? He had produced a show for MSN's October relaunch and gotten a big push from the attendant press coverage. (Envious competitors didn't realize how hard Leshem had had to fight behind the scenes to get PR for the show.) How did he do it?

Leshem's "fabulous relationship" began with a cold call. He had been talking to David Traub, who Leshem liked to call the "patient zero" of the multimedia world, since so many projects and companies could be traced back to him. Traub didn't produce much multimedia product himself, but was incredibly well connected and spent much of his time putting people together behind the scenes and working deals. Traub told Leshem he ought to call a guy at Microsoft named Marty Levin.

Leshem's dealings with Microsoft and Second City were in the best Hollywood tradition—playing a shell game with the rights to a property. First he made a call to Andrew Alexander to get permission to pitch an interactive Second City show. (Leshem still didn't own the rights.) After getting a grudging OK from Alexander, he called Microsoft and used Second City to get Levin's attention. He pitched five or six ideas for shows, but the one that interested Levin the most was a satirical news show à la *Weekend Edition* built around the Second City brand. Leshem and Hobbs worked days, evenings, and weekends ("Will and I slept under his computer for a week") to produce a one-hundred-page demo of the proposed show. Once he had a green light from Bejan, Leshem rushed back to Second City and finally negotiated a deal for Second City's digital rights.

Leshem and company rushed into production, opening offices in a shabby Santa Monica office building, rock-throwing distance from the Santa Monica Freeway. As part of the deal, Leshem had to agree to sign over all rights to *Second City Headline News* to Microsoft. (The *Second City* brand rights were excluded from the deal.)

Microsoft's hard-nosed insistence on owning all the rights to the content on its network grated on many developers in L.A., New York, and San Francisco. It was another example of Microsoft using its wealth and presence in the industry to take advantage of the creative community—and of their ignorance of entertainment-industry culture.

Bejan was sensitive to criticism about the ownership clause. He understood how creators felt about giving up the rights to their creations; he was a writer himself. But he defended Microsoft's position because ownership was a matter of risk and who assumed it. One could compare online entertainment to other mass media at similar points in their histories, he said. In the early 50's, CBS president Frank Stanton spent $1 million to get Jackie Gleason to make a season of *The Honeymooners* on CBS. Paying that kind of money for a show in the early days of television involved a great deal more risk than paying Jerry Seinfeld $600,000 per episode in the '90s. Stanton had no indication at the time whether CBS would make its money back on Gleason's production, so it was "fair and equitable" that CBS took ownership of the copyright and underlying intellectual rights for the first three seasons. (Gleason eventually bought back the rights.)

Leshem was happy with the deal he made with Microsoft. He felt he was fairly compensated, liked the people, thought they were very smart and that they treated him with respect. Marty Levin, who oversaw the show, gave him "good notes" and understood what was inherently funny. Many of the best pieces poked fun at Bill Gates. One time they did a Gates story that was "totally over the top." "You can put that up," Levin told him, "but if he reads it you're going to have a hard time." Leshem toned down the piece.[24]

He also appreciated the marketing muscle that Microsoft could use in promoting his show (if he fought hard enough), like hiring comedian Dennis Miller to guest host *Second City Headline News*. Miller was so impressed with the show's material that he hired away one of Leshem's writers, Josh Weinstein, who currently writes for *Dennis Miller Live*.

While Leshem's relationship with Microsoft was off to a promising start, the relationship between Microsoft and Paramount Digital Entertainment was heading south fast.

A Clash of Titans

MSN was giving David Wertheimer endless headaches. The relationship between Paramount and Microsoft was quickly becoming a clash of titans. Each company represented the best and worst of its respective industry cultures. Microsoft was a wealthy, aggressive software company with a youthful, entrepreneurial culture. Paramount was an old and venerable Hollywood studio, steeped in entertainment tradition and part of a huge, debt-ridden media conglomerate, Viacom.

As it happened, Microsoft's decision to embrace Internet protocols had serious consequences for Paramount. Wertheimer got the bad news early in 1996 from Paramount's Microsoft account representative Sandi Thomas, who worked for Peter Neupert, vice-president for strategic partnerships in Microsoft's interactive-media division. For months Paramount had been developing sites for *Star Trek* and *Entertainment Tonight* using Microsoft's Blackbird technology. Blackbird was a content-development tool that enabled one to build graphics-enriched content for MSN's online service. Unfortunately, Blackbird wasn't based on the Internet's open standards. "You guys have been our premier Blackbird site," Wertheimer was told. "Well, we're shelving Blackbird. You're going to have to rebuild *Star Trek* and *Entertainment Tonight* incorporating Internet protocols." Wertheimer was stunned. This was going to cost a fortune. Revenues would be lost due to the delay in launching the two sites. From that moment onward, 1996 became a fire drill.

By early 1996, MSN had a new set of managers. The new regime looked at all the content deals in place and, like inheritors of their siblings' investments, concluded that Microsoft had cut a very bad deal with Paramount—overpaying for the properties and allowing Paramount to retain too much control. The blame fell heavily on the previous MSN management. Now the new regime considered Paramount to be a legacy deal they couldn't support. The relationship between PDE and MSN, already tumultuous, became even worse.

After the relaunch of MSN in October, Wertheimer tried to improve the *Entertainment Tonight* and *Star Trek* sites. To do so, he needed statistics on how the sites were doing. Paramount was the only content provider on MSN whose advertising wasn't being sold by the MSN sales force. Microsoft had a host of tools for selling advertising, figuring out advertising space, and placing orders. When Wertheimer asked to have access to those tools, the MSN advertising group refused.

Microsoft was playing a game of tit for tat that revolved around intellectual property. The Redmond giant had learned from their experience with Paramount that media companies were very protective of their brands and jealously guarded their intellectual properties. Well, Microsoft could be as protective and hard-nosed about its own intellectual property—in this case, the source code that went into its advertising tools. Paramount would have to request the stats from the MSN advertising group if it needed them. When Wertheimer tried to request stats or place ads, the MSN advertising group suddenly became inaccessible. Managers were hard to reach and messages were filtered through assistants. The poor communications between PDE and MSN advertising caused a delay of as much as two weeks to get an ad through the system and onto the site. Everything about the arrangement seemed to be set up to fail.

Wertheimer was committed to making the relationship work. He made numerous trips to Redmond, trying, often in vain, to convince the MSN management to work with his people, not against them. At one point, he thought he made a crucial breakthrough. Bob Bejan was receptive.

Brandon Tartikoff Wants to Play

At AOL the relaunch of MSN was countered with a show of confidence. Publicly, people like Leonsis and Fink told reporters that MSN was following "last year's strategy" of buying shows. Privately, no one could afford to take Microsoft for granted—not with the hundreds of millions of dollars that Microsoft was prepared to invest in its content efforts. But the folks at AOL knew Microsoft might become distracted by the multiple initiatives it was pursuing in multiple markets. If pressed, Ted Leonsis admitted that if he and Steve Case or Bob Pittman had to go a round against Bill Gates and Steve Ballmer, they'd get their asses kicked. "But we're not going up against Bill Gates and Steve Ballmer," Leonsis smiled. "We're going up against Bob Bejan and Laura Jennings."

Leonsis had another reason to feel cocky. Both he and Fink were convinced that Scott Zakarin and his partners could carry the medium to the next level. Scott understood the importance of community building through his deft use of *The Spot* board. He'd pioneered the idea of using audience input to shape a show and build a following. Scott was an entertainer, not a geek creating content to show off whizbang technology. Scott had a proven online hit.

Scott had deep Web experience but could not carry the freight needed to fulfill Leonsis's expansive vision by himself. The plan was to pair Scott with an entertainment insider who had access to everyone in Hollywood. A player who could justly claim to know a thing or two about television and mainstream entertainment. Someone whose genius Leonsis could take and mate with Scott's genius. "Brandon Tartikoff," Ted Leonsis chuckled merrily to an associate, "wants to play."

In October 1996, Leonsis talked Brandon Tartikoff into entering a development deal with AOL Studios. Leonsis hadn't needed to do much arm twisting. Tartikoff had come away from his previous meeting with the 175 AOL programmers convinced he'd found a good sandbox to play in. This time he'd make good on the impulse that had inspired him to ask his station manager to let him go to a cable TV convention over twenty-five years before. This time he'd be a part of the cyberspace frontier town.

Unlike Scott, Tartikoff wasn't an entertainment wannabe. He was part of the bedrock of the Hollywood establishment. Few entertainment executives spent much time at all thinking about the Internet. The entertainment industry in Hollywood was a pragmatic and workaholic private club, and its denizens were wary of the online world. Typical of that pragmatism was the time Charlie Fink tried to convince Al Franken, a veteran of *Saturday Night Live* and author of *Rush Limbaugh Is a Big Fat Idiot*, to be a political commentator for AOL's *The Great Debate*. Franken's agent at CAA couldn't believe what he was hearing. "Now let me get this straight. You want to pay Al for twenty hours of work a month what he makes in one of his standard one-hour speaking engagements?" Franken later graciously called to personally pass. "You know Charlie, I'm a '60s liberal kind of guy . . . so I'm definitely going to go for the bucks here."

Tartikoff wasn't entering the world of cyberspace for the money. ("If people want to encourage me to toil in these vineyards," he said, "I really don't care that much whether I make zillions of dollars.") The Internet took time to master, and the financial rewards were so small that agents practically had their clients in choke holds to keep them out of new-media deals. "What Brandon did in sitting down and learning this medium is extraordinary," Charlie Fink later said. "Most of these guys can barely return their important phone calls. So to stop and learn how to use a computer, let alone navigate through the online jungles, is really an extraordinary act of will."[25]

Tartikoff was impressed by the Net's ability to provide direct access to entertainment-industry information. Being able to wake up in New Orleans—where he still maintained his primary residence—and get the *Hollywood Reporter* online delighted him.

He had another reason beyond money or techno-rapture for entering a development deal with AOL Studios. He felt that his colleagues in the entertainment industry would eventually follow him into the new-media space—and he wanted to get there first. "I know that when that convergence takes place, I'll already have run laps around other people in terms of my experience—in terms of what ideas work, and what doesn't," he said. "I'm going to do a thousand things wrong, and maybe a hundred things right. If the hundred things

I do right pay for the thousand things I do wrong, they'll let me continue to play."

Tartikoff came to his first meeting with Leonsis and Fink armed with a two-inch-thick pitch book. He had one idea for a show where he would hear AOL members' own pitches online. He had a special fondness for the pitch and had probably heard about thirty thousand by his count during his fifteen years in TV programming. (He'd once been pitched by Marlon Brando, who wanted to turn home movies of himself surrounded by naked Tahitian women into a special.) He had a tough time cutting back; what if he missed a pitch for the next *Seinfeld*-sized hit?

Tartikoff acquainted himself with the content on AOL and had become addicted to the Toshiba Powerbook Charlie Fink had given him. He felt he knew enough to know what was popular on AOL and why.

Tartikoff had an idea for Showtime he'd been developing as a miniseries that he wanted to pitch to Leonsis and Fink. *Beggars & Choosers* was a black comedy about working in network television, a serial replete with drama, comedy, and sex. "My homage to *Network*," he called it. The *choosers* in the title were the executives who chose which shows would be picked up by the network for the next season. *Beggars* were the independent producers who created the shows. Tartikoff had been a chooser at NBC. Now in his life as an independent producer, he was playing the beggar as well.

He'd kill two birds with one stone by developing an online version of the show, Tartikoff figured. He would give on-air shows depth by showing what the characters were doing the rest of the week. "The characters," Tartikoff said, "still have a life the other days you aren't seeing them." He could provide more backstory on the show's fictional TV network, and use video clips and company e-mail to give added color to the show's characters.

Because *Beggars & Choosers* was about network television, it would allow him to create "shows within a show." Tartikoff wanted to use AOL as a kind of "farm system" for developing and migrating shows from online to television, and vice versa. "If I found the next Jerry Seinfeld," Tartikoff explained, "I could put him in a situation comedy [on AOL]. I could get people to write it for me, film various pieces, and walk into [CBS Executive] Les Moonve's office and say, 'I want you to look at a six-minute tape, a minipilot. Forget the production values, just look at this guy.' I would be able to generate activity back in traditional media by experimenting with AOL."

One project that Tartikoff was invited to participate in at AOL was *Santa's Home Page*. For years, it seemed, people in the content business had talked about creating shows on the Web and licensing them to television. *Santa's Home Page* was the first online property to actually make the leap.

The story involved a geekish elf who had a taste for pizza and ambitions for "bringing the north pole up to speed" by introducing high tech to Santa's operations. The AOL site was an instant hit among kids, garnering over 3.5 million hits. Kids sent more than 50,000 e-mails to Santa—many sent after Christmas had come and gone. An army of AOL staffers volunteered to answer 20 e-mails a day for Santa. The site was AOL's fifth most popular content offering.

JC Penney had sponsored *Santa's Home Page* in 1995, its first year, and now Coca-Cola was set to sponsor the page for 1996. Leonsis and Fink approached Tartikoff to see if he wanted to get involved in developing *Santa* for television. Tartikoff said he'd get involved if he could also get a book version of the story for his publishing imprint at Avon books.

Once on board, Tartikoff worked closely with Fink on the project. He placed a call to Will Vinton (best known for the California Raisins and Nissan Barbie commercial spots) and paired him with a writer of *Santa's Home Page* to produce a TV-show "bible," or plan. The show was eventually sold to ABC as a Christmas special, which aired on December 12, 1997. *Santa's Home Page* became a textbook example of crossplatform promotion.

The site made a successful transition to television for three reasons. First, it was an unqualified success and had become branded for a sizable audience of children. Second, the characters were engaging. Ozzie was an elf with attitude, and Santa obviously carried a lot of water as a personality. Third, *Santa's Home Page* had a strong narrative spine, which meant that the property could be adapted to television with a minimum of trouble. All these factors apparently made *Santa's Home Page* appealing to the executives at ABC who ultimately bought the property.

Santa's Home Page reinforced Greenhouse's philosophy about what were winning strategies for online content, namely, appealing personalities. As Charlie Fink put it, "Since personalities worked for *Santa*, it ought to work for Real Fans [the Greenhouse's planned sports channel]; it ought to work at Electra [the women's channel]; it ought to work at Entertainment Asylum."

Charlie was looking for a way to get Tartikoff and Zakarin together—Greenhouse and Lightspeed had still not consummated their courtship. The opportunity came with *Beggars & Choosers*.

Mentor

Tartikoff was sitting in Charlie Fink's office one August afternoon in 1996 when Charlie picked up the phone and gave Scott Zakarin a call. Scott was in the middle of the *GrapeJam* press junket when the call came.

"Scott, I've got Brandon Tartikoff in my office. Brandon would like a walk-through of *GrapeJam*."

Scott—ever the technophobe—was the last person to walk anyone through a Web site. It was just as well that he was busy with the press. Scott grabbed Troy Bolotnick and had him call Charlie back and do the walk-through. After the demo, Scott cornered Troy. Was Tartikoff impressed with the site?

"He kept saying 'mm-hmm,'" Troy replied.

Scott and Tartikoff seemed to be entering each other's orbit even before the call from Charlie's office. Scott and his team had been preparing for the launch of *GrapeJam* and plotting their marketing campaign that summer when he had a conversation with Rex Winer at *Variety*. "If I'm going to get you on the front page of *Variety*," Winer said, "you've got to get a high-profile Hollywood alliance like . . . say . . . a Brandon Tartikoff." What Winer didn't tell Zakarin at the time was that he knew of Tartikoff's interest in online.

Shortly before the call from Fink's office, Tartikoff had taken a meeting with Mark Zakarin, an executive at Showtime and Scott's older brother. Tartikoff had come to Showtime's Westwood offices to talk about *Beggars & Choosers*, mentioning that AOL was interested in doing the show. "I don't know if you're aware there are these shows like *The Spot* online . . . " Tartikoff began to explain to Zakarin.

"Do I know about *The Spot*?" Zakarin shot back. "My brother created *The Spot*!" Tartikoff "was very impressed with you," Mark told his brother afterward.

In October, Scott got a call from a William Morris agent named John Maas, who represented Brandon Tartikoff. (Scott was being represented by William Morris agent Lewis Henderson.) Tartikoff had an opening in his schedule, Maas said. Could Scott arrange to meet him for lunch?

Yes, he was free for lunch, Scott said. (He did in fact have a conflicting lunch date scheduled with a friend at American Cybercast, which he swiftly canceled.) They agreed to meet at Ca Del Sole, a popular industry lunch spot near Universal Studios. As Scott prepared to leave for the lunch wearing a T-shirt and jeans, his wife shrieked. "You're wearing *that* to meet Brandon Tartikoff?!" She insisted that Scott at least put a nice sweater over the T-shirt. Since they were both at the Lightspeed house and there wasn't time for Scott to hurry home, a sweater was pulled off the back of a Lightspeed staffer.

Scott arrived at the restaurant first and waited. Tartikoff walked in and quickly expressed his admiration for what Scott had done in the new medium. "I wish I could take what's in your head and understand it," Tartikoff told him. Scott peppered him with questions about his television career. "Was it true, he asked Tartikoff, "that he had had second thoughts about airing the *Seinfeld* pilot? Was it true that . . . ?" After Scott sated his curiosity, the two got down to business. For the next two hours they talked about online entertainment, television, and celebrities. Scott tried out his Marlon Brando impression, which was quite good. Brandon told out-of-school stories about people in the industry. Midway through lunch Brandon handed Scott a five-page treatment for *Beggars & Choosers*, asking for Scott's thoughts about turning the treatment into an online show. Scott took this as a sealing of their working relationship.

A short time later Tartikoff came out to the Lightspeed house to meet the gang. He loved the house and even stood in front of the *GrapeJam* cam with a HI MOM sign.

The pairing of Tartikoff and Zakarin was unusual—not simply because of Tartikoff's stature in the entertainment industry, but also because mentoring itself was almost unheard of in the Internet business. The industry was still very new; there wasn't an old guard for the simple reason that the industry hadn't been around long enough for there to be one. Those people who had enough experience to qualify as mentors were too focused and/or burned out on their own stuff to mentor anyone.

For Tartikoff, the role of mentor was instinctual. He had once considered taking a year off to teach at a university. But that would have meant dealing with 130 or so students, out of which there inevitably would be only 4 or 5 he'd want to pair himself with. Being able to focus on Scott satisfied his urge.

Tartikoff understood why Scott had chosen the Internet path as his way into Hollywood. If he were twenty-one again, he mused, he might have taken the same pathway as a more direct route into the business than "slaving away at the same paltry salary" at a local TV station as he had done. Any medium that allowed you to use your judgment skills and programming instincts to please an audience was applicable to the tube.

Scott saw, firsthand, Tartikoff's exalted status in the entertainment world a few months into their collaboration. Tartikoff's health problems dictated that he work at home most of the time, though he and Scott continued to meet, talk regularly on the phone, and exchange AOL instant messages (IMs). One day Scott sent Brandon an IM asking what he was up to. Tartikoff IMed back: "I'm trying to finish up this memo for [Michael] Eisner," the chairman of the Walt Disney Company. "Oh really," Scott shot back, "tell Mikey I said 'hi!'." Tartikoff's response popped up on the screen a moment later. "Mikey says 'hi'." Scott suddenly realized that Eisner was at the Tartikoff home.

Business Models

I'm stupefied by the lack of business models. You may be on the first wave, but it's crashed on this island and you're Robinson Crusoe looking around for Friday with a deal memo.

— new-media consultant Kevin Stein (1996)

While Scott Zakarin and AOL continued to flirt with each other, *GrapeJam* consumed more and more money, threatening to sink Lightspeed. *GrapeJam* generated good numbers for an episodic, but compared to the search engines or major content sites like Pathfinder, they were dwarfish. It became apparent in the fall of 1996 that *GrapeJam* couldn't pull down the kind of advertising bucks needed to defer the cost of production.

Early on the team had assumed that advertising revenue would at least cover the production costs of the show—not an unreasonable notion in early 1996 when they had launched the company. Projections were that advertising revenues would grow beyond the $55 million generated in 1995. Ad sales did grow for the industry—but given the choice of buying ad space on a lot of small Web sites or a smaller number of ads on a few heavily trafficked sites like Yahoo, advertisers went for the latter.

Maybe *GrapeJam* would have to be shut down—at least until someone could be found to sponsor the show. The work-for-hire side of the business, on the other hand, was better than ever and offset most of their losses. People were beginning to approach Lightspeed to develop shows for them. One way out of their financial straits was to try to develop *GrapeJam* as a television series.

The idea had an irresistible appeal. But television was a mirage, tantalizing yet always out of reach. Just as the executives in the television world didn't understand the Net, the pioneers of online entertainment didn't fully appreciate how difficult it would be to break into the clubby world of television, or how challenging it was to adapt Web properties for the tube. The Web was a world where you made up the rules and where sloppiness, errors, and miscues were part of the medium's genial informality. Television, in contrast, was a tightly structured and rule-bound medium, where even the length of time allotted to running the credits was specified to the second. Yet, for all that, the vision was too compelling not to try. Television was the *deus ex machina* that would save them all from financial collapse.

Madeleine's Mind: The TV Series

On a clear November afternoon in 1996, Thomas Lakeman stepped into Josh Greer's office and dropped a bible into his inbox. This wasn't a Gideon's companion that Lakeman was dumping on his boss. A "bible" was an overview of a television series—premise, characters, backstory, and summaries of individual episodes. Lakeman had just finished the bible for *Madeleine's Mind*. *Madeleine* might not have conquered Hollywood, but Josh and his team did begin to get more meetings with creative types, including Sam Raimi, the creator of *Dark Man*, who expressed an interest in turning *Madeleine* into a TV series.

Developing *Madeleine's Mind* as a series was motivated by economic necessity. The first episode of *Madeleine's Mind* hadn't made any money. Lakeman had started production on episode two and needed to find a way to finance it. He began looking for a sponsor. The negotiations started that spring with MCA had gone nowhere.

The original Ant Farm team of five shrank to three: Thomas Lakeman, Daniel DeFabio, and Robin Gurney. Episode one had taken the team of five twelve weeks to complete, from writing the story to creating the animation to the final packaging of scenes. Episode two used more complex technology, such as Shockwave 5.0, and consisted of two new scenes each week, representing about a month of production time. They were able to produce the show more quickly this time because they had learned many lessons from the first episode, and the tools for creating an animated series were getting better and more powerful all the time.

Luckily, they found another group at MCA that was willing to sponsor the new episode. An Intel media-buying group (not the investment group) also bought an advertising/sponsorship package. When *Madeleine II* launched that September, it had been fully paid for in advance. In addition to advertising and corporate sponsorships, Josh Greer also wanted to generate licensing fees and other revenues from a television series based on the Web site.

Josh and Thomas soon discovered that having sponsors was a mixed blessing, and trying to adapt *Madeleine* for television nearly impossible. Intel had set two contradictory goals for Digital Planet to achieve with *Madeleine*: to attract a large Web audience, and to showcase the latest in Web technology—in particular, to promote the use of VRML, a 3-D Web technology that required huge amounts of processing power and powerful Intel chips to work.

The first episode of *Madeleine* had tested the audience's patience with plug-ins and interminable downloads. Episode two ensured that only the most technically savvy and patient viewers would stick with the series. VRML in particular was a problematic technology that all but guaranteed that the audience for the series would remain small.

Intel had also insisted that Episode two contain product placements, such as having Madeleine use a PC equipped with an Intel Internet telephone. The premise of *Madeleine* had been that there was a sinister side to technology—or as Lakeman put it, an "exploration of technology as a left-handed gift that is a curse unless you master it." Intel, however, objected to depictions of technologies as being anything but benevolent. Ironically, the evil organization that pursues *Madeleine* was inspired by Lakeman's experiences working with Intel, which he referred to as a "paranoid organization into mind control." Intel's sponsoring *Madeleine* was, in Lakeman's view, like getting a grant from the National Endowment for the Arts so you could do a performance piece called "piss on the flag."

Another problem was that the webisodic involved a story arc in which Madeleine eventually mastered her psychical powers. But you couldn't have that degree of plot resolution in a TV series—where would the show go? As it happened, the Ant Farm team never had to face that dilemma.

The Fifth Beatle

Despite its enormous costs, two arguments could be made for keeping *GrapeJam* pumping, one practical and one emotional. First, Lightspeed's work-for-hire gigs generated from the team's episodic shows—first *The Spot*, then *GrapeJam*. The shows advertised Lightspeed's expertise and creativity in the online realm—the part of the business model that actually brought in revenue. The second reason for keeping the webisodic going was that Scott Zakarin and company wanted to maintain the buzz they generated for themselves with *The Spot*. They loved the creative freedom that came from putting on a Web show every day and the rush from interacting with their fan community.

Scott and Troy Bolotnick began looking for ways to trim ballast and cut costs. Putting on a live event every day, as they had been doing, was expensive, so they were cut back to two a week. The "Sour Grapes," an interactive social rant à la Dennis Miller, was also an expensive production, mainly because it aired five days a week. *Why don't we cut back to three shows a week?* they thought. People didn't notice the cutback, but they did remark that the Sours were getting better. These cutbacks stabilized things for a while, and a crisis was temporarily averted.

There was still one other financial card they hoped to play: getting the Greenhouse to invest in Lightspeed. One important obstacle had to be overcome before the Greenhouse would consider pumping cash into the company. Charlie Fink told Scott that the company needed a "business presence." Though Scott had owned and operated his own companies in the past, he was certainly no suit. Troy had taken on the responsibility of managing the company's accounts, but he was a self-taught accountant at best and didn't qualify. What Lightspeed desperately needed was a CFO who could put systems into place and build a real business infrastructure. Charlie Fink had just the person.

Charlie knew Carl Genberg from his days at Virtual World, where Carl had worked his way up from controller to acting CFO, taking a major role in the company's transition from location-based entertainment to game development. Though he was only twenty-nine, Genberg had already amassed a long résumé, with stints in investment banking and management consulting prior to his five years at Virtual World. Carl had a mature demeanor beyond his years. Charlie thought he probably achieved adulthood by the age of eleven. Carl was born in Sweden and had the friendly, cool, and efficient manner associated with that country.

Genberg was in the process of leaving Virtual World and interviewing with a number of new-media companies when he got the call from Charlie. "We're really interested in investing in Lightspeed Media," Charlie said, "but they don't have anyone in their company that can give us a business plan."

Carl drove over to Lightspeed to take the meeting—experiencing the shock of all first-time visitors in finding himself in a residential neighborhood. Scott wore a T-shirt and jeans—as he did on almost all occasions. He leaned back in his chair and sipped a soft drink, squinting at the slender, Nordic young man with pearly teeth and pointy chin. "Charlie tells me I need to hire you," Zakarin said, taking a swig. "Can you tell me why, because I really don't know."

"Well, I really don't know either," Carl began. "Can you give me a P&L [profit-and-loss] statement?"

"What," asked Scott, "is that?"

"That's the first reason you need to hire me."

Scott called Troy, who managed to print out something that approximated a profit-and-loss statement. Genberg studied the figures. He was pleased to see that at least an effort had been made to log expenses and revenues. Their P&L had been a creditable effort, but it was clear that Lightspeed had been running a pretty sizable operation without any real accounting or business experience. It was like guessing how much money you had in your checking account when paying bills. But Genberg quickly saw that despite the lack of sophistication, the misposted entries, the huge expense of producing *GrapeJam*—despite it all, Lightspeed had a positive cash balance. "Hey, you guys are making money."

The meeting ended on a pleasant note—but no commitments. Scott invited Carl to stick around while he interviewed a Playboy Playmate for an acting gig on *GrapeJam*. Yes, Carl thought he could get used to show business.

Carl continued interviewing, talking to big companies like Disney. But the heavy corporate atmosphere at Team Mickey didn't sit well with him, and he began making the rounds at the new-media start-ups. Josh Greer interviewed him for the COO position at Digital Planet, but nothing came of it.

Still interviewing, Carl began to come over to the Lightspeed house one day a week to clean up the books—pro bono. He wanted to learn more about the Web business in general and about Lightspeed in particular. Genberg's regular visits prompted some curious responses. "So are you working for us or what?" That depended. If he was going to work for a small start-up, he decided, he wanted to do it as a partner, not an employee.

Taking on a fifth partner wasn't an easy or comfortable move. But Scott and the four had been impressed with Carl, recognizing their own deficiencies in financial matters, and saw the advantage of having "Math Boy" (as they liked to call him) on the team. They made Carl an offer, which included an ownership share in the company. Rich would later speak for the others when he said that bringing Genberg in "was the best decision we ever made." Genberg would smile and say "I'll always be the fifth partner. Kind of like the fifth Beatle."

Lightspeed's relationship with the AOL Greenhouse developed apace. The team produced a show for the Greenhouse that ran exclusively on Love@AOL called *Score*—a game of virtual dating. A new man or woman would be introduced each week and inserted into some dating scenario. A text-based conversation would begin. The member would have multiple-choice responses to select from. Depending on the choice, he or she would get closer or farther away from "scoring" with the potential date.

Score was the Lightspeed team's first experience working directly with the Greenhouse, mainly with Bill Schreiner. Like Charlie Fink, he came from the entertainment industry (television and film), and had recently joined the Greenhouse creative team. (*Score* was his idea.) He understood the needs of creative people and didn't attempt to micromanage the creative process or to get into the minutiae of production—which put Scott and the team at ease.

Scott and Troy got their first taste of Ted Leonsis during a visit to Vienna, Virginia to discuss a project called *Celebrity Graveyard*—later renamed *Hollywood Legends*. They were in the middle of a meeting with Greenhouse executives when Leonsis, unannounced, barreled through the conference-room door and swept into a seat. He began warmly, complimenting the Lightspeed crew on their accomplishments. "Scott, you guys did it. You guys did what everybody else was talking about. You'll forever be remembered that way."

He quickly switched modes. Despite having missed most of the meeting, he began to summarize discussion points, speaking in blunt, sing-songy Brooklynese:

"Okay, we're talking about you guys doing *Hollywood Legends*." *Check mark in the air.* "We're talking about possibly investing in your company." *Check mark in the air.* "Okay, show me what you got."

Scott and Troy made a brief presentation.

"Great," Leonsis said. He stood and turned on the Greenhouse executives. "*Talk* to these guys. *Make* something happen."

Then he departed as suddenly as he appeared.

Later that visit, Fink broke the news that the Greenhouse was no longer considering investing in Lightspeed. This was grave news. Despite their efforts to trim expenses on *GrapeJam*, Scott had been hoping that an investment from AOL would lighten the burden. Charlie delivered more disappointing news: the Greenhouse wouldn't be doing *Hollywood Legends* after all. Scott was beginning to get aggravated. His team had busted their asses to put together a proposal for *Legends*. Now he wondered how serious AOL had really been about the project. Two major body blows. Scott wasn't good at hiding his emotions.

"Don't despair," Charlie said, "we have another project in mind for you."

"My Personal Bosnia"

During Thanksgiving of 1996, Brandon Tartikoff discovered a lump in his glands while shaving. The lump turned out to be a reoccurrence of his Hodgkin's lymphoma, a third appearance. Tartikoff knew what that meant; getting blasted with chemo, hair falling out, weakened immune response. The lymphoma, Tartikoff would later tell Scott Zakarin, was his "personal Bosnia."

When Ted Leonsis learned of Tartikoff's illness, he sent his friend an e-mail message, offering heartfelt wishes on behalf of himself and his wife. Tartikoff sent back a response: "Thanks, that means a lot to me. I'm about to step into the ring with Mike Tyson." Leonsis sent a spirited reply to this post: "Fuck Mike Tyson. Be like Evander Holyfield. Go into the ring and push him around. Mike Tyson is a wimp. First time he got hit hard on the nose, he backed down. That's what you have to do with this."

Tartikoff replied, "Thank you very much. By the way, I've CCed Mike, who is a friend of mine, on your note. If I had Bill Gates's e-mail address, I'd CC him too."

"You didn't tell me about Bill Gates. Kick *both* their asses!"

Despite their deep concern for Tartikoff personally, it was unclear what impact his illness would have on Leonsis's plan to build and launch major content networks for entertainment, sports, romance, and women. Tartikoff expressed supreme confidence, but it was inevitable that the regime of chemotherapy he faced would curtail his schedule. Would he have the strength to guide their efforts?

Speeding American Cybercast

We took radio people and tried to make them TV people. That didn't work. Now we're trying to take TV people and make them Net people. It defies the law of natural aristocracy.

—Watts Wacker

Under the creative and strategic direction of Russ Collins and the executive management of Sheri Herman, American Cybercast grew very rapidly in 1996 (it adopted the call letters AMCY in October). Herman had a talent for winning over investors and spent much of her time on investor relations. She also recruited a number of executives from the traditional entertainment industry, and below them an assortment of Web producers, programmers, artists, and the like.

AMCY had grandiose ambitions to build the company into a quarter-billion-dollar online network and produce a dozen online shows by the year 2000. Intel and CAA were on board first. Telecommunications, Inc. and Softbank, among others, soon followed.

The company staffed and structured itself unlike any other start-up, due to the high caliber of TV executives they hired and the high salaries they paid. Like at many new companies, AMCY executives focused a lot of their time and energy on cultivating relationships with the investor community. To some observers, it seemed that the intensity of that focus was often to the detriment of the shows AMCY sought to produce.

A few fans of *The Spot* had been aware of the tensions building during late 1995 and early 1996 between Scott Zakarin and Fattal-Collins/AMCY over the creative direction of the show. After Scott severed ties with the company, fans noticed changes in the characters' diary entries and in the feedback they received: diary musings sounded more superficial; e-mail responses felt canned. AMCY management was dumbing down the characters to make them more accessible to a mainstream audience. It was apparent that the show lacked the attention and energy that had made it so popular. Meanwhile, new shows were being developed and launched.

The first show AMCY created and produced was *Eon-4* in April 1996. *Eon-4* was produced by Scott Nourse and Eric Barnard and was based on a movie script written by science-fiction writer Rockne S. O'Bannon. Sponsored by Apple Computer, *Eon-4* followed the adventures of two scientists who traveled through the galaxy in search of the source of a mysterious radio message from an interstellar civilization. What began as a concept-driven sci-fi show, in keeping with creative changes at the company, evolved into a sexy sci-fi show. The next show, *The Pyramid*, based on an idea Collins developed, was a webisodic about "lust, distrust, and software." The action took place in a fictional company called Global Oasys, which produced new-age software programs for things like dream control and astrological forecasting—a company that seemed oddly reminiscent of the show's corporate sponsor, Intel. The fourth and final show was *Quick-Fix Theater*, which provided a venue for celebrities like Spalding Gray and RuPaul to offer up content vignettes and other byte-sized entertainment.

AMCY management steered the shows toward what they considered to be the mainstream. There was nothing wrong about wanting to make the shows more appealing to a broader demographic—how else could the company hope to build an audience large enough to make the business models work? The problem was that management lost sight of what made shows successful Web properties. The result was simmering fan discontent, which boiled over into open revolt in November when AMCY fired Jeff Gouda. Gouda had been one of the last links to the original *Spot* team under Scott Zakarin. "He was the most interactive person on their site," John McKay, an engineer and fervent *Spot* fan, told the *Los Angeles Times*. "By getting rid of him, we felt as if our input didn't matter anymore."[26] Debbie Myers, the senior vice-president of production, said that Gouda's firing had been prompted by financial rather than creative reasons. Soon after, *Eon-4* producer Scott Nourse resigned because of creative differences over his own show. His director and associate producer left as well.

Among dissident *Spot* fans, Harry Zink was the chief agitator. He organized a fan boycott of the site. Some disgruntled fans found that their messages of protest were not being posted to *The Spot* board. Zink created an alternate site where *Spot* fans could post their complaints.

The protest board was inundated with messages after its first weekend, and protesters claimed the site got 2,000 to 3,000 hits a day (*The Spot* was getting 10,000). Myers called later and tried to talk Zink into taking down the site. Zink said that if Myers listened to the fans, AMCY could still get them back. Over the next three weeks the protest site logged more than 5,000 messages. Zink noticed that one individual posted frequent messages of support for AMCY management on the protest board. Suspicious, he traced the messages to the sender's originating server and straight back to the desk of an intern at AMCY. He immediately called and confronted the intern. The hapless intern was too stunned to speak. (The call landed Zink in hot water with his colleagues for what was seen as a violation of privacy.)

AMCY management tried to suggest that the campaign had been, as the *Los Angeles Times* put it, "the single-handed effort of Zink." They claimed that he had been embittered for being turned down for a job at the company and that he was scheming to launch his own Web show.

On December 12, 1996, a meeting was set up between the AMCY production staff, Debbie Myers, and representatives of the fans—minus Harry Zink. But by mid-December the fan revolt would be overwhelmed by events. AMCY was running out of money—fast.

Earlier in the year, AMCY executives, armed with $6 million from assorted investors, felt they had two choices in pursuing their goal of creating a major online network. They could husband their resources and grow slowly over a period of years, perfecting their shows, allowing the technology and business models to work themselves out—in other words, stick with the original business plan. The second choice was to build rapidly, burn through their money, and either make an initial public offering with a $250 million valuation—or crater.

Collins and his associates knew that AMCY would never generate enough revenue from advertising in the first two or three years to be profitable. So from day one the issue uppermost on management's mind had been, "How do we fund this thing?" Company executives were mindful of the spectacular run-ups for IPOs like Yahoo's and Netscape's. Many entrepreneurs were seized with IPO fever at this time, and some likened the seemingly inflated values of Internet companies to a modern equivalent of the tulip craze. AMCY and its board of directors decided to increase their spending and go for the IPO as a way to bring in a lot of money fast.

By September of 1996 the IPO window began to close. Wired Ventures had attempted an IPO and failed in a spectacular fashion—twice. *Wired*'s troubles were a signal to many that Wall Street was beginning to get skittish about Web start-ups. At this point it was not too late for AMCY to shift back to the go-slow strategy. Instead, the board decided to blow through the shrinking IPO window before it closed altogether. Hiring and building continued.

Beyond the desire to generate wealth, there was another reason for wanting to get big quick. As a small first mover in the online entertainment space, AMCY was vulnerable. Larger competitors like Microsoft, AOL, or more traditional media companies could move in, hire away the company's talent, and steal their audiences. Building up the company offered some protection from AMCY's predatory neighbors.

Meanwhile, the company prepared for the launches of *Pyramid* and *Quick-Fix Theater* in October. Before the launch Sheri Herman invited AMCY staffers to her Hollywood Hills home for an intimate get-together over pizza and Chinese food. Nearly everyone was there. The vibes were good. People shared their ideas and enthusiasm for the company's shows and AMCY's future. (Some felt Herman may have thrown the soiree to dispel the sense that management was distant from the people developing the shows.)

Shortly after Herman's get-together, the company threw a huge launch party at the offices of Fattal-Collins for *The Pyramid* and *Quick-Fix Theater*. The room was thick with the Hollywood crowd. Roger Clinton showed up, among others. The party was a success, but the launch was marred by technical snafus.

There were other problems as well—like low levels of traffic to the site. Just as *GrapeJam* had become lost in a sea of webisodics, so had AMCY's shows. A webisodic wasn't like a half-hour television show, which required little more of a viewer than to show up for thirty minutes a week. A webisodic had to be visited regularly to keep up. Visitors could expect slow downloads, a lot of text to absorb, and challenging territory to navigate. Being a fan required a significant investment of time and attention. Only the most diehard fans could sustain the level of effort needed to stick with the shows over a long stretch of time.

The audience for webisodics didn't grow very fast, and what audience there was was being splintered among the hundred-odd webisodics in operation. As a result, hits were down for the new shows, and even for *The Spot*. AMCY failed to deliver the level of hits it had guaranteed to its advertisers and had to give money back.

Nonetheless, the building and hiring continued. Scott Siegler, a well-liked and -regarded television executive, came on board as president of the company's entertainment division. Shortly after, a dozen staffers were cut loose. (Some speculated that the layoffs were needed to pay Siegler's salary.) The Web demonstrated its extraordinary capability to empower a fan base. AMCY management faced a raging mass of pitchfork-wielding fans. Things were getting ugly.

While the advertising pinch had hurt, the more troubling issue was the change in the mind-set of the investment community. It became clear that the IPO wasn't going to happen. Management decided instead to go for another round of financing.

In the past, AMCY had been a magnet for investors; Collins and Herman spent most of their time telling potential investors no. Now, suddenly, the investors were nowhere to be found. One of the original investors into the company offered to inject more money into AMCY, but only on the condition that a second investor could be found. The scramble began.

All the Major Tenets of Entertainment

By the fall of 1996, Scott Zakarin was getting anxious about finding new sources of revenue for Lightspeed. The fixes to *GrapeJam* had stanched the flow of red ink, but the company still needed either an investor or another major client. Things were looking promising with AOL, but nothing had solidified.

Lewis Henderson, Scott's William Morris agent, arranged for the Lightspeed team to make another go at pitching Microsoft. Scott, Troy, and Carl met with Jamie Fragen, who headed up the Los Angeles office of M³P, MSN's production entity. (This time there was no pretense about Bob Bejan attending the meeting.) Scott and Troy were hopeful that they could give a major boost to Lightspeed's work-for-hire business by selling shows to MSN. They pitched several ideas to Fragen and her producers, including a kids' show called *Lab Rats*. Scott tried to sell the community-building aspects of the shows they pitched.

"We don't believe the Web is about community," they were told.

Scott was speechless. If the Web wasn't about community, then what was it? Did they think people got online to interact with the technology? They could do that with a CD-ROM. Community was the only thing that really set the Web apart from computer games, encyclopedias, and other software.

Scratch MSN from the buyers list.

Within weeks of the MSN meeting, Scott and Troy made the trip out to Vienna, Virginia for the *Hollywood Legends* meeting, hoping that there might also be progress on getting the AOL Greenhouse to invest in their company. This was the meeting where Charlie Fink had delivered the two body blows: *Legends* was a no-go, and Greenhouse was no longer interested in investing in their company.

Having sent Scott and Troy reeling, Fink laid a sheet of paper on the Greenhouse conference-room table. The page was Greenhouse's basic grid for a network that would encompass all the major tenets of entertainment. Scott managed to get his bearings and to focus on the paper. His eyes widened.

"This is great," Scott said. "Can I do it?"

"Yes . . . as long as you're willing to do nothing else."

"You mean work exclusively for AOL?"

"Yeah."

Scott turned the offer down cold. The memory of his involvement with American Cybercast was still fresh in his mind. But the economic realities of the online entertainment business soon pressed in on him. His competitor Josh Greer was at that moment making a second run to raise financing for Digital Planet. (He hoped to raise at least $2 million and maybe as much as $5 million.) Greer's company had been locked in a boom-bust cycle that made life nerve-wracking for everyone.

The deal Charlie was presenting had attractive aspects. Building the kind of entertainment network Greenhouse was proposing was the closest thing to doing pure entertainment that was likely to come along. The Entertainment Asylum would feature local listings for TV and films, news, and communities built around entertainment themes.

Charlie seemed especially sensitive to the team's concerns about creative freedom. "It's gotta fit our models and it's gotta be successful," he'd say. "But it's not gonna work if you guys aren't happy with it." If the Lightspeed team came on board, Scott insisted they be given the resources to make the venture successful.

The two parties began to explore the what-ifs. Scott did not want to create content exclusively for Rainman, AOL's proprietary environment. Lightspeed was dedicated to life on the Web; producing inside AOL's firewalls was not their style. Apparently that would no longer be a problem. The Greenhouse wanted the entertainment network to have a presence both in Rainman and on the Web. The conversation came around to the idea of Greenhouse not simply investing in Lightspeed, but acquiring the company outright. Eventually the terms of a deal were worked out.

For Scott, Troy, Rich, Laurie, and now Carl, producing *The Spot* and *GrapeJam* had all been like some Mickey Rooney/Judy Garland movie. *Hey, we can put on a show! And we'll get all the grown-ups to come!* In joining AOL, they would be creating a network rather than just a show. Scott would have to think like a network programmer rather than an executive producer, and the others would have to think like production executives rather than writers. Managing fifty to seventy people (the projected staffing) was an order of magnitude different from managing sixteen. Could they build this entity and still hang on to the old house spirit?

Almost immediately, the clock began to tick.

Internet Time

1996 was the year when people in the industry began to feel the effects of Internet time. The industry was growing and changing at an unprecedented, overwhelming rate. It meant picking up the paper each morning and finding five new technologies, four new mergers, and seventeen other things happening on the Internet that could organically change the essence of one's vision. No one dared take a vacation—or even a long weekend—for fear that everything would be different when one got back. Working in the Internet industry wasn't a job; it was a way of life. For the twenty-somethings who worked in the business, the distinction between home and workplace blurred. Even the smallest start-ups maintain well-provisioned refrigerators. Some had basketball courts. One Web developer, W3-Design, had a masseuse who came in to rub down the staff. "Maybe these folks don't need to rest," Jim Jonassen of the Larkin Group observed. "Maybe they're so relaxed and having so much fun on the job, they don't need downtime."

Life moved so rapidly in Internet time that the only way to survive was to crowd as many activities into the same space of time as possible. "We are beginning to change ourselves to parallel process, to multitask, to do many things at once," Jeannine Parker said. "If you are going to be part of the new collective human mind [of the Internet], you have to be able to do this."

Scott and his partners were certainly living life at Internet speed. They had begun the year by walking away from *The Spot*. Scott thought he could leverage his brand identity and continue with a new, self-funded company, Lightspeed Media. He hoped that the company's webisodic, *GrapeJam*, would eclipse *The Spot* and evolve into a television series. As the year progressed, he discovered that life for a self-funded Web entertainment company was fast becoming untenable. Online entertainment was still a medium in search of a business model. While the Internet audience was edging toward mass-market numbers, most of the eyes and advertising dollars were flowing to the search engines and not to content sites. In terms of the entertainment niche, the Web was getting to be a crowded place. *The Spot* had inspired hundreds of imitators. Microsoft, with its cache of billions, relaunched the Microsoft Network with a full slate of Web shows in an effort to differentiate its service from AOL. The vastness of the Web, and the difficulty in getting noticed, meant that the old entertainment fundamentals, which the Internet was supposed to have overturned, counted after all: marketing dollars, distribution, brand identity.

AOL was playing catch-up with Microsoft, preparing to develop its own new major content offerings. As the last days of 1996 ticked off, Scott made the decision to give up his independence and make a deal with AOL, taking his partners with him. The opportunities would be huge, not the least of which was being able to work with Brandon Tartikoff, who would play a major role in the endeavor.

What no one suspected was that in the first weeks of 1997, even before Scott's deal had been announced, AOL would face its greatest crisis. In response to the challenge posed by Microsoft's flat-rate pricing policy, AOL adopted its own flat-rate pricing plan—with devastating consequences. By mid-January, AOL members would be howling from coast to coast.

1997–1998: Entertainment Asylum

Deal Memo

Scott Zakarin thought he had what every online entrepreneur coveted: access to AOL's 8 million households—almost mainstream distribution numbers—and a presence on the Web as well. It doesn't get better than this—at least in the online world. Money had always been a limiting factor at Lightspeed, as they trimmed *GrapeJam* to make payroll. He now had enough working capital (in theory) to pursue a grander vision.

While the Entertainment Asylum wouldn't be about pure entertainment, it would come close. *The Spot* and *GrapeJam* had been about empowering the audience, letting them touch and be touched by the characters Scott and his team had created. They would do the same for the Asylum. But being acquired by a company like AOL spooked them. Because of its size, the company had corporate trappings—particularly when compared to the genial anarchy of a start-up. Mindful of his experience with American Cybercast, he told the Greenhouse he had to have enough independence to fulfill their vision for the entertainment network. Danny Krifcher and Charlie Fink told him that although they would not be unfettered, the team would have a great deal of creative latitude. *We* (Greenhouse) *will make suggestions and you tell us when to back off on creative issues*, was the way Scott remembered it.

What made going with a large company like AOL more palatable was that they were actually being acquired by a much smaller, more entrepreneurial company within the AOL family. AOL Studios was a separate operating division within the company, of which Greenhouse was a wholly owned subsidiary. Greenhouse Networks looked and acted like an independent entity, had its own facilities, and made use of the AOL Studios sales force. Greenhouse Networks looked like a start-up, with all the scurrying about and confusion associated with the breed. As events unfolded, illusion collided with reality, creating all kinds of problems downstream.

One issue emerged as a red flag signaling the complicated relationship between Leonsis's AOL Studios and Bob Pittman's AOL

Networks: distribution. Distribution was equated with the amount of attention one's site garnered from AOL members. Attention was a function of the "amount of real estate"—the size of the button—on Rainman, AOL's proprietary online environment. The bigger the button, the more attention, the greater the distribution among AOL's members.

Distribution, or real estate, was a precious commodity for AOL Networks. Real estate could be sold or bartered, and there was only so much of it. It became clear that Asylum would only get what Scott called "a pinhole" on Rainman. Members would see no Asylum button on the opening screen, nor on the channels page. The Asylum button would be buried inside a generic entertainment channel.

The deal wasn't solid yet. Scott had a deal memo, not a contract. There were still months of negotiations ahead before contracts were signed. This deal, like the one with NBC a year earlier, could blow up. Scott and the Greenhouse agreed that, pending the acquisition, Lightspeed Media would begin development of the Entertainment Asylum on a consulting basis. The job would be immense for a sixteen-person company. They'd have to stop taking new work and allow existing contracts to run out. That put Scott and company in an uncomfortable position. If the AOL deal did indeed fall through, Lightspeed could be left with no clients in the pipeline and no revenues.

Scott and the team had other anxieties. Just as they had signed up with AOL, two great crises were breaking, one with their former employer, the other with their prospective one. Both crises would have consequences for their future in ways they could hardly have guessed.

Crisis #1: AMCY Craters

AMCY had burned through nearly every cent of its $6 million. A plan for massive layoffs was put together. Buzz Kaplan, AMCY's vice chairman, sent an e-mail to Sheri Herman asking her to make sure that Russ Collins saw the layoff plan. In one of the missteps that now seemed to plague the company, the message was accidentally CCed to everyone in the company. Not surprisingly, staff morale, buffeted by the fan revolts and first round of layoffs, broke down completely. The rumor was that the company would run out of money on January 15. Management had been denying that the company was in financial trouble for weeks.

Debbie Myers decided to tell her staff the state of things. While Russ was in San Francisco looking for an investor, Myers (it's unclear if on her own behest or Herman's orders) went on the fan boards and sent humiliating appeals through the media, asking fans to try to find investors to keep the company alive. She pleaded with fans to "e-mail *Variety* and *Hollywood Reporter*. Contact Bruce Haring at *USA Today* . . . contact Jennifer Tanaka at *Newsweek*. . . .Let's send a message of support for 'EON 4,' 'The Spot,' 'The Pyramid' and "Quick-Fix Theater.' Your passion may sway a firm's mind into investing into the company. . . ."[27]

All these efforts were for naught. Russ told everyone to take Friday, January 12, off. That Monday, Jan 15, he met with the staff and informed them that AMCY was indeed laying off most of its staff, severely cutting back on its programming, and filing for Chapter 11 protection. AMCY was broke and owed its creditors hundreds of thousands—some said millions—of dollars.

Shortly after the press-plea fiasco, Josh Greer was brought in for a meeting to discuss the possibility of Digital Planet taking over production of *The Spot*. Sheri Herman and Scott Siegler were in the meeting. Siegler had an oversized hourglass on his desk that he'd gotten for working on *Days of Our Lives*. The sand had run out. Macintosh computers were lined up and covered with plastic tarps like a row of body bags. Josh saw the same care-worn, shell-shocked face on Herman that he had recognized in himself so many times during the past months— a yet-one-more-thing-falling-apart look. The two walked off alone for a few minutes and Herman confided to Josh that things at AMCY were "really bad."

Greer had always been on good terms with Herman and enjoyed her company. He wanted to comfort her now, give her a pep talk. "Sheri, believe me, I've been hours away from closing my doors a dozen times," Greer said. "You just have to hang in there. Things'll work out. Don't give up." But by then the ax had already fallen. The next day the announcement was made that Herman was leaving the company. Josh never saw her again.

AMCY executives, while scrambling for an investor to bail them out, had turned to Paramount Digital Entertainment. Of the four shows, Wertheimer was only interested in *The Spot*, if it could be bought at a fire-sale price. But in the end there was no real enthusiasm for the deal, and Paramount passed. Scott Zakarin made a widely publicized play to buy back his creation, but the offer was rejected.

Utilizing a loophole in the corporate bankruptcy laws, Russ Collins and Scott Siegler set up a new corporation called CyberOasys (the name of the fictional company in *The Pyramid*) and bought back AMCY's remaining assets for $114,000, thus avoiding having to pay the company's many creditors. *The Spot* continued to be produced by a volunteer staff from home until it, too, disappeared from existence when CyberOasys pulled the plug on July 2, 1997. (As of this writing, the show is still archived at www.thespot.com.)

In Russ Collins's view, AMCY had become part of the "coral structure" of the industry, one among a growing number of Internet companies that began to fail that season, marking a consolidation of the industry. For some, the company represented a good idea that had come too early, while others felt the start-up was an example of the industry's Achilles' heel—weak management. Still others said AMCY's demise was a morality tale about the folly of the Internet IPO craze and the greed that fed it. "Everyone has their own take on American Cybercast," Collins would recall wistfully. "It will become part of the lore of the Internet."

The aftermath of AMCY's implosion was devastating. Industry watchers ignored the fact that AMCY was done in by its IPO gamble and management problems. They felt it was the concept of Web entertainment itself that had failed. Procuring investment in entertainment-oriented content from the venture-capital community had always been a hard sell—particularly in Hollywood, a town that many perceived as being fiscally irresponsible. AMCY had nonetheless managed to get the venture capitalists and technology companies to invest in its business, so when AMCY blew up, it soured a group that was already skeptical about content.

In the first years of the Net, the geeks had been in the ascendancy; it had all been about technology and empowerment. Then the ponytails had taken a commanding position, and content was king. Now the suits were moving in on the Net, taking the dominant position, dictating that the Net was, after all, about the business of business.

Entertainment could exist in this new landscape, but in a supporting, as opposed to a leading, role: "Entertainment is being leveraged by almost everyone," Charlie Fink said at the time, "from news outlets to retailers....You also see retailers like Eddie Bauer using tools imported from the entertainment industry—set design, mood, and music to enhance the shopping experience."[28] The role of entertainment was being reinvented; its purpose now was to make information or commerce more exciting and enjoyable. Bob Bejan would claim that even watching one's stock portfolio online had entertainment value, stretching the term to the point of meaninglessness.

In the wake of the changing market, content developers retooled their mission statements and "About Us" pages. An example was CyberStudios, which had launched in October 1996 as an "independent studio created specifically to produce original, revenue-generating, entertainment programming for the Internet." But by March 1997, the spin on CyberStudios' promotional literature had already shifted to "Themed Commerce Environments on the Internet."

The Palace was not a content company, but one that marketed a platform for 2-D, avatar-laden chat. The company felt compelled to broaden its customer base by repositioning its products for the teleconferencing and corporate-training markets. Even a Web magazine like MSN's *Slate* began touting the utility of its features, like a section aggregating the lead stories from U.S. newspapers.

Despite these adaptations, high production costs, small audiences, and low advertising rates associated with original content made the business model increasingly untenable for small, independent players. Content companies, which found it hard to survive on their own, were being picked up by larger media companies and brands with deep pockets. Scott thought that AOL would provide him with a safe haven. AOL's access crisis of winter 1997 would quickly disabuse him of that notion.

Crisis #2: AOL Busy Signals

Back in 1996, AOL was experiencing what one insider called a "killer churn rate." For every three persons who signed up for a membership, two would quit after the free trial period ended. The company's stock price was as low as $24, and it wasn't clear whether AOL would survive. Focus group after focus group yielded the same result: people didn't care about quality content, they wanted $20 per month, "all you can eat" access to online services. Up to that time, AOL had been charging an hourly rate of $2.95; some heavy users of the service ran up bills of hundreds of dollars a month. In comparison, MSN had just switched to the $19.95 per month flat-rate pricing structure, in line with many of the nation's Internet service providers. AOL had been forced to follow suit, abandoning its hourly rates and implementing its own $19.95 per month pricing structure. AOL executives had known that the all-you-can-eat pay plan would create a surge in demand, and probably a degradation in customer service. They would deal with the problem as it arose, they thought. But actual demand became so great that many members couldn't access the service. Newspaper and TV stories appeared showing angry members canceling their accounts. AOL was becoming synonymous with the busy signal. Competitors seized the opportunity to steal away disgruntled AOL members. State attorneys general banded together to investigate the company for fraudulent consumer practices, thus putting AOL executives in legal jeopardy.

Like millions of other AOL members, Ted Leonsis was fuming. He couldn't get through. Unlike the other millions of AOL members on this particular day, Leonsis wasn't trying to log onto his AOL account; despite the busy signals, he could dial an employees-only 800 number to get onto the service immediately. Leonsis was on the phone waiting for airline reservations. He'd called one of the airlines and been put on hold. "I've been waiting half an hour," Leonsis barked when the customer service representative came on the line. "I apologize, sir. By the way, you were waiting three minutes and eighteen seconds."

Leonsis loved to tell the story, the point of which, he explained, was that AOL's service troubles were not as severe as most people thought. Just as that three minutes and eighteen seconds had felt like a half hour, he believed AOL's access problem was more a matter of perception than reality, and he (Ted the unflappable) had the stats to prove it.

What Leonsis couldn't explain away was how the switch to flat-rate pricing had dealt a blow to the studio's business model. Until that time, the Greenhouse had shared revenue from hourly access fees with content developers. They would now have to shift to a more advertising-based model. Without the guaranteed revenue of hourly fees, AOL Studios began to hemorrhage money.

AOL executives quietly made the decision that Leonsis should start looking for investors or buyers for AOL Studios, or at least Greenhouse Networks. The sale would give AOL a much-needed influx of cash, while providing AOL Studios with a level of investment capital needed to fund its ambitious plans.

In anticipation of a future sale, Greenhouse executives began to take steps to brand the company as a separate entity. A logo—a green swirl—was designed to brand the company. Executives dropped references to AOL when discussing the Greenhouse with the press. While Scott and his partners were absorbed in developing a plan for the Asylum, Danny Krifcher packed his bags and went on the road in search of investment partners.

Apollo vs. Dionysus

Entertainment people think about storytelling. They think about talent. They think about all these things which have nothing to do with interactive data-driven models.

—Halsey Minor

Brandon Tartikoff and Scott Zakarin began to collaborate in earnest, beginning by fashioning what they hoped would be a strong vision for the Asylum. Tartikoff believed that personality would be critical to their success. "It's a very cold medium," he said, "unless there's something there to warm it up for you." He sent Scott a memo elaborating the point. "To break out personalities and characters," Tartikoff wrote, "we've got to try to have at least three times the number of personalities in order for at least the most memorable ones to emerge and stick."

This philosophy ran counter to the point of view popular in Silicon Valley: that personalities were unnecessary obstacles that stood between users and the information they wanted. Leading figures in the valley, like CNET's chairman and CEO, Halsey Minor, believed that personalities didn't fit into the interactive, data-driven models of the Net. Entertainment people thought that "the right thing to do is bring Howard Stern online," Minor once said in a different context. "Bring a big personality [online] because TV is about personality—big personalities." This in fact was precisely what Tartikoff believed the Net needed.

Tartikoff and Scott weren't the only people in the business who thought the medium needed warming up. Four hundred miles to the north, in the heart of Silicon Valley, personality had been an issue some months earlier at Excite, the Internet search company. Specifically, the personality of Barbara Feldon.

Barbara Feldon played Agent 99 in the '60s TV series *Get Smart*. She had the kind of sexy, cozy voice that conjured images of silky sheets. Stacy Jolna thought Feldon's voice would be perfect for Excite's Marimba channel guide. He shared his thought with Excite cofounder Joe Kraus. Kraus was not exactly sanguine about the idea: "Stacy, you're absolutely out of your mind."

Excite was the number-two Internet search company in the market (after Yahoo), and its success had been built on the notion that people wanted to find and download information as fast as possible. At the same time, Push Media offered an interim solution to the frustrations of narrow bandwidth. Once described by Wired magazine as "the radical future of media beyond the Web," Push was based on the idea that content companies could automatically deliver content to PCs—much as the morning paper is pushed or delivered to your doorstep. Long download times could be avoided by delivering large files while consumers' computers were idle. Problems with the core technology and doubts about Push's actual value to consumers doomed the paradigm—at least in the marketplace of the late '90s.

Kraus understood that Excite needed more experience producing multimedia content for the days when greater bandwidth was available. Designing an Excite Marimba channel guide would be the ideal way to experiment with the Web as a multimedia platform. A personable, dark-haired twenty-six-year-old who looked like a young Republican, Kraus was an ex–poli-sci major steeped in the valley's techno-ethos. Kraus and his colleagues were trying to morph Excite into a media company. As part of that effort, Kraus brought in Jolna, an ex-journalist and CNN documentary producer, to be the executive producer of Excite's Marimba channel guide.

A handsome man in his forties with small warm eyes and flecks of gray in his dark hair, Jolna had the right credentials for producing what in effect would be Excite's broadcast channel on the Web. As a journalist operating in television and print media, Jolna's whole career had involved taking the essence of people's stories, whether in business, entertainment, or politics, and communicating them to a mass audience. He strongly believed that the mass market didn't have the same fascination for technology as did the residents of Silicon Valley. Many people, in his opinion, viewed technology as inorganic and even a little frightening. If the Web was ever to be a mass medium, the technology had to be given a human face. The best way to humanize the medium was to give people a little giggle and push their emotional buttons. Barbara Feldon's voice was the way to do it.

Feldon had worked with Jolna in his days at CNN when she did voice-overs for the news network. Even thirty years after her role as Agent 99, Feldon was still a strikingly attractive woman. Jolna told her about the Internet, Marimba, and Push. "Wow, that's so magical," purred Feldon, who knew next to zero about computers. "I'd love to be that voice."

Kraus resisted the notion of using Barbara Feldon's voice—or *any* voice—for the channel guide. "Why would anyone need a voice on this thing?" he said. Feldon didn't mean anything to Kraus; he had heard of *Get Smart*, but the show had gone off the air a year or so before he was born. "Consumers don't care if you have Barbara Feldon's voice," he told Jolna. All consumers really cared about was getting their information quickly. Excite's slogan had been "We want to be the shortest distance between the consumer and what they want on the Web." Multimedia razzle-dazzle was one thing, but Kraus was convinced people didn't want to be bothered with voice-overs. Kraus hated the proposal, and he was sure consumers would hate it too. So he shot down the idea.

Jolna was not ready to toss in the towel. He managed to work down the price a bit and came back at Kraus. "At least let us tape some voice-overs and see how they sound in the product," he pleaded. Kraus could see how badly Jolna wanted to try his plan. As much as he disapproved, he was convinced that Excite's future was in the media space. This was a period of experimentation, and that meant not shutting the door on ideas too quickly—even silly ideas like some voice from a '60s TV show that none of his peers could remember. So in the end, Kraus grudgingly allowed himself to be talked into the try-out.

"This is a place where people love the machinery and engineering aspects of life," Jolna said. "Silicon Valley wants you to engage in a mechanical process." Hollywood and the news, entertainment, and information industries, on the other hand, "try and get as far from the technology and machinery as possible. TV and movies do everything they can to hide the magic from the consumer." The collaboration of the industries was literally a marriage of opposites. "The thing about two people getting married," Jolna said, "is you never know what the kids will look like."

The time arrived for Kraus to stroll over to Jolna's office to see the demo for the Excite channel guide. The demo had been a struggle every step of the way. The art director had been an easy sell, but the engineer on the project had rolled his eyes at first, though he eventually came around and in the end had become an enthusiast. Jolna loaded the software. "Welcome to the Excite Channel Guide," came the voice of Barbara Feldon, as warm, whiskey, and sexy as Jolna had hoped. Jolna clicked on a button. "Channel surf." He clicked on another button. "Add a channel." More buttons. "Previews." "Subscribe." Purr. Purr.

Kraus was not overly impressed. "Well, that's OK, but be sure you put a kill switch on the audio," he said finally. "After anyone hears that, they won't ever want to hear it again."

"On the contrary," Jolna countered forcefully. "People like warm and fuzzy. *People are going to love this voice all the time!*" In the end, Kraus got his kill switch. He also agreed to take the channel guide on the road, where he could try it out on some audiences.

When Kraus came back a couple weeks later he wore a big grin on his boyish face. Barbara Feldon, as it turned out, was a big hit on the road. Kraus was surprised at how many people immediately recognized the Feldon voice; in fact, the recognizability of the voice was one of the things that excited people the most about the product. He told Jolna that "everyone thought the coolest thing about the channel guide was that Agent 99 was the voice of the product."

After Jolna completed the project and left Excite, he bought Joe Kraus an Armani tie. Kraus seldom wore a tie at that time, but nonetheless donned the unfamiliar accessory with a suit for a debate between Yahoo, Infoseek, and Excite held at the Hyatt-Rickies. Jolna had included a note with the tie: "According to *Newsweek*," the note read, "within the next five years, Silicon Valley is going to be run by guys in Armani suits. Welcome to the brave new world."

The conflict over adding a touch of human warmth (Barbara Feldon's purr) to Excite's Marimba channel guide was only one engagement in a continuing battle between Hollywood ponytails and the Silicon Valley geeks for the soul of new technology. It was a philosophical struggle as old as Western civilization. What motivated people, their minds or their emotions? Which was closer to our true natures—the cerebral ideal of Apollo or the pleasure-seeking tradition of Dionysus? It was certainly true that people wanted information from the Internet—and wanted it fast. Most people didn't spend endless hours online. As Robert Seidman of the *Online Insider* newsletter (www.onlineinsider.com) put it, "the mainstream isn't going to give up beer, fishing, bowling, inline skating, sex, golf, skiing, swimming, music, and so on to spend gobs and gobs of leisure time online."

Maybe Seidman had it right, but it was hard to believe that people were that practical and utilitarian in their online habits. "You have to generate an emotion to generate a click," Charlie Fink once said. The case was made that original content could generate more clicks—attract more eyeballs and longer visits—if the content was compelling and entertaining enough.

Seidman was wrong about one thing: plenty of people were spending gobs and gobs of time online in the pursuit of at least one utterly Dionysian activity: cybersex. There was an explosion of user-generated porn in cyberspace. It seemed that eventually everyone would be naked on the Internet.

Vision Statement

"Complete. And completely unique," was how the vision statement opened.

Scott Zakarin had sat down and brainstormed with everyone involved on the project, sorting, arguing, discarding, and talking through ideas for the site. Scott met often with Tartikoff and Fink to define the philosophy, shows, features and capabilities of the entertainment network. His head fit to burst, he punched out a rough fifty-page draft.

The vision statement reflected Scott's own single-minded obsession with the genres of entertainment as much as it described the Asylum's potential audience. "Everyone loves entertainment. A person's identity is literally made up of favorite movies, TV shows, and music. Our entertainment choices define who we are—they give others more information about our personalities than our nationalities or religion."

Scott believed the Entertainment Asylum would eliminate the traditional talking-head interview on TV, the way television and movie listings were presented, the way late-night talk shows interacted with stars. While he could not and did not ignore what their online rivals were doing, the Asylum's true competitor was television itself. They weren't gunning simply for E! Online, but also for E! Entertainment Television. He poo-pooed Microsoft and its expressed goal of creating three-to-five-minute entertainment experiences. "Our philosophy," Scott said, "is that the entertainment channel [Asylum] is a lot of things. A place you can hang out at for hours. A resource you can use for two seconds."

The Asylum would offer up more than entertainment news, TV and movie listings, reviews, and other entertainment-related information. Themed content would be organized into shows. The shows in turn would provide a base for growing communities. If the Asylum was Manhattan, then the shows would be the little communities that made up the city—the Upper West side, the Village.

What made the Web different from television was audience empowerment, chat, and, above all, community. The essence of online, in Scott's view, *was* community—shared experience and empowerment.

"It's a real-time experience. Why do we go to the game, when we can see it much better at home? . . . For the high-fives and beer, the cheering . . . for the sense that we can affect the outcome somehow by being there."

Scott felt Microsoft's three-to-five-minute model was too confined to foster a truly interactive or social experience. "What's the oldest form of entertainment?" he'd ask. "Sexual intercourse. It's totally interactive." People wanted to make love to their favorite celebrities—in the sense of connecting with and provoking them. The Entertainment Asylum would pierce the barrier separating the stars from their fans.

Content Plan

Rich Tackenberg referred to the development of the content plan as the time when the team "minutiaized the minutiae." All sixteen members of the Lightspeed team participated in the development process. The Greenhouse had come up with the original concept and grid, and Scott had cranked through a top-level view of the site. Now it was time to take those concepts and turn them into a detailed design document that would please the Greenhouse and AOL and provide a roadmap for production. At the same time, the team would have to develop a game plan for transforming their group of sixteen stalwart Lightspeeders into an Asylum production organization of fifty to seventy people.

As a first step, Scott and the Lightspeed team broke into several groups and began brainstorming and fleshing out show ideas, without regard for practicality or reasonableness. The team took this potful of concepts and sorted through them, combining some notions, eighty-sixing others. There were proposals for action shows, gossip shows, a show that focused on "the biz," sci-fi, pulp, and others. What they had was a big jumbled mess of content that needed to be refashioned into a seamless, logical unity that would be easy to understand and navigate. The team walked through the material from the point of view of a user. Whatever seemed complicated or ambiguous was scrutinized. Scott's technical myopia came in handy here. *Make it simple for me. I want to click one button, not three. Why can't I see all this stuff in one screen instead of three?*

Brandon Tartikoff was pitching his own ideas during occasional meetings and phone calls. He thought they needed hosted shows. That made perfect sense to Scott; he'd always thought *The Spot* had been a hosted show of sorts because the characters spoke directly to the audience. What if *The Spot* characters worked on the Entertainment Asylum? Not the actual characters, since American Cybercast (or what was left of it) owned the rights to the show, but characters of that ilk? Brandon liked that idea and began to list various archetypal fictional personalities.

Why not real people? Scott suggested. Have a team of real folks who go out and do interviews, make appearances on the various shows, and otherwise operate as loose cannons on the site? This idea would eventually become the Screen Team.

"The Screen Team," the content plan read, "is a group of real people, all of whom are highly identifiable and promotable. They talk like real people and have strong opinions; they are people with whom you can identify, and who you will grow to trust for entertainment advice." They would "conduct interviews, give movie and TV reviews, and join in general discussions on boards throughout the site." It would be as if Tara, Lon, and Michelle from *The Spot* were on the entertainment beat. Naturally, Scott had Laurie in mind for the team. Jim Wise from *GrapeJam* was another. The Screen Team would differentiate the Asylum from its competitors, of which there were several.

The Competition

It's like fighting a war on virtually every front, every moment of the day.

—Stacy Jolna on competition in the Internet business

One of the early online entertainment news sites was *Hollywood Online*. Stuart Halperin and his partner Steven Katinsky began pitching the idea for a movie site to the online services in the early '90s. (Like Josh Greer, Halperin worked in Universal's marketing department.) Halperin and Katinsky launched *Hollywood Online* on AOL in 1993, when the service, astonishingly, served only 500,000 households. By 1995, *Hollywood Online* had also launched on the Web, providing movie and video guides, Hollywood news, and other features. The company was eventually acquired by Times-Mirror.

MrShowBiz, another entertainment news site, launched in March 1995. Susan Mulcahy was a New York journalist and *New York Post* alumna (she wrote page six of the paper) when she decided to take a hiatus from daily journalism and move to Seattle to work on her writing. She was soon brought on board at Starwave, ex-Microsoft co-founder Paul Allen's Web-development company, to build an entertainment service. Mulcahy spent three months hiring staff and developing the concept for the service. She thought the name of the site would be key. In late 1994 and early 1995, the Web was awash with sites and service providers that had techie names—*compu*-this and *info*-that—something she wanted to avoid. She wanted a name that had personality and that evoked a kind of retro Walter Winchell/Stork Club ambiance. *MrShowBiz* was the one that stuck.

Mulcahy and her partners had a rough time in the early going. Despite their industry contacts and journalistic credentials, the studios were often uncooperative. "We already have our own Web site," was the typical response. It was a struggle just to get a press kit. Often, the people at the studios didn't have a clue what Starwave and *MrShowBiz* were—or even what the Net was all about. Even brandishing the Paul Allen name didn't help—until Allen made a much-publicized $250 million investment in DreamWorks.

Mulcahy and her staff eventually overcame resistance from the studios, and the site grew and built a respectable level of traffic. By early 1997, *MrShowbiz* had a staff of twenty-five full-time employees, plus a list of stringers and contributors. Then it attempted to inject contests, humor, and some not-always-gentle mocking of celebrities into the entertainment news mix. "Celebrity Plastic Surgery Lab" was a game in which the visitor could pick and choose among the facial features of a group of celebrities—say, the cast of *Seinfeld*—and create their own composite celebrity.[29]

The next major launch of an entertainment news network—and the one to beat in terms of brand recognition, technical sophistication, and traffic—was E! Online. One Wednesday night in early 1996, Jeremy Verba got an urgent call from Halsey Minor, the chairman and CEO of CNET. Verba was working for Technology Ventures, TCI's venture-capital incubator. Minor had just signed a joint venture with E! Entertainment Television. They wanted to build an online equivalent of the cable network. He needed someone who understood both cable television and the Internet. The pool of people who had that kind of background was very small. Verba had been working in both worlds during the past six months at TCI.

Shortly after, Verba flew out for a meeting at CNET's offices on Chesnut Street in San Francisco. Within two weeks, he had quit TCI and was working for CNET. Halsey sealed the deal when he told Verba to consider what people were looking for on the Net. Setting aside porn for the moment, the top three categories on search-engine logs were sports, entertainment, and computers. ESPN was going to own the sports category. CNET would win the battle for the computer category. But entertainment was up for grabs. There wasn't any big play in the entertainment space—just some small plays like *MrShow-Biz* and *Hollywood Online*. The opportunity was ripe for an existing brand to come in and claim the space as its own.

Halsey hired Verba as a vice-president of entertainment ventures at CNET. E! Online was actually supposed to be the first of several additional online ventures that Verba would build. The plan was for Verba to hire the management team for E! Online, get the venture up and going, write the business plan, then move on to the next online venture for CNET. "There's a nice operating leverage. CNET had built all these tools and an entire back end," Verba remembered. At one of the board meetings he put up four candidates for president of E! Online. The board considered the names, then turned back to Verba. "Why don't you be the interim president and see how it goes?"

Like so many of his colleagues in the online space, Jeremy Verba had an eclectic résumé. He majored in architecture at MIT in the early '80s, and had taken courses at the Sorbonne as part of an MIT exchange group. "I wasn't a great architect, but I loved building." So he abandoned architecture and went to work on Wall Street. There, he absorbed an education in the workings of the investment-banking and corporate-finance worlds for a couple years, then quit and went for a long and leisurely trip around the world. Back home in Toronto he combined his architecture and business backgrounds and went to work for a real-estate-development firm. He also began to pursue his interest in entertainment. He wrote sketches and scripts with friends, learned more about performance in Second City improv workshops, and took more entertainment-type classes.

When the real-estate company he worked for went bankrupt, Verba went back to business school, where he earned a degree in management. After graduation he worked for two years at Reiss Media before moving over to TCI's recently formed Technology Ventures, where he'd been hired to work on the @Home project. @Home was a pioneer in the field of cable modem services.

Verba's new boss explained what @Home was all about to him. "That's great. Can I see a business plan?"

"A business plan is a great idea," his boss replied. "You're going to write it for us." Verba spent the next eight months on the effort. Though he had a business background and knew the economics of cable, he knew nothing about the Internet. Eight months later when Minor called him, he'd gotten up to speed.

E! Online launched in August 1996. It was never intended to be an ancillary online operation of the E! cable network. The idea was to use the strength of the E! brand combined with the promotional power of the television network (then available to over 40 million homes) to launch a category leader in the new medium. That meant building content specifically for the new medium as opposed to repurposing programming or content from E! Entertainment Television. MTV and Showtime had tried to build ancillary sites on the Web using repurposed content, an approach Verba wanted to avoid. "If we were seen as just a marketing arm for E!," Verba observed, "E! Online would fail." Verba set about hiring an independent editorial team, which included Lew Harris, the former editor-in-chief of *LA Magazine* and past entertainment editor of *People* magazine.

Verba agreed with Halsey's view that as bandwidth increased, sites that "owned video assets" and that had an ongoing ability to create video would be the winners. E! Online had plenty of video assets and infrastructure thanks to its association with E! Entertainment Television. The use of video clips and webcasting would be one of E! Online's major strengths.

What most concerned Scott Zakarin, Charlie Fink, and the others was E! Online's potential for crossmedia promotion. Unlike Asylum, the site could get heavy airplay via E! Entertainment Television. It was a huge advantage that so far hadn't been fully exploited.

All of that made E! Online a formidable opponent. AOL had a bigger overall brand and more online distribution, but the Entertainment Asylum would lack the "brand incumbency" that E! Online enjoyed. Thousands of people were already in the habit of getting their entertainment news, TV programming information, movie reviews, and gossip from the more established site. The one aspect of E! Online's operation that Scott and his team would follow closely was their experiments with streaming video.

Video streaming was the technology that allowed video images to be downloaded in real time from a Web site to a viewer's computer. In the Web's early days, video files couldn't be viewed until they were fully downloaded—often a lengthy process. In early 1997, Real Networks came out with RealVideo, a streaming media product similar to its popular RealAudio. RealVideo allowed video files to be viewed at the same time they were being downloaded, much as a television image is seen at the same moment it is being broadcast. Streaming video (the generic term for the technology) promised to transform the Web into a video broadcast medium.

Streaming video images on a computer screen were about the size of a Central European postage stamp. Small, unclear, and "jerky" as they images were, they represented the outer frontier of the Web.

Who Am I to Argue with Brandon Tartikoff?

Work continued apace on Entertainment Asylum. Scott Zakarin and Brandon Tartikoff evolved a distinctive style for working together. Tartikoff would pitch an idea: "How about blue?"

Scott would think about it: "Blue is nice, but blue doesn't work well online."

"What about red?" Tartikoff would shoot back.

Scott would create a character to host the *Comedy Clinic*, one of the Asylum's shows. "I don't like this character," Tartikoff said.

"I'll throw it out," Scott replied.

"Don't," Tartikoff shot back. "I also didn't like *Hill Street Blues* at first."

Like any media heavyweight, Tartikoff possessed a gargantuan ego, though he carried it with considerable style and tact. But in the online sphere, he willingly checked his ego at the door. Once Rich Tackenberg found himself in a passionate discussion with Brandon about real versus fictional hosts. As Tackenberg forcefully made his points it dawned on him that he was arguing with one of the greatest programmers in TV history. *Who the fuck am I to argue with Brandon Tartikoff?* he thought. But there he was, and Tartikoff was listening intently.

The Lightspeeders put together an organizational chart and structure. The group feared evolving into a bureaucratic, corporatized structure, although the final organization ended up being fairly hierarchical anyway. The five partners in particular knew they worked well together and wanted to replicate that model as the company grew. They created a series of small teams that would be given a lot of latitude to take the original show ideas and run with them. The teams would grow around the original Lightspeed staff, with the partners functioning as a top-level team responsible for watching and coordinating the whole operation. No upper-management bullshit, no middle-manager chickenshit, not a lot of approval process. Hang on to the advantages of a small company. At least that was the hope. Once the content plan and organizational structure were finished, the team took the plan to Vienna to let the AOL accountants have at it.

By February the attacks on AOL over its monumental access problems picked up steam. Having tied his fate to AOL, Scott was worried. Everyone was beating up on the company. Other Internet service providers incorporated busy signals into their commercials to slam America Online and siphon off its members. The company's enemies smelled blood. Could AOL management take the heat? How was Ted Leonsis holding up under the pressure?

Studio God

While boarding a flight from Los Angeles to San Francisco that February, Scott spotted a familiar-looking man of about forty with glowing gray-blue eyes. Scott was flying up to AOL's World Play game company to see how they could tie game development into the Entertainment Asylum. At first he thought the man might have been someone he'd known in the film business. The man looked and dressed like a film guy. After a couple minutes his mind clicked. *Wait, that's Ted Leonsis.* Scott walked up and down the aisle a couple times before he convinced himself that it was Leonsis. *Yes, it's definitely him. But what's he doing sitting in coach?* Scott immediately thought of his ongoing negotiations with AOL and how this would make arguing for first-class flights really tough. He approached Leonsis in midflight.

"You're Ted, right?"

"Yes."

Leonsis was friendly and effusive when he recognized Scott and told him how much confidence he had in small Internet start-up companies. In fact, he was thinking of investing in some of them himself. He picked up the *Wall Street Journal* and began to handicap the day's stories. "You see this story?" Leonsis pointed to an item about Disney acquiring a share of Paul Allen's Starwave. He seemed unperturbed by the class-action lawsuit that was being filed by state attorneys general against AOL. Scott was impressed by Leonsis's confidence and felt reassured about the decision to go with AOL. "He's cooler than I could ever be," he said afterward. The more pressure on AOL, the cooler Leonsis got.

Scott told Leonsis that he considered him to be a "studio God," a remark that left an impression. The fact was, Leonsis was beginning to *feel* like a studio executive. While driving to Pasadena he worked through a stack of messages on his cell phone. He discovered that people didn't hide behind their assistants when Ted Leonsis phoned—they took the call. Leonsis's hero was Hollywood's last mogul, former MCA chairman Lew Wasserman. Back in the days when the studios owned theater chains, Wasserman had been the ultimate integrator, working all sides of the creative and business equation—a packager of talent, a creator of content, a financier, and a distributor. It reflected Leonsis's own ambitions. He too wanted AOL to own as much of the value chain as possible.

Leonsis's confidence in AOL Studios bucked the growing anti-content sentiment in the industry. The *Wall Street Journal* had stated that content was dead. "I loved it," he said. "I was thrilled. Because in '85 the *Journal* wrote an article that said cable content was dead. So Turner went for it," and CNN became wildly successful. He was confident history would prove the *Wall Street Journal* wrong again. His certitude extended to the company's access crisis. "We thrive," Leonsis said, "in this paranoia-crisis stage." AOL was so important now that "if people can't get on, they sue us."

Leonsis's bravura aside, the access problems of that winter had turned into a full-blown crisis of Tylenol-poisoning proportions. AOL shifted into rapid-response mode. The company purchased or leased thousands of modems to handle the added demand. As the new modems came online, service slowly improved and the crisis abated. The money for those modems had to come from somewhere, and Bob Pittman promised to ransack the company in search of the needed resources. "I told people I was Robin Hood," he told the *New York Times*. "I would rob from someone else to get what you needed."[30] One of the targets would be AOL Studios.

Leonsis got the news that AOL's arch rival, the Microsoft Network, planned to cancel as many as ten of its twenty Web shows—including *15 Seconds of Fame* and *475 Madison Avenue*—and to lay off almost one hundred temporary workers.

The *Los Angeles Times* quoted Bob Bejan as saying that "The role of labor in media is accordion in nature. . . . You gear up when you need people. Then you gear down. Finally, we are doing that." And, after all, MSN's budget had not been cut, and many of the temporary workers would doubtless be rehired for future productions. MSN's show cancellations, Bejan continued, were similar to what the television networks did every season: drop some shows and add others. In fact, MSN would be launching fourteen new shows to replace the ones being dropped, shows that Bejan promised would be "light-years better."[31]

MSN just didn't get it, Leonsis said. MSN was fixated on shows when it should be thinking about communities. One didn't build a community in a ten-week season. "AOL would never cancel a show after ten weeks."

They Are *Not* End-Users

The shake-up at MSN came as a surprise to many in the industry and, coming so soon after the AMCY debacle, cast more doubt on the appropriateness of pure entertainment as an online genre. *Fifteen Seconds of Fame*—one of the shows that was axed—was based on an idea by Jon Kimmich and Ed Yip. Kimmich had been a programmer in Microsoft's original interactive TV group. The two thought it might be fun to have a site that located clever and unusual Web sites created by Internet users. That original notion evolved into a show in which MSN subscribers would send in funny personal stories that could be used as fodder by comedians Charlie Fleischer (the voice of Roger Rabbit) and Stephanie Miller.

Bejan had been enthusiastic about the idea because it "smudge[d] the line of collaborator and spectator."[32] One of the better stories submitted by subscribers was about a travel agent who thought the island of Molokai was populated by leprechauns. The engineering crew on the site backed up Fleischer and Miller's bantering with Hawaiian music and the sounds of rain-forest fauna.

Sometimes the show worked, but more often it didn't. *15 Seconds of Fame* simply wasn't interactive enough to be compelling. Bejan believed the show would have worked better if there had been a wider pool of participants. Like all of MSN's content offerings, the show was trapped behind the network's firewall. The shows needed to live on the open, free Web, where they could breathe.

The news was not all bad for MSN that winter. On January 22 the company announced an exclusive relationship with Jim Henson Interactive, a division of Jim Henson Productions, the creator of the Muppets. The deal called for the development of family-oriented entertainment programming. In March, the Walt Disney Company signed with MSN to distribute its new online service for kids, *The Daily Blast.*

It was obvious that MSN was shifting strategies, developing programming for women and children in hopes of finding passionate core audiences. Like almost everyone else in the industry, Bejan believed that children—the so-called Generation N (Net)—were still forming their media-viewing habits and would be more open to interactivity. If MSN could capture those young eyes it could take a big step toward strengthening its online brand. But Microsoft was discovering that it needed more than hundreds of millions of dollars to make it in online entertainment.

The effort to recreate a Hollywood production studio inside the corporate campus of a software company like Microsoft was daunting.

One could assemble a staff of producers, artists, and technicians, make liberal use of entertainment metaphor—refer to the Redmond West production pit as the "back lot"—even open development offices in L.A. and New York. But the fact that Microsoft was located in Redmond, Washington, not Burbank or Hollywood, was hard to overcome. Even in the age of the Internet, location still mattered. Once again, Microsoft paid the price for arrogantly insisting on centering its important operations in the Pacific Northwest. Being distant from Silicon Valley had contributed to its underestimating the importance of the Internet in the early '90s, and now the distance from major media centers hurt the company in its content initiatives. Even *Slate*'s editor, Michael Kinsley, admitted that though "it's very helpful to be surrounded by people who are always surfing the Web . . . it would also be great [to be in Washington, D.C., and] to hear, 'Hey, have you heard the latest on Newt?'"[33]

The physical layout of the Redmond offices, with its cubicles and other corporate trappings, seemed better suited for geeks than ponytails. Creative people had different space needs than computer programmers did. Ponytails worked collaboratively much of the time, but they also needed time alone so they could replenish the creative well. Cubical floor plans were more appropriate for a Dilbert cartoon than a Hollywood-style imagination station.

Engineers would foam at the mouth when they heard ponytails complain about limits on their creativity. To them, listening to consumers and slavishly following their current preferences and wishes made innovation impossible. Wasn't the sameness of Hollywood product—the unending string of sequels and remakes—proof of Hollywood's creative bankruptcy? The audience never asked for sound on film. The impetus for digital special effects in film did not originate from market research. Whenever a new technological paradigm emerged, Hollywood had to be dragged in kicking and screaming.

If there was one thing the new-media industry had suffered from, ponytails countered, it was too much innovation for innovation's sake. Building content to showcase technological features shifted the focus from the inner logic of the content to something exterior to it. Often this meant moving content away from the very things that made it compelling to people. Frames, for instance, might be a nice way to create a windowslike environment within a Web site. By 1997 everyone seemed to be using them; they were an elegant technical solution to an interface problem, making for easier navigation of a site. But they also made for a less immersive user experience. The boxiness of the display reminded people that what they were viewing was, after all, a Web site.

Geeks' and ponytails' perceptions differed the most regarding audiences. They didn't share a common word for the people who ultimately consumed the fruit of their labors. Engineers referred to the people who used their products as *end-users*, a term that irked media people no end.

"They're not end-users," Matti Leshem said, "*they're not end-users!* An end-user is someone who denotes, *I'm going to give them something to use, they're going to use it, and that's the end of the relationship.*" Leshem preferred the term *clients*, people that he listened to very carefully and whose needs were vital to his survival. Since developing *Second City* for MSN, Leshem said he had become "very tied in to what [my clients'] needs are. Why? Because I know if they don't like my show, my show is going to go off the air." Engineers didn't understand audiences. "The designers who make Office '97 are more like surgeons. My father comes into the surgery, the guy opens up his heart and does what he thinks is best. He closes it up and that's the end of the discussion. He's not really asking my father's input on stuff."

This internally focused expert approach didn't work for the production of interactive entertainment. "If you're some schmuck who comes from the technical side," Leshem continued, "and you approach content development the way you approach writing an application, you're going to be out of luck."

Matti Leshem's *Second City Headline News* had survived the February cancellations at MSN, but not unscathed. In an attempt to increase the show's traffic (i.e., ratings), Leshem and his team had renamed the show the *Second City Naked News* [emphasis added]. The page showed two attractive, suitably nude news readers sitting behind a desk. The anchorwoman held a sheaf of script pages strategically in front of her ample chest.

Meanwhile, Leshem did not want to depend on a single show, or even on MSN, for Cobalt Moon's survival. He had other projects in development, like *Angel House*, that had been optioned by MGM Interactive. *Angel House* was based on an idea by Tim Bennett and Dave Sheridan, the latter being the creator of *Buzz Kill* on MTV. It was another show designed to appeal to the hale and horny segment of the Internet audience. A male student is sent to a Big Ten university by his parents. He uses all his money to buy computer equipment and ends up with no place to live. He finds shelter in the basement of a sorority house. This student, who is something of a geek, has wired the house with "cams" (digital cameras suitable for webcasting), enabling viewers to select and maneuver cameras throughout the sorority house. In a sense, the show was a throw-back to Leshem's *Hilton Head Homicides* days, when his audience could wander from room to room picking up pieces of action. The show also seemed inspired by the cam craze on the Web. A growing number of people were setting up cams in front of their computers, in their bedrooms, and in other rooms of their houses to broadcast their day-to-day activities over the Web, activities that were often crushingly boring and occasionally titillatingly sexual. Ultimately, MGM Interactive let the option lapse, and *Angel House* never went into production.

Leshem's most ambitious product, *The King of Television*, was designed to run on WebTV. The character-driven product featured a jolly monarch (Paul Goebel) as its personality element and used a short list of questions to discover a TV viewer's tastes in programming. (The product was inspired by Goebel's extensive knowledge of television trivia.) The show also included a TV trivia game and enabled viewers to chat online while viewing television shows. As of this writing, *The King of Television* hasn't found a buyer. Leshem found more success working with Fujitsu, which selected Cobalt Moon to develop virtual worlds using Fujitsu's avatar-based Worlds Away software.

Leshem's affection for Microsoft was tempered by the fact that, like the major studios, the company could be difficult when it came to issues like ownership, control, and money. Still, he felt he was being treated well and paid well—Cobalt Moon would receive more than a million dollars during *Second City*'s one-year run.

On the other hand, there was a price to be paid for the Redmond giant's big-kitty gambler spirit. Although there were people at Microsoft who understood "the business"—people like Bob Bejan, for instance—most didn't. Surprisingly, the major problems for the show were technical rather than creative. Leshem had even had to struggle with simple things like getting his show "propped" on MSN's servers. ("Propping" referred to the process by which new information—text, graphics, audio, or video—was incorporated into a show's computer files, making the new material visible to viewers visiting the Web site.) The root of the problem seemed cultural. In the entertainment world, when the curtain rose at 8:00, it rose at 8:00. "These guys," Leshem complained of the engineers, "five or six hours later, they might have looked at a couple of files." Imagine if NBC was set to launch its fall season on September 8, and on September 7 it announced that it would be delaying the fall launch for three weeks! Microsoft simply wasn't an entertainment company.

With the exception of his show runner and head writer, Leshem's creative staff now consisted almost entirely of television and joke writers. On a typical afternoon, the writers would sit around a battered conference table amidst spit balls, yellow pads, diet soft drinks, Evian bottles, and three-by-five cards, working out the next episode of *Second City*. Holed up in his office with the door closed, Leshem could hear peals of laughter.

He hired experienced writers because—contrary to the prevailing opinion about the value of user-generated content—he firmly believed that content should be created by people who knew what they were doing. Leshem hated when the masses made media—it was wrong and boring and literally filling up space. He fumed that he had spent his whole life since age eleven in the constant pursuit of becoming an excellent media artist, whether through theater, film, video, or interactive. So it might be all and well for some guy to put up a Web site about his girlfriend or dog to please himself, but it detracted from what he and other experienced media people were trying to do.

Sometimes the people he hired from the TV business didn't work out. He hired one producer who had impressive television credentials with a list of award-winning shows and specials on his résumé. But the producer couldn't wrap his head around how to manage all the disparate elements involved in producing interactive entertainment. "So I fired him," Leshem said.

"He thought he could fire off an order and come back in two hours and it would be done." That might be OK in television, where the production processes were seamless, but it was unworkable when it came to producing interactive content. Everything was so interconnected, so organic, so improvisational. Cobalt Moon wasn't a factory producing widgits. "The collaborative, fluid approach is built into the architecture of the stuff we're making," Leshem would say. "You can't do it any other way." That collaborative, inventive effort didn't happen by itself; it required someone who could nurse the process along.

Not that he thought collaboration should be a smooth and collegial process. Far from it. "I believe in creative abrasion," he'd say. "I foster that. Everyone is very passionate about their ideas here" at Cobalt Moon. "When people are fighting over ideas, I start to dance with joy, because I realize we're going to get a great product."

Leshem loved feeling part of a revolution. There were a lot of entrepreneurs in the business who had "big cojones." He was sure that "old media guys" looked upon online entertainment and pioneers like himself with a mixture of fear and envy.

Leshem only got it half right. Most "old media guys" didn't worry about the Internet or even think about it much. Despite all the news stories about how the Internet would transform the world of entertainment, most executives were too embroiled in the day-to-day warfare of take-no-prisoners film or television production to give much notice. Those who were fearful, said new-media consultant Kevin Stein, would relax "if they knew how lame the Internet was and what a small universe it occupied."

Too Many to Battle

People in the content community might complain about Bob Bejan's seemingly imperious manner, but David Wertheimer wasn't one of them. He liked Bejan and saw him as a creative individual with a good heart. What Wertheimer liked about Bejan was that he got excited about things. He'd leap out of his chair during meetings and yell "YES! That's a GREAT idea!" The two were on the phone almost every workday. Wertheimer would call Bejan's office from his car at 5:30 A.M. on his way to the gym and Bejan, who lived and worked in the same time zone, would inevitably be at his desk at that early hour, and often wouldn't leave until 8:00 in the evening. They both wanted to work through the corporate bullshit and make the troubled relationship between their two companies work.

During these early morning conversations, they talked about

combining the strengths of the two companies to bring content on the Web to a new level. One idea was inspired by *Duckman*, Paramount's animated television series about the adventures of a "wise-quacking" detective. While Wertheimer's team had writers and artists from the original series, there seemed no point in simply repackaging the show for the Net. Instead, they decided to give Duckman a moonlighting gig as the "hip, sassy, offbeat" host of the *Microsoft Network Good Time Hour* on MSN's Channel 5. The show made ample use of animation and RealAudio soundbites for Duckman's three monologues a week and visits by Cornfed, Mambo, Aunt Beverly, and other *Duckman* characters. The show was canceled after a few months when, like so many other MSN shows, it failed to find its audience. Despite the poor ratings, Wertheimer felt *Duckman* had an adult, *South Park*ish, sensibility that was a natural for the medium.

One idea Wertheimer and Bejan discussed was a show that would present a new kind of online narrative. The concept would have been expensive to produce, a serious obstacle given advertisers' growing reluctance to back original content offerings. Bejan flew down to L.A. and met Wertheimer at the Sky Room of the Mondrian Hotel to discuss the terms of a deal for producing the innovative webisodic. They talked for five hours. Bejan had brought an MSN executive who had been part of the team that negotiated the original deal with Paramount. Wertheimer suspected that the executive had climbed on the "we got a bad deal from Paramount" bandwagon. Bejan and Wertheimer bounced ideas back and forth for what would have been a one-of-a-kind show. The two were creatively in sync. While their enthusiasm for the project grew by the hour, the MSN executive seemed bent on exposing every possible wrinkle in the deal. At the end of the evening, Wertheimer and Bejan reached an agreement and shook hands. The paperwork would be sent down from Redmond the next day, Bejan said.

When Wertheimer came in to work the next morning, he had a message from the MSN executive. "We want to change the deal," the executive said when Wertheimer returned the call. As he listened, it became apparent these weren't small details the executive was haggling over, but unacceptable changes that altered the whole basis of the deal. Wertheimer concluded from the episode that despite their efforts to build a good relationship between their respective companies, Bejan simply had too many people to battle within Microsoft.

Closing the Deal

Scott Zakarin's deal with AOL was announced on March 10, 1997. The Greenhouse would acquire 100 percent of Lightspeed Media. Lightspeed's current talent and assets would be assumed and managed by Greenhouse Networks. Brandon Tartikoff would, in *USA Today*'s phrase, "spearhead the company's next wave in entertainment as chairman of the new entertainment network."[34] As the new President of Programming for the Entertainment Asylum, Scott would build a West Coast studio with as many as fifty to seventy employees.

After three days of wrangling in Vienna, Greenhouse executives had approved Lightspeed Media's content plan. At this point the deal was inching to a close, but some issues remained unresolved. This acquisition differed from others in that AOL Greenhouse Networks wasn't buying Lightspeed Media for its assets, processes, or proprietary software. All AOL really wanted was the people, primarily the five partners.

Still, the nature of the acquisition made the valuation of the company, in Carl Genberg's opinion, somewhat esoteric. Genberg, Danny Krifcher, Charlie Fink, and AOL Studios general counsel, Paul Baker, went through a few rounds of looking at comparables (valuations for similar entities), but none of them were really applicable. Not surprisingly, Greenhouse started the bidding way low and the Lightspeeders way high. Eventually, the two parties found each other in the bearable middle. Scott and the team would have to walk away from a viable business painfully built over the period of a year. Greenhouse would have to pay what amounted to a signing bonus (buying Lightspeed) just to get into the game with Scott. Since Lightspeed's other contracts were fast running out, Carl insisted on and got a breakup fee if the deal fell through. It wasn't much—enough to pay the bills for a month or so. By April, nearly all the outstanding issues in the deal had been worked out.

Ironically, the Lightspeeders fought down to the wire for an all-cash deal. Luckily, they lost. The value of the stock they were forced to accept would increase more than sixfold during the one-year holding period imposed on the stock (i.e., unable to sell their shares). On the other hand, they gave up the right to approve the final production budget. Greenhouse would have final approval. Later the two sides would be at each other's throats over budget issues.

Things looked solid enough to begin executing the content plan in April. They had little choice. The original plan had been to close the deal in January, start production, and then launch in June. Things would have to get rolling now if there was any hope of launching by autumn. The worrisome thing was that autumn was several months off. Their competitors' hold on the fans would deepen. Charlie told a reporter that a new-media manager had to divine where the world would be in six months, build a product, and hope to be where the puck was going. But the Asylum's original business plan would be a year old by launch time—an eon in Internet time.

Most of April and May were consumed by hiring and staffing. Thanks to the publicity surrounding the Lightspeed acquisition and Tartikoff's involvement, Scott and Troy were inundated with résumés. Troy now had the opportunity to hire real technical people; back at Lightspeed they had had to farm the programming out to contractors. Scott made it a point to hire people who had strong backgrounds in film production. He liked their creative sensibilities, even if some of the new hires had limited Web experience. Scott would later joke that so many film people worked at the Asylum that he could flip a switch and transform the operation into a film-production company. There were times when Scott would have loved to flip that switch.

As the staff started to swell, one thing became certain. The Lightspeed house on Madison Avenue had to go.

Hayden Tract

Scott Zakarin loved the new office building because it *looked* like an Asylum. The building was a grayish blue concrete structure with de rigueur exposed steel beams and bolted sheets of Plexiglas. The steel-plated entrance door was built into a corner of the building with an edge that conformed to the edge of the building. As a result, people would miss the door altogether and have trouble finding their way into the building. One time, representatives from Intel, CAA, and a company they represented came for a meeting at the building. The seven attendees arrived one at a time. Whenever an attendee entered Scott's office, he or she complained about spending ten minutes wandering outside trying to find the door. Each time, Scott would turn to Troy and say, "We've got to do something about that." They put up a sign, but the door stayed as it was.

The 20,000-square-foot facility, which had been the home of IRS Records, stood at the corner of Hayden and National, ground zero in Culver City's burgeoning Hayden tract—informally known as multimedia gulch. (IRS Records still had the second floor, and for the first few weeks the Asylum team and IRS Records shared the same reception area—to the confusion of all.) Scott knew his new neighbors in the tract well and had been on friendly terms with all of them. Staff members from the companies got together regularly to play softball. The only team the Asylum could beat was Nick Rothenberg's W3-Design.

In keeping with the etiquette of the culture, the online pioneers avoided explicit displays of competitiveness, though a fierce undercurrent ran through their relationships. In the early days of the Web-development industry, competition wasn't such a big thing. "Everyone could take a slice [of business] as big as they wanted," said Michael Mascha, the president of W3-Design. There was a kind of collaborative culture where everyone felt they were building something important. In 1994 and 1995, people like Rothenberg and Mascha welcomed their competitors' efforts and saw them as potential educators of the market. Most of the Fortune 500 companies didn't understand the Web, and the more people spreading the word, the better it was for everyone. By 1997 competitive edginess was evident among Web developers. The market had gotten crowded. Still, things had not deteriorated to the point where people did vicious things like steal employees from each other. "We're precipitously close to falling over the edge," said Rothenberg, "but nobody has gone to that edge yet."

Rothenberg, for one, still felt that he could pick up the phone and call Josh Greer regarding some work with a major studio that Digital Planet had had as a client. "Hey, what's your experience?" Nick could ask if someone on his staff could talk to someone on Josh's staff for a couple hours and "just get briefed on some stuff so we don't have to go through the learning curve." Here was a precious asset that a competitor had, and yet there was still enough residual good feelings that Josh would be willing to help out. *Why should the other guy suffer through what we suffered?* They were all a band of brothers and sisters in a way. "We saw the Web-development business," said Greer, "as a very subversive way to get some of our content and technology ideas across."

Scott's deal with AOL changed the competitive dynamic in one regard. Scott had AOL's now 9 million households in his back pocket and had come to Hayden not as a competitor, but as a potential *distributor*. In the early going, the Asylum would produce most of its own content, but as the operation established itself and found its voice, the mix would change and more deals would be made with independent production companies.

Meanwhile, the acquisition deal with AOL finally closed. Scott, Troy, Rich, Laurie, and Carl had hoped and dreamed about the day they would put pen to paper. All of them had been living hand-to-mouth for months. Troy had mentally moved into a new apartment, bought new furniture, made investments, and filled his new place with spanking-new consumer electronics from Fry's.

When the day came to sign, all five partners were so busy that they begrudged having to pile into a car for the trek to their attorney's office in Century City. Everyone gathered afterward for a celebratory dinner at Zenzaro's in Santa Monica. Brandon Tartikoff, ill from chemotherapy, held up his glass and told everyone how happy he was to be associated with the Asylum effort and how confident he was that they would be successful.

They barely had time to enjoy the perks of acquisition. The new modems that brought AOL back from the brink had to be paid for, and—unbeknownst to the Asylum team—Bob Pittman was about to take an ax to their budget.

Honey, I Shrank the Budget

Scott and his team were in the midst of enacting their content plan and building the Asylum's infrastructure when Charlie broke the news in May that the budget for the site would be scaled back. Bob Pittman had shaken down AOL Studios for its share of farthings to pay for modems.

They were unprepared for the cut. It was as if Lightspeed were building a house and had laid the foundation only to be told that the house to be built atop that foundation would now be smaller than they'd planned. Ultimately, the budget would be cut by more than half.

If the budget cut had come in one fell swoop, it would have been painful, but Greenhouse and Lightspeed teams could have found their bearings and moved on. But the cuts came in the worst possible way— incrementally, bit by bit over a period of months. Charlie would assure Scott that the latest budget figures were final and solid—only to have to return a week later, red-faced, with additional cuts. The manner in which the cuts were made underscored a growing reality: Greenhouse and its parent, AOL Studios, were less autonomous from AOL Networks than anyone thought.

Scott got more pissed with each passing week. He, Charlie, and Brandon had worked hard to create a blueprint and vision for the kind of site that would be cutting edge and commercially successful—a category killer. Now the elements of that vision were being sliced off, one piece at a time.

The cuts impacted several key elements of the content plan that Scott and his team had developed and which Greenhouse had approved. The marketing budget took an immediate hit, which would make it even harder to find good distribution on AOL Networks.

The cuts also affected the level of technical support that Asylum was receiving from AOL. This would put the delivery of a publishing engine, the development of "Asylum Shops" and the building of "VR Station"—*Studio i*— in jeopardy.

Publishing engines provided the tools that enabled developers to create templates so that Web pages wouldn't have to be recoded every time there was a design change. Not having a publishing engine would make building a Web version of the Asylum much more labor intensive and error prone.

"What do rare autographed scripts, the latest soundtracks and videos, the clothes that Susan Lucci wore last season on *All My Children*, movie tickets, boxers signed by Brad Pitt, and movie posters have in common?" the content plan read. "They're all for sale in the *Asylum Shops*." *Asylum Shops* would be an important revenue source, and impulse buys would be facilitated by making items "available for purchase right on the page in the show or tenant [sic] where it is featured." The *Asylum Shops* were a throwback to Scott's Scream Queen schemes in the days before he conceived *The Spot*.

The likelihood of losing these elements of the plan were bad enough. What frustrated Scott the most was when the suggestion was made that he cut Studio i—Asylum's video infrastructure—from the plan. Given their decimated budget, there was no way Leonsis would pay the $500,000 to build the video unit, he was told.

"The station [Studio i] is equipped with broadcast quality audio and video, so that the live events can easily end up on a cable channel or home video just as easily as they will broadcast across the Internet," the plan read. "The hottest stars and coolest industry insiders can take advantage of the unique freedom they have at [Studio i] to create off-beat and original content . . . "

While Scott was upset by the probable loss of all these elements, losing video would be a disaster from both a creative and business standpoint, in his view. They'd need video to entice celebrities into coming to the site. Video was integral to the Asylum vision and the ex-pression of its personality. AOL seemed to be reneging on the vision. "*The site's going to suck*," Scott fumed.

The budget issues amplified other tensions between the Asylum and Greenhouse crews. Asylum was the largest entity that Greenhouse had ever overseen, and Greenhouse executives were flying by the seat of their pants in terms of long-distance managing. The Asylum crew acted with a level of independence that sometimes belied the fact that they were part of a much larger corporate entity. "You've gotta give us some kind of schedule," Charlie told Scott and Troy at one point. "We've got to know what's going on, some milestones, something we can do."

"We've spent as much time educating those who were managing us," Troy said, "as they have managing us."

Another source of tension was the clash of cultures between the Greenhouse and the Asylum. The Asylum team was used to operating like a film crew. Film production was a highly structured and disci-plined business, and a film crew operated like a small army. While mid-level staffers (in this case the Asylum producers) had a lot to say regarding the development of their shows, decisions at the top were discussed and made by a very small number of people. Film productions, needless to say, are not democracies. The chain of command is alive and well in Hollywood.

The style at Greenhouse Networks, on the other hand, was one where everyone got to feed the group. Meetings bulged with managers and assistants from marketing, licensing, production, and finance. Greenhouse's attempts to be inclusive seemed to slow things down and struck Scott and the others as not being a good use of time.

The loss of Studio i ate at Scott. Without the studio there would be no interactive video webcasts of live events, celebrity interviews, or Screen Team antics. Video was the key to the medium's future. This was one battle he was determined not to lose.

Leaping Ahead of the Curve

The Asylum wasn't the only content company trying to keep pace with the new technologies coming out of Silicon Valley. New content-authoring tools, video-compression technologies, and upgrades of existing tools appeared on a daily basis. The geeks were working hard to make the Web a more dynamic and compelling experience for users—a point that Steve Jobs drove home the previous December at a conference.

Jobs used the occasion of a Business Week Technology Futures conference in San Francisco to fire a shot across the bow of the Hollywood establishment. "We are headed for a train wreck," he told the crowd.

Jobs brought strong credentials vis-à-vis the convergence of entertainment and technology industries. As the chairman and CEO of Pixar, he had presided over the creation of *Toy Story*, the world's first totally digital film and a billion-dollar blockbuster. "Steve Jobs gets it," Halsey Minor of CNET observed. "Steve Jobs has a lot of flash and a lot of Hollywood and he really gets technology." Some insiders believe Jobs benefited from the dumb good luck of having John Lassiter, *Toy Story*'s creator, on his team. When Jobs acquired Pixar he seemed much more interested in the company's image rendering technology than its content, leaving Lassiter, Ralph Guggenheim, and their content-development group alone.

As he spoke, Jobs scolded the entertainment industry for making poor use of the dazzling tools and features being furnished by Silicon Valley. He feared that Hollywood would be unable to keep up with the ever-evolving technology. The result, he warned, would be a technically breathtaking—and breathtakingly dull—online world.

When David Wertheimer heard about his old boss's speech, it made him pause. He knew where Jobs was coming from; he himself had spent years working in the Valley, and he comprehended the geek mindset like few others in Hollywood. But he had also worked long enough in the entertainment business to understand the point of view of the consumers of these dazzling tools that people like Jobs and his tribe were peddling.

Wertheimer believed that for media or entertainment companies, technology was a boat anchor. Once you made your technology choices—dropped anchor—you were stuck in the water. It was very difficult to stay on top of the dizzying stream of technologies that flowed from the office parks of Redwood Shores, Palo Alto, and Mountain View. Content producers were constantly mired in the problem of how to deliver an entertainment experience with today's technology. As soon as development on a Web show like *Entertainment Tonight* began, a new and better technology would appear. By the time the site launched, even better technologies would be available. Keeping current was a nightmare. It had become so prohibitively expensive to produce content that the cost of production often far outstripped the ability to make money. The richer the entertainment experience got, the more difficult and expensive it was to produce. "You create really great content," he said, "throw it up on the Web, and you're cash-flow negative—almost guaranteed."

Jobs's observations notwithstanding, some content developers were actually trying to leap ahead of the technology curve. "We design shows for technologies that don't exist," was one of Matti Leshem's favorite lines. "By the time the shows are sold, the technology invariably does exist. When we designed *The King of TV*, we had no way to stream graphics as efficiently as we do now. Just didn't exist. We had a great idea for a show," but the necessary technologies were not available. While Leshem and his team of programmers, designers, and comedy writers were in the midst of production, a product called Media Splash appeared, which presented the solution they needed for streaming graphics.

Phil Flora worked the same way when he produced *Generation War,* the world's first feature-length movie made entirely on a personal computer. Others had used digital cameras in film or TV production, but Flora's project was distinct in that all the scenes involved digital, as opposed to real-life, sets. The technology Flora needed to render his story did not exist when he began the project in 1992. "I had been playing around with the first version of Adobe Premiere and an early version of Autodesk 3D Studio," Flora remembered. "The early versions of Adobe Premiere didn't do composites without halos. You may have seen some of those early computer games where actors had halos; that was because of Premiere. It suddenly occurred to me that with another version or two [of Adobe Premiere] it would be possible to do a movie on all-virtual sets in a PC. I assumed they would fix Adobe Premiere before I needed it." In fact, a third of the way through the production, Adobe released the necessary update. The strategy pursued by Leshem, Flora, and others was comparable to painting yourself into a corner, hoping that someone would build a doorway by the time you got there.

The pursuit of this constantly changing technology was what Rod Swanson of Electronic Arts once called "technostress" and "technolust." *Technostress* referred to the anxiety that came from having to keep up with changing technologies; identifying new tools and learning to use them was an endless process. *Technolust* described the infatuation with what was new and expensive. People in this industry, hot for new technology, stumbled from one new thing to the next, so that everyone was constantly on a learning curve. The never-ending learning curve defeated efforts to attain mastery. A violinist took twenty years to become a master. Would there have been any violin virtuosos if the violin itself was constantly changing and evolving?

Direct IPO

Despite Jobs's criticism, no content company made a greater effort to exploit emerging Internet technologies than Digital Planet—nor suffered more for it financially. If Scott Zakarin was feeling squeezed by the Asylum's shrinking budget, it was nothing compared to the cash-flow anxieties that Josh Greer was experiencing. Josh's plane trips to the Bay area and New York in search of investors had yielded nothing. Intel had long forgotten about them. Josh talked to just about everyone in the venture-capital community. The reality was that Digital Planet was an undercapitalized company that wouldn't show a profit until the following year, at the earliest. Nor did the company have the kind of management depth that investors looked for; from the management standpoint, it was basically Josh and Thomas Lakeman. The company also lacked the business infrastructure to absorb the kind of money it so desperately sought. *Madeleine II* had garnered a devoted but small audience. While there were distant prospects for creating content for broadband, Josh faced up to the cruel reality that Digital Planet had to give up on its plans to be a creator of original content.

He now had to give serious thought to the future direction of the company. The Web-development space had grown enormously since the days when Digital Planet was among the few firms offering such services. The industry had entered a shake-out and consolidation. On the positive side, the team had major ongoing work for the U.S. Postal Service, Allstate Insurance, and Warner Brothers. They were also keeping the company afloat with work designing DVD interfaces. The outside world viewed the company as a highly creative design shop. But the consolidation made the future uncertain. Josh had high ambitions for growing the company, so he focused their efforts on venture capital.

After months of fruitless searching for partners willing to address their immediate cash-flow needs, Josh was desperate for a miracle. Direct IPO seemed like one. Michael Terpin, a public-relations professional, and Mark Perlmutter, a former CFO, stockbroker, and financial planner, launched Direct IPO in early 1997. The firm was in the business of enabling Internet companies to make public offerings directly over the Internet—in essence, using the Net to make an appeal for investors directly to Internet users.

A press release was issued on April 5, 1997: "Digital Planet, a longtime leader in the field of entertainment industry Web site development and content creation, will use the Direct IPO Web site to offer its self-underwritten Regulation A offering directly to Internet users via the nation's first direct public offering of an established Internet firm." Digital Planet was the company's first client.

Digital Planet's unorthodox IPO looked like a desperation measure—which, in fact, it was. The IPO process in any company meant diverting a huge amount of resources. When so many top people in a company were devoting their time to getting money, it raised the question of who was running the store. Just days before, Josh had finally settled on a COO—Thomas Lakeman, his head of production, who had already been managing the company's day-to-day affairs.

Josh had already publicly committed to Direct IPO when the FCC sent a letter of complaint. Direct IPO had run afoul of a technical provision of the law when the company posted a press release about the arrangement on its Web site before Digital Planet could register their offering with the SEC. Greer had to make an embarrassing public withdrawal from the process.

The fiasco put Josh into a tailspin. He began to think that he'd have to sell the business. If they were going to survive, they needed to stop taking $10,000 accounts and go after the six-figure work. One account they targeted was Mattel's Barbie site. Going after that client had been a huge drain on them; they'd spent $50,000 to $60,000 to create a prototype (Mattel had given them a $25,000 budget). The contract to create this huge online destination would be awarded that September, which would have been perfect because it would have given them the cash flow they needed. As usual, things were delayed.

Wiggle Room and Growing Pains

With the contracts finally signed and sealed, the Asylum crew was now executing in earnest along two curves. The first curve, building company infrastructure, meant hiring people, assembling teams, and identifying areas of responsibility. The second curve, site infrastructure, involved acquiring computers, phone lines, networks, and video-production equipment—the tools they would need to produce the Entertainment Asylum. Ideally, those two curves would be identical. Asylum had thirty days to staff up by 500 percent, move into new offices, and set up networks, computers, and phones. Of course, the ideal didn't happen; infrastructure was lagging far behind the rising head count.

The team was hampered by AOL's corporate procedures and processes. Those procedures and processes were designed for a large company traveling on a normal growth curve. But the Asylum growth curve was anything but typical. AOL's policies regarding its phone-answer-center operations, content creation, and digital-network infrastructure were restrictive for a start-up building as fast as the Asylum. "It's hard for a big company to wiggle its toes," Troy later said. "We are the toes and we need to wiggle like crazy."

Large corporations managed millions of dollars and vast resources, which required systems of accountability and checks and balances. Everyone knew that going in, but the Asylum team now saw that the devil was indeed in the details. Back at Lightspeed, if the team needed a new computer monitor, hey, someone got in a car and drove to a computer store and bought one. Now if they needed a computer, someone had to fill out an AOL requisition form, which would then wend its way through five or six different approval layers before ending up at an AOL corporate purchasing group.

The layers of accountability at AOL slowed other processes as well. If Troy needed help from an AOL technical group, the request had to go up through the Greenhouse, AOL Studios over to AOL Networks, down to AOL systems operations, then filter through one of a number of groups, such as network operations and Web operations, before reaching the desired desk. Worse than the circuitous route such queries required was how much time was consumed by the process. Time was the enemy.

AOL wasn't the only corporation struggling to adapt its structure and processes to fit the demands of Internet time. Pathfinder, Time Warner's content portal, was plagued with organizational problems from the start. The site featured the online versions of Time Warner publications like *Time*, *Fortune*, and *People* magazines, as well as Net publications like the highly regarded *Netly News*. Pathfinder was structured like many media corporations, with separate technology and editorial departments and a hierarchical chain of command. A request for technical assistance had to navigate through the chain on the editorial side, then be fielded through the head of the technology department before finding its way to the person who could fix the problem. The response cycle was too slow for a site like Pathfinder, which published on a daily basis. A major glitch like a server crash could be devastating.

AOL's procurement processes resulted in delays in the acquisition of more than computers. They also had trouble getting office furniture in a timely fashion. Scott commandeered the company's one good couch (which had originally been his), a black-leather affair that had been in Troy's office. Troy bought lawn furniture as a replacement— fodder for an endless week of jokes from visitors ("Hey, nice couch, Troy."). Visitors in the reception area had one uncomfortable chair to sit on, until someone brought in some dowdy "granny furniture" that clashed horribly with the building's postindustrial ambience.

Greenhouse executives were aware of the challenges of dealing with AOL's corporate systems, and did the best they could to speed things along. That responsibility usually fell to Charlie Fink. Charlie had a tough job. In anticipation of being acquired, attempts were made to run a tighter ship at AOL Studios, with more disciplined and centralized decision making. That meant less autonomy for the Asylum than Scott and the others had been led to believe. Charlie had to reconcile Scott's need for autonomy with a constantly changing situation on the ground in Vienna. He tried to be supportive of the Asylum team's demands, but he found himself getting more blustery by the day.

The budget cuts imposed on AOL Studios and the Asylum had

intensified the search for an investment partner or buyer. The prospect of being acquired was the bright spot amidst their frustrations with AOL's corporate systems. The hope among Scott and his team was that when investors were finally found, their budget problems would be eased by an infusion of cash and they would become part of a smaller, faster-moving company—so said Danny Krifcher. The Asylum crew would regain their independence.

By one AOL insider's reckoning, the chances were 49 percent that Greenhouse would be acquired, 49 percent that all of AOL Studios would be bought, and 2 percent that Steve Case would get nervous about selling off the family jewels.

Of course, there were advantages to being part of a big corporation, too. AOL had been in the online business since the '80s. As Troy later wrote, "the experience of having published tens of millions of pages has made AOL a great and easy place to create" in that "the basic tools you need to be creative are, for the most part, established and available." "If you want to get into online commerce," Carl Genberg noted, "you can talk to the AOL marketplace person. You can get a quarter million dollars' worth of consulting advice over the phone for free."

Meanwhile, the staff continued to grow. New faces appeared in the bright white halls of the Asylum building. Usually, Troy was involved in all the interviewing and would introduce new hires (freelancers) at the weekly staff meeting, sharing details about their backgrounds and easing their way into the group. As the build-up continued, Troy began delegating personnel matters, so that one morning he came to a staff meeting and found several people he didn't recognize.

Rich Tackenberg later posted a checklist of things to look out for that meant your start-up was becoming a large corporation:

> *You refer to many of your coworkers as "Big Guy," because you can't remember their names.*
> *You continually refer to the UPS delivery man as "the new guy." . . . New staff members continually refer to you as "the UPS delivery man."*
> *If your company abruptly changes where they order their pizza from, you will put the old pizza joint out of business. Not an exaggeration.*

IRS records finally vacated the second floor, and Scott, who had been in temporary quarters, moved into a large office that had (on a clear day) a line-of-sight view of the HOLLYWOOD sign. Hollywood remained largely aloof from the online world, and for all the attention he'd garnered from his status as an online pioneer, he still stood outside the Hollywood mainstream. Conquering and co-opting Hollywood was what the Entertainment Asylum was all about. To do that he needed streaming video.

Battling for Studio i

"If the Entertainment Asylum doesn't have streaming video at launch time," Scott told Charlie Fink, "I'll quit." Scott felt his stand was a principled one, that having touted the Asylum as a cutting edge content network, his reputation was now on the line. He felt that restoring the marketing budget, getting technical support for a publishing engine and Asylum Shops were all crucial to their success. None of that would happen. Now, he pressed to get Studio i's $500,000 budget reinstated.

Listening to all this, Fink's patience was getting as thin as his hair. This came at a time when, budget-wise, AOL was (as one insider deftly put it) "as tight as an anal sphincter."

On AOL's side there were questions as to why the company should dish out precious dollars—which could go to buying more modems—for unproven concepts like e-commerce and streaming video. That Spring, e-commerce transactions for 1997 were projected by some analysts, such as Chris Stevens of the Aberdeen Group, to total between $1 billion to $3 billion by the end of the year—a growing but still modest figure. Consumer concerns about the security of online credit card transactions made online shopping anything but a slam dunk as a business model. Budget worries made AOL reluctant to be an e-commerce innovator, at least in the case of the Asylum.

If e-commerce was a promising but untested business model, Webcasting streaming video was even more uncertain—particularly for AOL. AOL's 9 million members couldn't get streaming video through Rainman, and far fewer members would attempt to access the site through AOL's gateway to the Web. The decision to nix Studio i reflected AOL's ambivalent attitude toward the Web and its uneasiness with cutting-edge technologies. *Don't confuse the mass audience with new technology choices. Keep it simple.* "The geeks don't like us," AOL CEO Steve Case told a *Time* magazine reporter. "They want as much technology as possible, while AOL's entire objective is to simplify."

As far as AOL was concerned, streaming video was a "PR driver not a business driver." "Why not wait until Greenhouse Networks or

AOL Studios nailed down additional financing, and pay for the video studio out of that?" Charlie suggested. Scott was not moved by that argument. The suggestion had come too late, to his thinking.

Scott and Troy's desire to use streaming video was heightened by the fact that the competition had already gotten a jump on them. E! Online had incorporated media streams into its site, and had even begun webcasting entertainment events. Even if they launched Asylum immediately, they'd be behind the curve.

Charlie was aware of E! Online's webcasting experiments and thought they were "dogs." He also knew that Jeremy Verba had farmed out the technical side of the webcasts to Boxtop Interactive, a major L.A. Web-development house. "Why don't we do the same?" Fink proposed. They could contract with Boxtop to do a video test twice a month. Fink thought the "work-around" would provide an interim solution until financing came through.

Scott stood his ground. He believed that the site's success depended on having a credible presence on the Web, and that meant having the latest available media-streaming technology. They prided themselves, through their various incarnations as *The Spot* and *Grape-Jam*, of being at the edge of—or even a bit beyond—the technology curve. "We give people a reason to upgrade their browsers and technology," Troy said. *The Spot* used page layouts that hadn't been done on the Web before. *GrapeJam* had Net-radio programs, webcasts, and a Palace 2-D chat site. Troy in particular was used to producing for a technically diverse audience; many *Spot* and *GrapeJam* fans had used powerful T-1 lines to access those shows at work while others used slower connections at home. Lightspeed produced for both groups. They intended to do the same thing at the Asylum, though the technical challenges would be far greater than anything they'd attempted before. Anything that deviated from their stated vision would be mortifying from a professional standpoint.

Charlie Fink, on the other hand, felt Scott wasn't being sensitive to the problems the Greenhouse faced involving budgets, the search for investors, and its relationship with the rest of AOL. He could have his video, but not on the scale that they had planned on. Scott was thinking like an artist, not like a president of programming.

For all his techno-dyslexia, Scott wanted to push the technology as far as the audience would accept, because the further he could push it, the closer the site would get to being like interactive video. On some level, all the Web pioneers wished they were working in television.

Sneaking Out with Brandon

Scott's first impulse was to follow up on his threat and make video a deal-breaking issue. It had the potential to blow up in everyone's faces and send them running for the lawyers. He had one powerful ally, "a gun in his holster" that he thought he could count on.

Because of the recurring Hodgkin's lymphoma, Brandon Tartikoff had cut back on his Asylum activities. Many of his ideas had already been "front-loaded" into the concept of the site, and he had been a full partner in shaping it. His new role was to make phone calls, set up meetings with stars, agents, and producers for the Asylum crew, and be the glue that held the teams in Vienna and Culver City together. Tartikoff's name also gave the Asylum the patina of respectability that the fledgling production needed in the entertainment community.

Back in January, when the word about Brandon's illness and chemo treatments got around Hollywood, everyone in the entertainment community sent him a hat for the inevitable period of hair loss. Brandon's office received so many hats that he vowed to wear a different one every day. By April it became apparent that the chemo had not been successful. Tartikoff still had cancer cells in his system. Next he submitted to a stem-cell transplant, a radically more severe treatment, one that nearly killed him outright. It left Tartikoff's immune system weakened and vulnerable to infections. His doctors imposed a quarantine on him and prescribed rest. But Tartikoff was too type-A to sit and meditate.

The stem-cell procedure showed signs of success; his white-blood-cell count rose, but he had also acquired an infection that his doctors couldn't isolate. Tartikoff began to chafe under the isolation imposed by his physicians and to take meetings with people around town. In addition to his work with AOL, he also had a television show in development with Mark Frost (of *Twin Peaks* fame) and a development deal with Spike Lee at ABC. Tartikoff was also looking for books for his publishing imprint. There were movie scripts in the works. Tartikoff's wife, Lilly, would get so concerned about her husband's unwillingness to slow down that she repeatedly tried to pull the plug on his e-mail and phone. Each time Tartikoff reconnected them.

Scott tried to be respectful of Brandon's time. But Brandon seemed to gain energy from their sessions and didn't want to stop working. Despite the illness, Scott and Brandon's relationship continued to develop. Scott was a young turk in a new industry that was still inchoate and trying to become "what it's supposed to be," and Tartikoff loved that. Scott, for his part, revered Brandon like an older brother. (His real older brother, Mark, was almost exactly Brandon's age.) He studied the way Tartikoff handled himself in various situations. Tartikoff understood the ego dynamic and social structure of Hollywood. On one occasion, Tartikoff was dealing with the handler of one of the business's greatest stars, who was asking for more "exclusivity" for his client than the Asylum could provide. Scott observed how Tartikoff dealt with the situation. He should not worry about exclusivity, Tartikoff told the handler. The Asylum was going to be like Mt. Rushmore and his client was going to be like George Washington. Sharing Mt. Rushmore with Lincoln, Jefferson, and Roosevelt didn't diminish Washington's stature. In fact, the presence of the other presidents made Washington's head look even *more* impressive. It was a masterful performance that left Scott breathless.

Another time, Tartikoff told Scott he could get Tom Cruise for the Asylum. Cruise was a hockey fanatic. Why not call the L.A. Kings and get Cruise to do something online with them to promote *Jerry McGuire*, Cruise's latest film? While the Cruise idea never materialized (Cruise had a schedule conflict), Tartikoff instinctively knew all the angles for building ties with high power celebrities.

Months of working together did nothing for either of their technical talents. One time Tartikoff wanted to upload a file for Scott to review. "Let me show you something." When meeting at the office, the two could always count on having plenty of technically oriented people around. On this occasion they met at Tartikoff's home. The two sat together in sweats on a couch. The laptop was balanced on Tartikoff's knees as he tentatively clicked and tapped keys. For some reason, the desired file wasn't uploading. "Let me try," Scott said. After half an hour of fumbling with no results, they gave up. "We're the future of Interactivity?" Scott asked incredulously.

One day in June Scott and Brandon met in a restaurant to catch up on Asylum business. "Let me tell you about my health thing," Tartikoff began. "I'm under house arrest for the next three weeks." Once again, his doctors had forbidden any meetings. Normally, Tartikoff never laughed out loud, something that frustrated the comedian in Scott no end. Now Tartikoff was snickering like a thirteen-year-old. *What was so funny?* Scott realized that Brandon was snickering "because he'd snuck out of the house."

Scott took the opportunity to pour his heart out to Brandon about the video issue. The site would be inferior without video, and Tartikoff wouldn't want to put his name on the final product, he told him. They needed video to bring the Asylum alive, to bring out the site's personality and to forge a compelling connection between celebrities and their audiences. His instinct was to pick up his ball and walk away from the court.

Tartikoff agreed to fight for the Asylum crew on the video issue. But he also told Scott that battling head-on over the matter was not the best way to win. Scott would make more headway if he could show AOL what they would be losing if they didn't move aggressively to build an audio/video infrastructure for the Asylum. Brandon was a consummate player of the Hollywood corporate game. Most often making a frontal attack was about as effective as guiding your plane kamikaze style into someone's aircraft carrier—a messy and ultimately futile gesture. Much better to approach your enemies like a master of aikido. Don't confront. Look for indirect means to get what you want. He used that approach when his doctors and Lilly pleaded with him not to meet with people. He'd sandwich in meetings on the drive back from the doctor's office instead of heading straight home as he should have.

Showdown

By June things were getting tense between the Asylum team and their counterparts at Greenhouse Networks. Tartikoff talked Scott into taking a more diplomatic tack regarding the media-streams issue. Distribution, the publishing engine, e-commerce, Studio i, and a host of other issues had to be sorted out.

Danny Krifcher, president of Greenhouse Networks, was in town to check out the new Asylum building and see how things were developing. Despite being pegged as the "money man," he had a deep enthusiasm for what the Asylum team was attempting to do. Scott was out of town, but saw the visit as an opportunity to make headway on the streaming-video issue. He and his partners would carefully orchestrate what Krifcher would see and hear.

Krifcher and the Asylum team held a meeting in the main conference room shortly before lunch. Rich walked Danny through some of the site's production work on the computer, describing what the site would and would not be capable of delivering technically. Then he gave an update on what their competitors were doing. Rich downloaded an archived, streaming-video webcast of E! Online's coverage of the *Batman and Robin* movie premiere in Westwood. The video was technically crude—as was all Web video. The E! Online folks had missed the mark, in Rich's opinion, by presenting a linear program with limited interactivity. None of that really mattered. The important fact was that E! had done the webcast at all—and done it a full *four months* before the Asylum's scheduled launch. Their competitor had also covered the *Evita* premiere and had plans to Webcast more movie premieres and entertainment events. No doubt they would get better at it. "This is a freight train barreling out of control into our station," Rich told Krifcher.

E! Online had leveraged the E! Entertainment Television brand to land a place along the red carpet at the *Evita* premiere. The idea was not to simply repurpose the television broadcast of a movie premiere, but to actually add a layer of interactivity and to take advantage of the strength of the medium.

For the *Evita* premiere, E! Online had two cams, one where the cars arrived and one on Ted Casablanca perched at the edge of the red-carpet runway. As Glenn Close's limo pulled to a stop, viewers e-mailed their questions. Someone in the editorial chair at E! Online sorted through the questions coming in and relayed the best ones to Casablanca, who in turn addressed them to Close as she strolled down the red carpet to the theater entrance.

Jeremy Verba was a big believer in webcasting; he felt it played to three advantages of the medium: immediacy, interactivity, and archiveability. Like Scott, Verba felt webcasting could engender a sense of shared experience among Web viewers. Cyber-media philosopher Douglas Rushkoff once said that the Web as a mass medium would evolve into a series of "be-ins," where people came together and had a shared sense of intimacy. Live events—even ones as seemingly trivial as a movie premiere—could be the focal point for such shared experiences. E! Online's Webcasts provided the opportunity for—or illusion of—interacting with celebrities, at least in the form of directing questions to them. The notion that Madonna fans out in the hinterlands could interview their favorite star had tremendous appeal. Finally, the team at E! Online noticed that there would often be a surge in hits for an archived movie-premiere webcast around the time that the film went into general distribution. A video webcast need not simply be a one-shot, live event, but could be a video asset that could have significant shelf life for weeks to come.

Scott respected E! Online's efforts but knew he could do the interactivity better. Fielding questions from viewers was something he'd done months earlier with *GrapeJam*'s NetRadio interviews. He imagined taking it a step further. He had created opportunities for the audience to influence the characters and story line in *GrapeJam*. He wanted to do the same at Asylum. He wanted viewers to be empowered to prod their favorite stars into performing in situations that blurred the line between fiction and reality. Playing with reality was what online entertainment was all about.

Scott was getting calls updating him on how the visit progressed. Krifcher had been impressed with E! Online's pioneering video webcast. Now as an afterthought—perhaps a calculated one—one of the Asylum members walked over to the room where tapes were stored and logged, came back with a video cassette, and dropped it into the VCR. Rich had teams shooting broadcast-quality video on an experimental basis. "I want to be able to produce TV for the Net," said Rich, "then cut back and follow the technology wave." The Screen Team members had been roaming around Hollywood with betacams shooting awards shows, interviewing celebrities, and trying out their shtick. This particular cassette happened to be of Jim Wise—one of the most talented members of the Groundlings improv group and a *GrapeJam* alumnus—interviewing Carmen Electra of MTV. His questions for Carmen were funny, cutting, and engaging. Compared to E! Online's production, there was more ad-libbing and comic banter for the camera. The Asylum team members stole furtive glances in Krifcher's direction as he watched the tape.

"That's it!" Krifcher intoned at one point. "That's the spirit we need to get across on the Entertainment Asylum!" Personality was what made the Asylum different from its competitors, and this video had shown that personality in a fresh way.

The implicit threat of a walk-out, combined with strong arguments for the PR value of having media streams on the Web version of the site, helped turn the tide in favor of video—at least within AOL Studios. That didn't mean that the Asylum team would get their video. The budget issues still carried the day, and the weight of the AOL bureaucracy still tilted against the idea. Finally, Ted Leonsis had to personally walk over to Steve Case's office and plead, a personally humiliating act for Leonsis, in order to get the $500,000 for the video studio. The matter did not end there. Just because Case gave the OK didn't mean that Leonsis walked away with a check. There was still AOL's capital-improvement process to grind through. In the end, Scott got his Studio i.

Doubts would linger at AOL regarding webcasting. In an interview for *Wired* magazine that was conducted that August and appeared in the November issue, Fink said: "We talk about webcasting here a lot, and we think audio and multimedia is going to be a big part of what we do going forward. Yet, it is totally unproven. The biggest webcast *ever* reached ten or twenty thousand people. If you're running your business on an advertising model where you're getting sixty dollars per thousand, an audience of twenty thousand is not going to cut it as a business model."[35]

Studio i would become Scott's test bed for interactive television. Audience empowerment wasn't just marketing hype; he believed deeply that something magical emerged when you put actors in a loosely structured concept and gave the audience the ability to shape that concept. Wonderful, spontaneous, unpredictable things occurred—hopefully. Studio i made them feel like they were building more than just another Web operation. It gave Scott and his team the tools they needed, they felt, to prepare online for the day when it really merged with television.

Distribution continued to be a problem. Apparently Leonsis was unable to get AOL Networks to give up more real estate. The Asylum didn't get a publishing engine. There would be no Asylum Shops. Still, tensions eased between the Asylum and Greenhouse teams as they talked things through.

Being sandwiched between the Asylum team in Los Angeles and AOL Networks had been rough going for Greenhouse executives. The politics were treacherous. The worst of it seemed to be behind them. Finally, things were flowing.

A tentative date of October 8 had been set for the Asylum launch—five weeks past the earlier target of September 1. Already it looked like that date would slip, too.

This Is Not a Test

Webcasting in general was becoming more ubiquitous. MSN had begun backing off from entertainment-oriented content, but one of the last pure entertainment shows that Bob Bejan launched employed webcasting in a new and innovative way. *This is Not a Test* launched at 10:00 P.M. EST on June 27, 1997, with Conan O'Brien as a special guest. The show was a weekly webcast hosted by Marc Maron, live from Catch a Rising Star, the New York comedy-club. It combined a live comedy-club audience with MSN's live online audience taking part in comedy sketches, games, and other interactive hullabaloo. Interestingly, one of the challenges the show faced was keeping the online and club audiences in sync—a big problem in an online environment where latencies could result in long downloads and slow connections.

This Is Not A Test had been developed in cooperation with Broadway Video, Lorne Michaels's production company and the producer of *Saturday Night Live*. Bejan was convinced that the shows were screamingly funny and that, week in and week out for fourteen weeks, the sketches worked in the online space. He believed the show was an "amazing technical accomplishment." Not that it mattered anymore. Again, the show was stuck behind MSN's firewall, limiting its audience. Even among MSN members, only 5 percent spent time in the Onstage area, where the network's heavily promoted entertainment-oriented shows resided.

However thrilled Bejan might be with *This Is Not A Test*, there was no escaping the fact that the tide had turned at MSN. Entertainment was on the way out. As Amy Harmon wrote in the *New York Times* a couple of months later, ". . . after spending some $1 billion chasing the evanescent business of entertainment and media, Microsoft is finding that the Red West products it likes best are those that bear the strongest resemblance to the pragmatic productivity software packages it already knows so well."[36] Shows that appealed to twenty-somethings, like *Mint*, were canceled, as were other pure entertainment fare . . . including Cobalt Moon's *Second City Naked News*. *Mungo*

Park—the travel show that sent celebrities to remote regions where they posted text, audio, and video dispatches—was shut down as well.

"Microsoft just doesn't get it," many said of its entertainment-content ventures. Instead of putting the shows on the open Web where they might find and grow an audience, *Second City, Duckman, Star Trek: Continuum,* and others were stuck behind MSN's firewall. Isolating the shows made it harder to build communities of interest around the properties. Forcing the shows to prove themselves in a ten-week season denied the show producers the opportunity to learn from their mistakes. Bejan's intention to use the metaphor of television to market the shows to a Web audience backfired. Identifying the shows so closely with television inevitably raised performance expectations that could not be met in terms of the vividness of the multimedia experience.

These criticisms were as petty as they were trenchant. No one could claim to have mastered the medium; all the pioneers were still experimenting. The truth was that MSN was never given the time to honestly fail or succeed. The fault could ultimately be traced back to Bill Gates and the different mind-sets of technology and entertainment executives.

Gates was a software executive, not a media mogul. How could one expect an executive who hadn't even owned a television set until very recently to provide the vision for a billion-dollar content venture like MSN? Bill wasn't a mass-media kind of guy, nor did he ever understand the Hollywood establishment that his company courted. He gave a presentation to an audience of Hollywood television executives in February 1996 and bombed badly. The well-heeled television crowd had come to hear how digital technology would change their industry in the years to come. What they got instead was Gates's warmed-over stump speech touting Microsoft's software products. The executives deserted the luncheon meeting in droves during the Q&A period.

There were people at Microsoft, like Bejan, who came out of entertainment and who understood that world. But the few who understood media were several layers down in the hierarchy and overwhelmed by a culture geared toward the production of software.

The pioneers of online entertainment had mixed feelings about MSN's floundering entertainment fare. In one sense it was payback for the company's haughtiness and arrogance. Like others in the industry, many feared the power that came from the company's monopolistic hold on PC operating systems and its (then) $9 billion war chest. "We may all be working for Microsoft one of these days," said Josh Greer. But these feelings were swept aside by the concern that Microsoft's troubles meant another nail in the coffin for online entertainment. The movement couldn't afford to lose another buyer—especially one as wealthy as MSN.

The folks at the Greenhouse could take heart from their arch competitor's troubles. They always felt that MSN's strategy was a year behind their own. They could only hope that they were a year ahead in the right direction.

Suits Move In

Scott knew that a lot of people were watching him closely. Back when he was president of Lightspeed, he only had to answer to his partners, staff, and audience. He had no investors, executive poobahs, or corporate bureaucracy to fret about. In his new role as president of programming for the Entertainment Asylum, things were much different. He had to be more careful in speaking to the press. He had to be mindful of the Greenhouse's position and of AOL's interests. He had almost sixty people depending on him. He was riding on top of AOL's largest investment in the creation of content.

Greenhouse executives began a search for a president and CEO, a Hollywood suit who could jump start the advertising sales effort and keep an eye on the cookie jar. The candidate would have to be someone who was comfortable with technology and entrepreneurship—not an easy ticket to fill in Hollywood. Many Hollywood execs were, in executive-search consultant Dana Ardi's words, "the gatekeepers of mature businesses who are holding on for dear life." Thanks to the unexpected explosion of the Internet, that was changing.

In 1997 more and more experienced executives from other industries and major brands started to migrate into technology and new-media start-ups. These were executives who were experienced and senior in a way that was uncommon among most new-media entrepreneurs. Many of these executives saw new media as an opportunity to move into a nascent industry and redefine it, to build their own companies. It was almost a no-lose situation. One could go into a start-up and build it, then get bought out and walk away with a lot of money. On the other hand, if the company went all the way—got to IPO—the potential was limitless. The more Internet start-up companies that crossed the $100 million—or even $1 billion—market-capitalization threshold, the more suits that flocked to the business. Gray hair made its appearance.

The executives who migrated to new-media companies often faced culture shock. "The change can be pretty dramatic," Dana Ardi observed in 1998. "I just placed a very senior executive from one of the studios into a new-media start-up company. He took a cut in pay. He doesn't have two secretaries anymore. He gets his own coffee. He used to have an office suite; now he'd settle for having a window in his office. Why does he do it?" she asked rhetorically. "Because he's building the company he joined from the bottom up and defining an industry space. He's challenging himself in ways he never could in his old company."[37]

After an intense search, Greenhouse hired Monica Dodi as president and CEO of the Asylum. Dodi would be managing the "day-to-day operations," the press release read, "forming alliances with key advertisers, establishing cross-promotional partnerships and overseeing marketing efforts to create a strong brand identity." Dodi was a Harvard Business School graduate who had spent nearly her entire professional life in start-up operations. She helped create MTV Europe—handling the business side and developing revenue, marketing, and promotions. She also had done stints building overseas operations at Walt Disney Company and Warner Brothers.

Dodi visited the Asylum in early July, just after the log jam had broken. AOL had been slow in supplying the growing operation with hardware and infrastructure. The computers had at last arrived, still in their boxes and taking up floor space. There weren't enough places for people to sit. Chaotic comings and goings. Fink and Leonsis stood talking about sales and revenues, assuming existential poses. People had serious expressions on their faces. The place looked like the beaches of Normandy after the invasion force had landed.

Pulp Cult Horror and More

Can you imagine what it would be like if on the set of his next movie, Steven Spielberg turned to his film crew and said, "For this shot, I'd like a close-up of our main character as he walks toward the camera," and his crew said to him, "That's a great idea. We'll need two months to design a camera, three months to build it, a few weeks to invent film and about six weeks to test the whole thing to make sure that the film and camera actually work together the way we think they should."

Welcome to the world of online production.

—Troy Bolotnick

In June, AMCY's *The Spot* finally shut down. Scott had *GrapeJam* retired from cyberspace in order to clear the decks for the Asylum. The

Asylum team didn't spend much time crying over *The Spot*'s demise or the shelving of *GrapeJam*. There was too much work to be done. The Asylum was now in full production. The daily drill went something like this: Working off the original content design plan, a producer assigned members of his or her team to write something, to research something, or to work with rights and clearances to find an image. The producer then might go and talk to a designer to find out how things were coming with a particular graphic and give input ("we need to change this background to blue"). Then there would be a short conference with the coder ("OK, these elements are coming over at 2:00 today. You'll have from 2:00 to 6:00 to put these elements together. Here are some of the new constraints that came along."). Later the producer might meet with the vice-presidents of production, Rich and Laurie, who in turn meet regularly with Scott and Troy to make sure the production was not violating some "big technical or vision thing."

Each show had its own particular spin and dynamic. *Hollywood Wire* had a template that had to be filled daily with entertainment news and gossip. *Wire* also ran editorial pieces that focused on different aspects of the industry, such as Jim Wise writing about what the casting couch was like for men in Hollywood.

The Biz was "*the* place to come for inside information about the entertainment business." An interesting feature of *The Biz* was the "Mogul of the Week," where Mike Medavoy or someone of that ilk would be invited to come and share his or her experiences with the online audience. Visiting moguls would be given a choice of twenty things to do during the week—open up their calendars to show what a mogul's typical day was like, upload their first "deal memos," post their baby pictures, or sit for an interview. The show was Tartikoff's idea. Film buffs excluded, how many people really cared what Mike Medavoy looked like as a baby? Hardly anyone, Tartikoff admitted, but "Mogul of the Week" would be a great way to build relationships with the power brokers around town. Those were the people who could send the stars Asylum's way.

A key to the whole Asylum concept was to give celebrities a safe, paparazzi-free environment in which to interact directly with their fans. Celebrities would also be given an opportunity to experiment with their own creativity. A rock star could read poetry, or an actor could sing a song—or plug an upcoming film, for that matter.

Pulp Cult Horror Highway ("A dark and mysterious ride through the wild side of entertainment") was particularly intriguing. It featured a cult diner with the likes of John Waters and Divine on barstools, in-depth treatments of films like *Bucket of Blood* and Orson Welles's *A Touch of Evil*. Adam Dubov was *PCH*'s producer. (Like the other producers, Dubov produced more than one show.) Dubov was a screenwriter, film director, and rock guitarist with a notable if offbeat entertainment pedigree. His parents wrote the pilot for *The Mod Squad*, and his father played heavies in '40s and '50s B-movies and noirs. The whole *PCH* team seemed to be a bit on the scraggly side. One Friday the 13th, the *PCH* crew went through the Asylum building hanging black balloons in everyone's offices. Managing Adam Dubov and the Asylum's other producers was the responsibility of Rich Tackenberg, who had assumed the position of vice-president of production. Rich was Scott's front line on the production side. At Lightspeed Rich had been very hands-on—putting shows together, working at a computer, maybe directing the activities of a few other people. Rich reviewed and coordinated the work of several production teams.

Less technical than Troy or Rich, Laurie worked on the "voice" for the whole site, meeting with the production teams, working on ad presentations, and interviewing celebrities as part of the Screen Team.

The burden of the Asylum team's prolonged negotiations with AOL had fallen on Carl. Once the deal closed, he spent much of his time as CFO, immersed in the often frustrating task of building sensible internal systems and infrastructure for the Asylum and getting the whole operation connected to AOL.

All the partners (with the exception of Carl) missed being deeply engaged in the creation of content. Rich in particular had taken personal responsibility during development of the *Comedy Clinic* show. Someone had come up with the idea of having chat-oriented post-mortem sessions following television shows so that viewers could come together and analyze comedies sketch by sketch. Rich had loved this idea and pushed hard for it during development. But because of his growing responsibilities, he handed it over to a whole new crew headed by Adam Dubov. He told them to take the show concept, keep what they liked, throw out the ideas they didn't like, and "make the show their own."

Some time later, the plan for the *Comedy Clinic* landed on Rich's desk. He began to read. *Oh my God, this is so different.* Rich stopped reading. He stepped out and got a cup of coffee and returned to his desk and braced himself. *OK, let's get objective,* he thought. The post-mortem chat rooms were gone. Producer Adam Dubov later told Rich that the feature didn't make a lot of sense; after all, people lived in different time zones and it might be tough to get people to meet immediately after the end of a TV show. What they had come up with instead was the metaphor of an office water-cooler poll. Audience members could vote on the aspects of TV shows that they liked or hated. Should Ross and Rachel have gotten back together?—that sort of thing. Poll results could be tabulated and dynamically mapped out to compare different shows. People could go as deeply into the polling results as they wished.

Rich had to admit that the polling feature was a better idea. The original plan that he and the others had created served as a starting point and "license to springboard" for the new production crews. Before, at Lightspeed, if Rich had ignored an aspect of production, the task didn't get done. He was discovering that if he ignored something, not only would it get done but it would come roaring in.

With the exception of Scott's, nobody's job responsibilities grew more than Troy's. Given the twin tasks of building the infrastructure of a new company and of overseeing the development of a large online production, he had more cares and frustrations than many executives twice his age. Troy hung up the phone and sighed. He'd just finished speaking with someone who was trying to break a verbal commitment on a licensing deal. As senior vice-president of production, Troy had sweeping responsibilities—including being part of the Asylum's licensing effort. (Troy would later hand off that duty to the new business-affairs person.) Troy wearily climbed the stairs and slumped into a chair in Carl Genberg's office and stretched his legs. "You know how we say we have to be great leaders," he asked Carl, whose desk was covered with spreadsheets, "and how great leaders roll with the punches, deal with problem situations, and turn on a dime?" Carl nodded. "I don't wanna right now," Troy continued. "I just want to sit and scream."

As the summer months passed, things began to get less frantic. The shortage of time forced them to make choices in terms of technology, design, content, and other features. "There's less time to go in several directions at once," Troy observed.[38] With each new week the operation and the final product came into focus. There were still weeks of production work ahead, but they could now get their hands around the task. Troy began to relax a little.

Whatever peace of mind they all felt was shattered by a phone call early one morning at the end of August.

Losing the Glue

At 7:30 A.M. on August 27, 1997, the phone rang as Scott lay in bed. It was Charlie Fink: Brandon had taken a turn for the worse. He was not expected to survive. Scott was stunned. Tartikoff had called ten days earlier and canceled a meeting, saying he didn't feel well. Scott hadn't heard from him in days, and didn't know that Tartikoff had checked in to a hospital.

Early that afternoon Scott got another call at the Asylum. Brandon was dead. To Scott, Tartikoff had seemed to be on the mend. "He's going to live. The question is, when is he coming back," he had maintained. Two days before, an article by Tartikoff had been posted on the prelaunch site. No one at the Asylum had realized that Tartikoff was battling for his life.

Surgeons had recently drained fluid from Tartikoff's lungs, and during his last visit to the Asylum Brandon had begun to get his voice back and "to sound like Brandon again," as Laurie put it. His energy level was rising. Hair was growing back on his head. Brandon was feeling better; he was coming back to make deals for the Asylum. Now, suddenly, he was gone—almost eleven months from the day they teamed up.

Tartikoff was buried on Friday, August 30, at Mount Sinai Memorial Park in Burbank. Two thousand people attended, including Jerry Seinfeld, Ted Danson, and Danny DeVito, to name but a few of the Hollywood elite who showed up to pay their respects. The hall in which the service was held was so crowded with mourners that even Brandon's friend Jeffrey Katzenberg couldn't get inside and had to cool his heels among the crowd that sat in chairs outside. Scott and Charlie were in the crowd as well. The obituaries naturally concentrated on his TV career, with only a passing mention of his relationship with AOL. Nobody had seen his online work—his last project.

Sunday evening, Scott and his wife, Debra, went to see Scott's brother Mark. Mark's wife had just given birth to a son, Ethan. Ethan had been born the same day Brandon died. Debra herself was almost four months pregnant. *The circle of life*, Scott mused. He'd lost more than a mentor. On the drive home Scott shared his feelings about Brandon with Debra. For the first time in as long as he could remember, he began to cry.

When Tartikoff died, Greenhouse Networks lost more than its titular chairman. His signing on with Ted Leonsis had been a sign that original content on the Internet ought to be taken seriously. Though his weight in the industry had diminished since his successful tenure at NBC, he could have taken AOL places that it could never have gone without him.

Leonsis and Fink couldn't help but think what would have been accomplished if Brandon had not become ill. Brandon had a thousand ideas, knew a thousand people, heard a thousand pitches. If he had been well, there was no telling what might have emerged from the partnership. Maybe another golden age. Maybe zip.

There was something else they lost that late August afternoon, something that would not become apparent until later. Brandon had been a key element in the family dynamics between the Asylum and AOL Studios. Like a revered don in a mafia family, he had been the wise elder that everyone turned to when there were problems and disputes. He had been the peacemaker, the person whose presence inspired all the players and kept them in line. Now there was a void.

Less Passive, More Active?

A new launch date had been set for October 27, and for once it looked like they would make it. Troy for one felt he had learned a lot about the medium in the past few months. He was less preoccupied about the specific format at the moment—the Net, the protocols, Push—and more concerned that the content they were developing would be "future-proofed." Anticipating the day when broadband network connections became common, they had shot everything in broadcast-quality video.

Troy was more enthusiastic than ever about the industry's potential to be a business. What they were doing at the Asylum was "mimicking the entertainment business, but it's not the entertainment business." Cyberspace wasn't as big as Hollywood, couldn't offer the salaries, budgets, or audiences yet. Hollywood insiders would have to adjust their thinking accordingly. But they should also realize that the Asylum represented where the business was headed. New technologies would transform the entertainment industry in ways none of them could suspect—film and music distribution, interactive festivals, or e-commerce.

As the launch date approached, the implications of having distribution to 9 million AOL members began to sink in for Troy. This was as close as anyone in the cyber world could come to a mass market at the moment. Greenhouse Networks would become what AMCY had meant to be but wasn't: an online entertainment network with immense reach.

The past ten months had been gut-busting. There were moments during the negotiations when they had thought of bagging it. Conflicts erupted regularly. They were entering a crowded market late in the game, and their strategic model was more than a year old—a disturbingly long period in Internet time. But at last they were ready to fulfill the vision that Scott had typed out months before. "We're bringing people closer to their favorite stars than they've ever been before," Troy said. "The way you could have a direct conversation with Tara on *The Spot* or with Meredith on *GrapeJam*, you'll be able to do that with David Ducovny or Jack Nicholson, or whoever comes into Studio i."

The question was . . . would it all work?

"Is the general population going to spend less time passively and more time actively?" asked media mogul Barry Diller. "I personally would be surprised if that were to happen."[38]

Launch Party

The launch of *The Spot* had been a brilliant piece of guerrilla marketing. *GrapeJam*'s launch had been on a more professional footing ($100,000 worth), staged by Cowan & Company, but hampered by Lightspeed's limited budget. With Asylum, Scott had the weight of the AOL marketing juggernaut behind him—and Leonsis spared no effort for the jewel in AOL Studios' crown.

Scott flew to New York to run the press gamut the week before the launch—generating wide coverage in newspapers and magazines throughout the country and overseas. The *Los Angeles Times* summed up AOL Studios' wager in the lead to its coverage of the site: "Ready for battle with its launch of Entertainment Asylum, AOL is venturing where others have failed. Hollywood is all eyes." To be successful, they had to win over a skeptical and easily distracted Hollywood establishment. With Tartikoff gone, they needed some sort of validation to maintain the deal-making momentum and to encourage a steady stream of celebrities to Studio i. To do that one needed a real Hollywood-style launch party, one befitting the community that Entertainment Asylum was attempting to get close to. Ted Leonsis opened up the checkbook.

Scott explained to reporters that the Entertainment Asylum was both an entertainment information *service* and *experience*. The network's content was built around the areas of movies, television, and celebrities. Genre-oriented sites were matrixed across those three domains. There was the *Comedy Clinic*, the *Action Explosion*, the *Drama Den*, the *Sci-Fi Zone*, and *Pulp Cult Horror Highway*. The network also had information services: The *Hollywood Wire* provided a steady stream of gossip and entertainment news, and there were guides showing the latest television and film listings.

Fan communities would be nested in the genres, and each site had its own bulletin board. The shows' producers and Screen Team members regularly seeded the bulletin boards with their own thoughts and observations.

Studio i was the centerpiece of the Network, offering up live events, interviews and simultaneous chat hosted by the Screen Team members. The lineup of scheduled celebrities was impressive: Mel Brooks, Carl Reiner, Tommy Davidson, Holly Hunter, and Robert Duvall.

The Asylum at launch was intended to be a diamond in the rough. The site would feed off audience input and evolve. Scott and the team planned to create new content offerings over time and to solicit more material from independent producers. If successful, Asylum would become a major buyer of original online content.

"The online world needs a hit entertainment property," David Wertheimer told Bruce Haring of *USA Today* shortly before the launch.

Wertheimer believed that AOL's huge audience made the Asylum an almost sure success. "It's a short putt."[40]

Night descended quicker than usual on the evening of October 27, and it was already dark when the party began at 6:00. Searchlights cut through a thin layer of fog that moved in after sunset. The early arrivals began to pull up to the entrance, where the reservation tables were supervised by Asylum and Greenhouse PR staffers Karin Mikaels and Anne Bentley. Richard Gere soon appeared on the innumerable monitors scattered throughout the Asylum's offices, creating the illusion that he had just entered the studio (in fact he was being interviewed from a remote location in New York). The Web version of the site was visible on numerous terminals located throughout the building—it looked better than the Rainman version.

Foggers and heavy industrial music provided the atmospherics. The offices and spaces were divided up, each for a different show or genre on the site. *PCH*, on the second floor, was the best realized. There was a buffet with a macabre candelabra, gargoyles, and a big, hairy bat with green eyes and a head that moved slowly back and forth. Creepy fingers moved next to the guacamole. A bug-eyed mannequin sat in an electric chair, periodically getting electrocuted. Also in the *PCH* area was a '50s-style pulp cafe with fat, campy waitresses in uniforms and too much makeup.

Downstairs, next to Troy's office, was the set for the *Comedy Clinic*. A bartender dressed in a lab coat and headband reflector served drinks.

The offices, halls, and outdoor courtyard quickly filled with partygoers. Leonsis held court in a hallway just off the courtyard, gesticulating as he spoke. Word circulated among the gathering that he was unofficially predicting Entertainment Asylum would reach a million hits per day within the first hundred days. A million hits a day would put Asylum well above the traffic of all its competitors. The launch party had already succeeded in one way: Asylum closed a content partnership with Universal (*Universal Monsters*) and advertising deals with Columbia House Music and Sony Films (*Starship Troopers*). Everyone kept track of the traffic, and so far the numbers were great.

Charlie Fink was typically expansive and genially rumpled in a black leisure suit and unbuttoned tab-collar shirt. In a way, he mused, his work with Entertainment Asylum was finished. Now it was the job of the sales force to try to pay for it. Charlie had the other content networks to worry about—Real Fans, Electra, and Love@AOL.

Leonsis had expected Steve Case to fly out for the launch, and Scott had worked a role for him into the improv show for the night, but quarterly financial reports were coming out and he decided to stay in Vienna. Bob Pittman had been invited as well, but also found business pressing. For better or worse, Leonsis would have the show all to himself.

While Laurie was interviewing Richard Gere via Studio i, several thousand people crowded into the studio's chat area. Only a couple dozen of the visitors came through the Web version of the site; all the rest were AOL members. The stats momentarily resurrected an old argument. *Just as we predicted*, Charlie thought, *most of the chat participants are coming from AOL.*

Well represented among the Hollywood starlets, agents, and producers were the members of the Los Angeles Web community—and some of Entertainment Asylum's direct competitors. Jeremy Verba seemed wonderfully bubbly given the circumstances. Ronald Frankel, the president of MGM Interactive, was on hand. Josh Greer showed up with a newly grown goatee. Matti Leshem also sported a goatee and broke out in a sweat as he worked the crowd. Of all the members of the "Mr. Clean crowd," Matti was the one who most closely resembled Scott. That night, a number of people came up to congratulate him, thinking he was Scott, for having a great launch. Jim Jonassen, the head of the Los Angeles New Media Roundtable, a key player in efforts to market Los Angeles as a new-media mecca, made his way toward Leshem and extended his hand. "Scott, congratulations." A little light went on behind Matti Leshem's small, dark eyes. He hardly missed a beat and seized the opportunity for a little fun. "Thanks Jim . . . but you know what? *Fuck* AOL! I'm tired of dealing with them. I'm walking away from this deal. . . ." Jonassen's jaw dropped.

The Screen Team and members of the Groundlings put on an interactive improv game show, a demo for what online interactivity would be like at the Asylum. Fink and Leonsis were roped in for some merciless roasting of AOL. Scott dedicated the show to Brandon Tartikoff.

The rest of the evening unfurled in typical Hollywood fashion.

Gregory Hines showed up for an interview and generated a suitable buzz among the crowd. Downtown Julie Brown, the newest member of the Screen Team, gave out a piercing shriek when the Italian model Fabio "goosed" her.

Troy and Rich, looking uncomfortable in suit and tie, were too immersed in technical aspects of the launch that night to socialize much. On the other hand, Scott could barely contain his excitement during this apotheosis of his career. He was everywhere. Dressed in black, his head was especially shiny and smooth this evening, almost like a new-born baby's. As the party wound down, he and Debra edged their way out to the tarmac to say good-bye to some of the guests. Scott must have wondered at how far he had come in the twenty-eight months since he launched *The Spot*. He had wanted to break through into the Hollywood establishment. He'd wanted to generate a little heat for himself. Now producers and agents were calling and pitching him. The biggest stars in the industry were showing up at his (well, AOL's) doorstep.

Leonsis walked into Troy's office and said how happy he was with the launch. He wanted to make the Web side of Asylum huge.

In a few months it would all be over for Scott and his fellow pioneers. Online entertainment was dead. In retrospect, they wondered whether the Asylum had arrived on the scene too late. Or had it come too early?

Shakedown Cruise

Of course, everyone thought things were fine—even Ted Leonsis. Maybe even Bob Pittman and Steve Case. The launch party was an unqualified success. The press was good. People were stoked.

Around the time of the launch, Ted Leonsis set a formidable goal for the Asylum team: 1 million page views per day within one hundred days of the launch. It was a lofty goal for a newly launched content-oriented site—all the more so because of Asylum's "pinhole" distribution on AOL. By comparison, Disney.com took three years to reach 2.6 million page views per day—and benefited from Disney's powerful brand identity and crosspromotion on the Disney Channel. The Asylum team rolled up their sleeves and got to work.

The Asylum had embarked on what was essentially a shakedown

cruise to discover what worked and what didn't with the public. Even before the launch party had ended, Troy could see where they needed to make changes. There was early feedback about the site's navigation, which was confusing to some visitors and not as transparent as they'd hoped it would be. Work immediately began to generate an easier way for people to move about the site.

They discovered that the animation program they used had a lot of bugs that resulted in slower-than-desired page downloads. There were technical problems with the message boards.

Many observers thought the site looked compelling, but some groused that Asylum had broken no new ground in terms of design, business models, or interactivity. Jupiter Communications analyst Mark Mooradian had not been effusive when he first saw the site. He thought Asylum's look was "impressive," but wondered if it wasn't a bit "clunky" and "bloated."

Every newly launched Web site was a work in progress. No one knew that better than Jeremy Verba, the president and CEO of E! Online. Verba gave his assessment of the Asylum one month after the launch. The toughest thing about launching a Web site like the Entertainment Asylum or E! Online, Verba said, was knowing what worked and what didn't. "I've been in jobs, businesses and industries where you have a good idea of what's the right way to go," he said. "You've done it before, you know what the client expects." But nobody really knew the correct genetic code for a successful Web site. Verba quoted *Los Angeles Times* publisher Mark Willes as saying that 80 percent of what one did in the media was right, but that to succeed, you had to find the 20 percent that was wrong—and find it quickly. "On the Internet," Verba noted, "most likely 50 percent of what you do is right. The other 50 percent is wrong. The Entertainment Asylum is a perfect example. I don't think Scott got a lot of it right. But he will. You have to be in the middle of it to realize what works and what doesn't. We are still trying to figure out the best way that our front door should look at E! Online. That sounds like a small thing, but it's a very important thing. After a year and three months, we're trying to figure what's the best way. We've changed the front door eight times."

Asylum Television

Scott focused his creative energies on the content coming out of Studio i, the most innovative and experimental part of the site. Scott was more than pleased with the "interactive and bizarre stuff" coming out of the studio—the same playful, anarchic spirit that had been evident in *GrapeJam*. "Open the microphone with an agenda and see how that agenda changes," Zakarin had said. In other words, engineer situations where real people can do unpredictable, entertaining things—and involve the audience in the mix. That same philosophy was being embraced in Studio i—none of which could be seen in its video format through the AOL version of the site.

Matt Wagner, who was performing the news for the *Hollywood Wire*, gave a perfect example of the kind of edgy improvisation that the Asylum team encouraged. Wagner was a handsome, lean actor with an engaging on-camera presence. For one webcast he interviewed actress Denise Richards from the movie *Starship Troopers*. Unbeknownst to Richards, the audience had been told that Wagner's goal for the interview was to get a date with her. Members of the audience fed Wagner lines to use on Richards in the pursuit of his goal. (Richards ended up inviting Wagner out for lunch.)

One of the early webcasts from Studio i featured Mel Brooks and Carl Reiner doing an interactive version of the two-thousand-year-old man, with the audience supplying the questions. On other occasions, Rich Tackenberg's camera teams roamed around Hollywood asking celebrities for their opinions on audience-selected topics, for instance, capturing Henry Winkler's thoughts on mysterious, UFO-related cow mutilations. What followed were shows featuring Screen Team crushes and flirtations. When Jenny McCarthy's show was canceled, Laurie impersonated her for an interview segment.

Some of the antics were reminiscent of what Ernie Kovacs or Steve Allen might have attempted if they'd had interactive technology in the golden age of television. Of course, some of it was magic, while some of it was just silly. What mattered to Scott was that the Asylum team was always experimenting with the medium. For Scott, interactivity wasn't simply the thing that differentiated the Net from everything else; he believed interactivity could be found in some form in all media, that the power of interactivity had been too little appreciated in Hollywood.

Eventually, he wanted to edge back toward producing another online narrative, giving the storytelling a new dimension from what he was learning from Studio i and other video escapades. In early February, Scott managed to line up Dustin Hoffman as a guest in Studio i. Scott had big plans: Hoffman would be the first major star to give a live interactive performance in a piece scripted by an online audience in real time.

Meanwhile, rumor had it that AOL was about to undergo a major reorganization. Charlie Fink was flying out to L.A. to hold an all-hands meeting with the Asylum staff.

The End of the First Wave

Matti Leshem would later recall with fondness the excitement and élan associated with being among the first wave of entrepreneurs who attempted to "create the concept of Internet entertainment." With the exception of Scott and the Asylum team, those pioneers found themselves continually scaling back their ambitions and expectations as the year 1997 progressed. The notion of building businesses around new and original forms of interactive entertainment became increasingly elusive, quixotic, and hopeless.

When the Microsoft Network canceled *Second City Naked News* in the early fall, Leshem and his partners lost their company's cash cow. The show had finally succumbed to MSN's shift away from entertainment and toward more information-intensive and useful sites. There was no point in attempting to create another interactive entertainment show because MSN was no longer a buyer of that kind of content. MGM Interactive had purchased an option on *Angel House*, but had allowed the option to run out. Faced with closing the company, Leshem did what he once vowed never to do—built corporate Web sites. Cobalt Moon won a contract to build an online insurance site for Alan Snyder of Answer Financial. The contract was lucrative and enabled the company to continue operations while Leshem tried to sell unsold properties like *The King of Television* and figure out what the company was going to do next.

Shortly before the Entertainment Asylum launch in October, Leshem got a call from a headhunter at A. T. Kearney. Would he be interested in a position in television? Leshem's thoughts about working in television were changing. Like everyone else, he saw the convergence of television and the Internet as an inevitable evolutionary development that would eventually unfold. He already had great credentials on the Internet side of the equation. Maybe it wouldn't be a bad idea to broaden his experience base by working in television for a while. Still, he was loath to abandon the company that he'd spent years trying to build, especially since Cobalt Moon was still profitable.

As it happened, this was no ordinary position in television. Barry Diller was preparing to make his first sortie into local television. He was looking for an editor in chief for a new and experimental television station in the South Florida market, one that would produce cutting-edge programming for the multi-ethnic Miami audience. Would Leshem like to meet Barry Diller? Of all the "old media guys," Diller (bald of head!) was the one that had intrigued Leshem the most.

By November, Leshem was engaged in heavy negotiations for the position. Peter Dekom, one of the most powerful entertainment attorneys in Los Angeles, represented him in the early phase of the negotiations. He would conference with Dekom while maneuvering his BMW convertible through traffic on Wilshire Boulevard on his way to his favorite sushi restaurant. (Leshem ended up closing the deal himself.)

He would have to give up his role in Cobalt Moon, pack up his family, and move cross-country. On the other hand, Diller was rolling out a new strategy that might revolutionize local television—and Matti would be heading up Diller's test-bed station, WAMI-Channel 69 in Miami. The station would produce local-flavor television programming geared to the cultural sensibilities of Miami's cosmopolitan market. Leshem couldn't entirely suppress his competitive instincts. If he were successful, Zakarin and his AOL deal would be small potatoes in comparison.

By December, Leshem and his new WAMI staff were working in an old building that had once housed an art gallery, creating programming for hip, young Cuban Americans. Cobalt Moon shut down within a matter of months.

As the 1997 holiday season approached, Josh Greer had to come to terms with his situation. The Direct IPO fiasco had been deeply embarrassing. The company had net earnings for two quarters, but no cash reserves to carry them from one payroll to the next. Investors were interested, but none made any moves. At one point Josh ran into the Reese brothers—major behind-the-scenes players in the media world. Jeffrey had been one of the creators of the Showtime cable network, and Randolf had worked with Barry Diller at Twentieth Century–Fox, later moving on to Disney television. Jeffrey Reese had been approached by WebTV to create a whole WebTV destination.

He in turn called up Greer to talk about hiring Digital Planet to help develop that site. Greer managed to steer the conversation into a discussion about acquiring Digital Planet outright. The discussions progressed to the point that by the first week of December, the parties sat in the same room with polished contracts, ready to sign. Jeffrey was excited about the deal. But Josh and the others' desperation for cash was evident to all. The Reese brothers got spooked and backed out of the deal.

When the Reese brothers walked away from the table, Josh was forced to lay off a quarter of his staff a week and a half before Christmas—without severance pay. Some of the folks he'd been forced to let go were people who had worked at Digital Planet from day one. Greer had had it.[41]

There had been many other opportunities to sell Digital Planet in the past. Greer had resisted all offers; he wanted to maintain control of the company, and so had turned down every bid. He'd resisted CAA's efforts to bring in another CEO to replace him, as often happened with other growing start-ups. Even hiring an outside COO had been impossible for him. The layoffs changed everything. The business stopped being fun. Josh went home and had a long talk with his wife, Lorraine.

As the old-time movie comedian Joe E. Brown once said, "the handwriting is on the floor." Josh had long expected that the Web-development business would enter a period of consolidation. The big brands—Nike, Ford Motor, and Procter & Gamble—would want big, sophisticated destination sites. He knew that Digital Planet would never have the cash flow needed to sustain the pursuit of those large accounts. It was time to sell. He'd finally achieved peace of mind about the prospect.

One week later, the unexpected occurred. Finally, Mattel made a decision on a contractor for its destination site: Digital Planet was awarded the very lucrative account. Suddenly, there was plenty of work for the company. His partners Jeff Gall and Thomas Lakeman now reversed course and pleaded with Josh *not* to sell the company. Josh disagreed. "Guys," he said, "all this does is put us at a different altitude. But it sets us up for the exact same problem six months from now." Josh pushed forward with the search for a buyer.

Kevin Wall was interested. He was the founder of BoxTop, a well-known Los Angeles Web-development company that had been acquired by iXL, a "worldwide Internet solutions company," in 1997. Wall was now the CEO of iXL's Los Angeles office. iXL was the kind of large Web-development company that Greer expected to emerge from the industry consolidation, and iXL was in an acquisition mode. Wall did a good job of wooing Greer, who spent some time with Wall and his family over Christmas in Palm Springs. Greer met iXL's executive group in Atlanta and was suitably impressed.

Lakeman and Gall were angry about the deal at first, and highly resistant to the proposed merger. "Listen," Greer told them, "the worst that can happen is that we'll be paid off and sit on a beach for a year or something. If that's the worst that can happen . . . " There was also the fact that Digital Planet was saddled with debt—debt that Josh had to personally guarantee. Lakeman and Gall weren't ready to cash out and felt the company was getting close to controlling its bottom line. The Mattel deal, they felt, would keep them solvent until the company could negotiate more favorable terms with a buyer. But Josh was worn down. He wanted out.

Greer signed the deal memo in December, but didn't close the deal until May 1998. iXL also acquired another Web company, Spin Cycle, at this time, and the staffs and assets of all three companies— BoxTop, Digital Planet and Spin Cycle—were moved into the Saban building in Westwood, where Greer was made the COO of the Los Angeles office.

Many of Josh's friends thought he would be ill suited to a corporate position. He had spent years resisting being sucked into a real corporate environment, after all. But Josh was tired. He now hungered for stability and had reconciled himself to the position, even convinced himself that he looked forward to it. The position promised him something that had eluded him since the Fall of 1994: structure.

In late 1997, Paramount Digital Entertainment finally made the decision to wean itself from the cold breast of the Microsoft Network. While shoppers were choking the malls trying to return unwanted gifts the day after Christmas of 1997, Wertheimer sat in his office, scheming how to take Paramount's big properties off MSN, change the business model, and achieve the change as seamlessly and profitably as possible. Wertheimer eventually steered his group toward a new business model that would be almost totally driven by advertising and licensing fees, a risky and dramatic shift for a company that for two years had enjoyed the benefits of a single-customer relationship.

Wertheimer spent a lot of time talking to advertisers, handicapped by the fact that Microsoft never gave PDE actual performance statistics for the shows that ran on MSN. That made it very difficult to provide potential advertisers with forecasts for the amount of traffic that *Star Trek: Continuum* or *Entertainment Tonight* might draw. He did manage to build a strong relationship with Marianne Caponetto, IBM's director of worldwide advertising. IBM became the charter advertiser for *Star Trek: Continuum* and began working with PDE in a technological collaboration. Through that collaboration, IBM helped develop the technological underpinnings of a *Star Trek* store, which launched later in 1998, featuring e-commerce with customization and agenting features.

Wertheimer and his team also continued researching new forms of storytelling for a variety of platforms—the Internet, digital television, and enhanced television. One idea they played with involved taking existing brands and making people feel a part of the brand, even if it was only in an online universe. "Through a variety of means," Wertheimer explained, "a fan would be able to follow stories between episodes, learn more about the shows, and engage in a totally different kind of experience than they would get on television."

By July 1998, Wertheimer entered into the last three months of his three-year contract with Paramount. His team had developed over twenty sites. Some of them, like *Duckman*, were as technically sophisticated as anything on the Web. He had been able to leverage the studio's major brands, like *Star Trek* and *Entertainment Tonight*. He'd wanted to do much more.

The reality was that—with the possible exception of Sony, Disney, and Warner Brothers—the studios didn't care much about the online business. It seemed that the studios were in the online business only because they felt they needed a presence there. The major studio management would wait for someone else to figure out how to make online work, if it were even possible. Whoever cracked the code would eventually have to come courting the companies and studios that owned the brands. For now, the Web seemed to stymie everyone. How did you aggregate an audience for content? Even when the content was interesting, how did you get the audience to come?

Wertheimer sat down at his PC and drafted an assessment of PDE and its future for Paramount's upper management. Many executives at Paramount questioned the viability of online entertainment. Wertheimer addressed these doubts in his report. Despite the poor traffic, he believed that the Internet was still destined to be an entertainment medium with the potential to empower audiences like no other. Technology made it possible to customize and deliver experiences and advertising messages with great precision—a powerful tool in today's increasingly fragmented media markets. As he had one afternoon almost three years before in Kerry McCluggage's office, Wertheimer urged Paramount executives to think in terms of what the medium could be rather than what it was at the moment.

The studio paid lip service to the idea. Wertheimer was offered another three-year contract. Though he liked and respected Lindheim and McCluggage, he knew it would be three years of the same. Paramount had too much invested in its motion-picture and television businesses.

These were still the early days. Back in 1948 Milton Berle created a breakthrough show that established television as an entertainment medium. Someone, somewhere (other than Paramount) would do the same for the Web. That was where Wertheimer wanted to be.

A visitor to David Wertheimer's office in 1998 likened the Microsoft Network's enormously expensive efforts to develop online entertainment to a disaster on a scale with the sinking of the Titanic. Wertheimer smiled. "We were the best content on a ship that sank coming out of harbor," he said. "Unlike the Titanic," Wertheimer added, "Microsoft never made it to the Arctic."

By the fall of 1997, Microsoft had decimated its entertainment programming, signaling a shift toward content that had more utility for MSN visitors. The entertainment metaphor was officially declared dead on February 26, 1998, when MSN announced that it was ending its remaining entertainment programming, such as *Underwire*, a site for women; *Satori*, a health-oriented site; *Cinemania Online; Music Central;* and several other sites. "Our research shows," Laura Jennings said in a statement, "that with the exception of games, pure entertainment is not what people find most valuable on the Web. What they're looking for are tools and services that enable them to get everyday things done faster and more easily online."[42]

MSN would shift its attention and resources to sites such as its travel-services site, *Expedia*, and *CarPoint*, a site that offered a database of information and reviews for car buyers. "We were romanced by the entertainment stuff," said Pete Higgins, vice president of Microsoft's interactive media group. "But we underestimated the value of software. And you know there really is something very sexy about creating a product that is useful to people and can help them live their lives better."[43] Microsoft would yet again begin to reinvent MSN, this time as a portal offering a bundling of Internet utilities and information services to Web surfers.

Bejan had the difficult task of closing down the M^3P he had built. The day the layoffs were announced, Bejan drove back to his Lake Washington home and spent hours walking around the lake's shoreline.

For a time thereafter, Bejan seemed to drop out of sight. Wertheimer, for one, had made phone calls and sent e-mail, all of which went unanswered. Rumors circulated that Bejan had taken an extended vacation. Everyone had assumed that his deal with Microsoft was too sweet for him to leave.

The Sacking

The search for investors to acquire AOL Studios was heating up by the winter of 1998. A year before, AOL's change from hourly to flat-rate pricing had wiped out a major source of revenue for AOL Studios. The urgent need to divert resources to the purchase or leasing of modems drove the company deeper into the red. Steve Case gave Ted Leonsis his blessing to find an investor for Greenhouse Networks or possibly all of AOL Studios.

Leonsis and Danny Krifcher had entered into talks with two potential investors, Bertelsmann AG and Madison Dearborn Partners, Inc. Bertelsmann AG, a German partner in AOL Europe, was one of the largest media companies in the world. Discussions were progressing to the point where the two companies were prepared to invest $200 million in AOL Studios in exchange for an interest in the company.

While all these discussions were going on, Bob Pittman was busy transforming AOL into the kind of company that Wall Street loves to love. Pittman brought what the *New York Times* called "a mature marketing vision" to the company.[44] His steady hand imposed a level of discipline that had been lacking during previous years. AOL was on its way to becoming one of the first blue-chip stocks in the new-media space. When fourth quarter 1997 statistics were reported for the company in early 1998, the results of Pittman's labors were nothing short of spectacular. America Online had earned $20.8 million for the quarter on sales of $592 million. Even more amazingly, the company's stock in February closed at above $110 per share, a threefold increase over the previous fourth quarter performance. There was more good news: advertising revenues soared, almost double what they had been. What's more, Pittman had maneuvered to sell off AOL's ANS Communications, Inc. to WorldCom, for which it received $175 million. Case and Pittman no longer had to rob Peter to pay Paul. The company's coffers were brimming.

With the need for cash no longer a threat, selling AOL Studios became less necessary and less attractive. In January 1998, it became clear that if the company sold the studio, "pooling rules" would mean AOL would forfeit significant tax advantages if it made any major acquisitions. Case and Pittman decided that it wouldn't be such a good idea to sell AOL Studios after all. But the current situation was untenable as well. AOL Studios was spending too much money. Entertainment Asylum expenses exceeded revenues to the tune of $400,000 a month. It would take two to three years for the operation to break even. (Scott thought they could have been profitable in one or two years.) That was if the site was successful. And Asylum was just the first of four content networks that Leonsis planned to launch. Worse, the AOL Studios sales force was often in competition with AOL Networks salespeople. Even if the duplicate units weren't going head to head against each other, they constituted a further waste of resources.

As Charlie Fink sat in his room at the Beverly Wilshire hotel on the evening of Tuesday, February 10, 1998, the jungle drums were beating outside his window, figuratively, if not literally. The natives were restless. *They knew.* Fink wasn't talking to the press, but there was no way sixty people would keep quiet for long. In fact, the word got out almost immediately. By the time *Daily Variety* and the *Hollywood Reporter* landed in in-boxes around town, much of digital Hollywood had already heard the grim news: Charlie Fink had fired forty employees of the Entertainment Asylum over the lunch hour that day. Scott, Troy, Rich, Laurie, and Carl were among the casualties.

The Asylum firings were part of an overall savaging of AOL Studios. Another sixty-five employees were laid off from the studio's gaming company, WorldPlay.

Fink was scheduled to be a panelist at the Network Entertainment World conference at the Beverly Wilshire on Thursday afternoon. He'd be joining peers like Lara Stein, who headed up MSN's development office in New York, Sriram Viswanathan of Intel's content group, Rick Markovitz of the entertainment marketing firm BBDO, and Hala Makowska, vice president of brand development at Time Warner Inc. New Media. The panel was called "What Do Buyers Want?" and would be moderated by Robert Tercek of Columbia Tristar Interactive. There would be no running for cover. While he had merely carried out the order to layoff, Charlie would be the one to absorb all the arrows—at least in public.

All the excellent financial news in January 1998—AOL stockholders were understandably ecstatic—was followed by a disquieting two-day interlude. Leonsis was accustomed to being on the receiving end of a barrage of e-mail messages from his boss, Steve Case. Suddenly, the e-mail messages stopped. "It was radio silence," was the way Leonsis would later remember it.[45] On a visit to New York, Leonsis's pager beeped. Steve Case was calling. It quickly became apparent that what looked like a 2 percent probability last summer had now climbed to nearly 100 percent. Case was having doubts about the deal with Bertelsmann/Madison Dearborn, and told Leonsis that AOL Studios would instead be folded back into the company.

The reorganization occurred the first week of February. Bob Pittman was promoted to chief operating officer of AOL, number two in the hierarchy. AOL Studios was brought under Pittman's authority. Ted Leonsis—who had so assiduously recruited Pittman during the summer of 1996—would now report to his former equal. Pulling the studio back into the "mothership" would allow Pittman to trim expenses. It would also bring the content-development wing under his direct supervision, where he could impose some of that discipline for which he had become famous. Leonsis, a proud and brash man, was devastated. Many thought he would quit, but instead he chose to hang on.

No one should have been surprised at his decision. "This is the biggest stage," he told reporters. "And no matter how many times we change, I still have the best seat in the house."[46] Leonsis was also a prisoner of his options. He owned an immense block of AOL stock.

Scott Zakarin was as surprised as anyone about the machinations in Vienna. But he was also unconcerned, at least publicly. The reorganization seemed to be unfolding on levels above him. There might be a storm raging on the ocean surface, but all seemed calm deep down in Scott's octopus garden. When Scott was contacted in Culver City Tuesday morning by a journalist from the *Hollywood Reporter*, he said that the reorganization would have no effect on himself or the Asylum's operations. Zakarin went on to tell the journalist that Entertainment Asylum had reached Ted Leonsis's goal of a million hits per day on January 31, weeks ahead of the one-hundred-day target.

The week of February 9 began with a small coup for Scott. Through mutual friends he'd managed to get Dustin Hoffman to agree to come in to Studio i for a session. Scott planned to have Laurie interview Hoffman. The broadcast (if that word was still appropriate) was scheduled for later in the week. Scott and Laurie did a promo for the interview that morning in Studio i, then collected Troy and Rich and headed out to meet Charlie Fink, who had arrived the night before, for lunch at the Sage Brush Cantina. Carl normally would have been included, but he had flown out to Vienna for a meeting.

Charlie was already at the restaurant when the four walked in the door. To Scott's surprise, Fink was sitting at a table with a "sweet-looking woman" who turned out to be from human resources at AOL. Charlie stood and the two hugged. Scott immediately sensed that something was wrong.

Charlie began by congratulating Scott for reaching a million hits a day ahead of schedule. He then added that it was a great accomplishment but that it didn't matter. The Asylum was costing too much money to produce. They would have to make cuts in personnel—starting with the senior management.

Scott was so completely unprepared for what was being said that he didn't understand the import of Charlie's words at first. In the first moment he didn't equate senior management with Troy, Rich, Laurie, Carl, and himself. In the next moment he worried that the founders were being split up—that some would stay and others would go. Then he got it. AOL was laying off *all* five of the original partners—in fact, almost everyone associated with Lightspeed—more than forty people in total.

The woman from human resources began to hand over envelopes. Scott was in shock as he received his own. (At that very moment Carl was being handed his own packet in Vienna.) Charlie gave Scott the option of going home or attending the all-hands meeting after lunch. Scott decided to attend the meeting, which lasted twenty minutes. Most faces registered shock. Scott thought some of the others knew what was coming.

Hoffman's people asked Scott if he still wanted the actor to do the Studio i session. Scott said yes. But instead of the interactive piece he had planned, Hoffman ended up doing a straight interview.

Scott went home and helped with his newborn son. Debra had given birth to Caleb Mason Zakarin six days before. Caleb's bris came the day after the layoffs.

1999 and Beyond

The Future of Entertainment: Siliwood Redux

There is a theory which states that if ever anyone discovers exactly what the Universe is for and why it is here, it will instantly disappear and be replaced by something even more bizarre and inexplicable.
There is another which states that this has already happened.

—from *The Restaurant at the End of the Universe*
by Douglas Adams

In April 1998, Steve Jobs flew to Las Vegas to address the National Association of Broadcasters. Those in the audience who remembered Jobs best as the archetypal figure of the PC revolution in the '70s and '80s couldn't help but notice how he'd aged. The leanness of youth was gone; his hair was thinning. He now looked more like someone's eccentric, sweater-vested father-in-law than the wunderkind of his early Apple days.

Jobs's address came between the failed efforts at online entertainment during the previous years and the cusp of the broadband era. He had come to say that Silicon Valley in general—and Apple in particular—still believed that the technology and entertainment industries needed each other. "The computer community knows nothing about entertainment," Jobs told the assembled broadcasters, implicitly acknowledging past and continuing misunderstandings between people in the two great industries. The '90s had seen a lot of "Siliwood" roadkill. What was past was past. Their best days lay ahead in the looming possibilities of broadband. Like a reconciling lover, Jobs had come to ask the entertainment industry to make another go at it with the valley. "We're dying to work with you," he said.[47]

The Second Golden Era

In an article entitled "The Second Golden Era," posted online just forty-eight hours before his death at Cedars Sinai hospital, Brandon

Tartikoff explained why he decided to join up with the Greenhouse. "As a Baby Boomer," Tartikoff wrote, "I had grown up in the golden age of television, but didn't get to the big dance till I was in my twenties, when a lot of the significant infrastructure had already been invented and laid down. I always fantasized how great it would be to hop in a Jules Verne time machine or even Michael J. Fox's 'Back to the Futuremobile,' set it for the year 1945 and be present at the beginning of that golden era. Now thanks to AOL, I get that chance."

In 1995, many thought a new era was unfolding in the history of entertainment, a golden age every bit as significant as the early days of cinema or television. The Internet was like television circa 1947. Like all pioneering times, the early Internet days were wide open, the barriers to entry nonexistent. The new-media business attracted some of the brightest and certainly the most entrepreneurial people in the entertainment, technology, and other industries. Pioneers like Zakarin, Fink, Bejan, Greer, Wertheimer, and Leshem had no road maps for creating online content. There were no books, courses, rules, elder statesmen, or success stories to guide them. They all made it up as they went along.

The Net offered a powerful new medium for reaching out to audiences, and a technology that was cheap and democratic enough to allow almost anyone to distribute content to the entire world, bypassing Hollywood's traditional gatekeepers. A relative outsider like Scott Zakarin, someone without money or access to Hollywood's grand aggregators, could take a simple insight and develop it into a whole new form of entertainment. Because of the power of the Internet, Zakarin was able to distribute *The Spot* to people around the world simultaneously and to involve them directly in the show in ways that were impossible in any other medium. "The Hollywood studios, publishers, all the information and entertainment distributors are the dinosaurs and the Web is the comet," was how digital moviemaker Phil Flora put it. "They are going to need to adapt really fast or become history." *Content* was king—not the studio heads or TV execs. The Internet seemed as pure a medium of artistic expression as they would ever have—if only there were time to master it.

Why Did Online Entertainment Fail?

It may be a conversation that has to continue for five, six or seven more years. It may be a conversation that's not fruitful.

—Denise Caruso on the dialogue between Silicon Valley and Hollywood[48]

Why did online entertainment fail? Why did the venture capitalists, Internet executives, media moguls, and technology potentates drop original content like a date with a venereal disease?

The Medium Had No Back Office

The Internet of the mid-1990s was like a fourteen-year-old whose growing body has outpaced his coordination. The Net developed faster in some ways than in others. New and innovative forms of content were being put out—including entertainment content—before the means for making money back on that content existed. Huge amounts of content could be downloaded for free by consumers, so those consumers were unwilling to pay subscriptions. Advertisers wouldn't pay enough for ad space to enable developers to make back the cost of producing content. While Web production costs were a fraction of what it cost to produce television shows or make movies, the costs weren't trivial. Even a technically unsophisticated early webisodic like *The Spot* could cost $50,000 a month to produce. The Entertainment Asylum burned up half a million dollars and more a month. How did you pay the bills?

One answer seemed to be e-commerce. One of Scott's earliest ideas had been to sell "Scream Queen" merchandise over the Web. But e-commerce was embryonic in the mid-'90s. Consumers were uneasy about using their credit cards online, and those who did got tired of reentering credit card numbers every time they wanted to make a purchase. Most Web developers had no experience with fulfillment operations. As Bob Bejan later put it, the Internet lacked the "back office" paraphernalia needed to be a business. Former Disney Internet czar Jake Winebaum believes the producers of online entertainment didn't give much thought to how to turn entertainment into a business. On the other hand, if Zakarin or anyone else had waited until the Net's financial underpinnings were in place, shows like *The Spot* would never have been created in the first place.

The 28.8 Net is an Information, Not an Entertainment, Medium

Entertainment content might still have succeeded as a genre, despite the problems with the business model, if it had drawn a large enough audience, enough eyeballs. But shows like *The Spot*, *GrapeJam*, the hundreds of webisodics inspired by them, the offerings on MSN, and even Entertainment Asylum garnered relatively small audiences compared to search engines like Yahoo.

The numbers were small in part because the narrow-band 28.8 Internet was (the pioneers all now acknowledge) more appropriate as an information and communication utility than as a multimedia platform. The narrow bandwidth of the Net was brutally limiting and undependable. "Transmitting information online," wrote Thomas Lakeman, "is like shoveling fleas across a barnyard: not half of them get there." *The Spot* and *GrapeJam* were text-driven by necessity, which demanded more of the audience than watching television, just as silent films required greater attention on the part of early moviegoers because of the absence of sound and spoken dialogue for moving the story. Film and television engaged the senses by bombarding the viewer with live action and surround-sound. On the Internet, vivid graphics, animation, and quality audio choked the pipes. Such audio as was available in streaming form sounded as if it came out of a cheap five-dollar radio. Video was delivered in a two-inch-square window and looked jerky and smudgy.

The pioneers were challenged and stimulated by the technical limitations of the medium. Zakarin, for one, had to set aside much of what he knew from filmmaking to accommodate the Net. When the opportunity came to use interactive video at the Asylum, he seized it, looking ahead to the day when the bandwidth would catch up to him.

Mastery of Interactive Media Art Forms Will Take Years

Even if bandwidth hadn't been a problem, producers were still puzzled about the nature of interactivity itself. Zakarin and his team were learning more about interactivity every day, throwing everything against the wall to see what would stick. The task was daunting; the medium might well take years to come into its own, and then maybe only after present-day toddlers, elementary-school kids, and teenagers—suckled on CD-ROMs, Play Stations, and the Net—grew up and entered the business. Bejan had said that the Net generation was learning the seven basic story lines of the medium, just as he had learned the seven basic story lines of linear storytelling from Saturday-morning cartoons. He reconciled himself to the fact that he'd never see the medium the way they did. He could be a Max Sennett, but he'd never be an Orson Welles.

If it would take years for interactive-media artists to come into their own, it would also probably take the audience years to become comfortable with interactivity itself. One of the consequences of the rapid roll out of the Internet was that interactive media and technology evolved much faster than the media habits of the audience. Interactivity was a startling new experience to an audience that had been conditioned by one hundred years of passive, linear media experiences like those in films, radio, and television. Joe and Jane wanted to veg in front of a screen. Interactivity seemed too demanding, too much work, too difficult to navigate to appeal to the exhausted American public in the mid-90s.

What was worse, the technology wasn't easy to use. Often it went awry. People would download plug-ins and find that they didn't work, or that they crashed their computers. The kind of outages and access problems that plagued AOL in late 1996 and early 1997 were unheard of in traditional broadcast or cable television. "The thing that worries me the most," Jake Winebaum said in 1998, "is the reliability of the Internet experience at all levels, from your local POP to the performance across the backbone and our own servers. All that adds up to a very inconsistent experience for people who are used to turning on their TV sets and watching the news." [49]

Culture Wars Among the Geeks, Suits, and Ponytails

Let's say one of our competitors [an Internet Search company] was to get bought out by a major Hollywood studio. I would just cheer. One more down! They're never going to make it in that environment. It's going to be hard for a media company to know how to interact with this beast of change they've just acquired.

—Joe Kraus, cofounder of Excite, April 1997

The technical and business challenges were, in some ways, the least of the obstacles facing the geeks, ponytails, and suits who tried to bring Hollywood to the Internet. At least those challenges were tangible. It was the intangible, interpersonal, and cultural issues that were the most daunting. The three groups approached the Internet with different visions, motivations, and problem-solving styles. Those differences often contributed to the false starts, miscalculations, and conflicts that sidetracked or derailed efforts to create entertainment in the new medium. Each group took turns taking the medium off track.

When the geeks held sway, too much emphasis was placed on what the technology could do rather than what audiences wanted, as was the case for early experiments in interactive television, CD-ROM, and plug-in-laden Web content like *Madeleine's Mind*. Microsoft executives saw content as a way to show off the company's tools and technology. The results could be technically spectacular—and creatively flat.

The ponytails approached content from the point of view of the story or the experience. But often what was inside a writer's head was something that would choke the technology. One could make a missile crash into the Chrysler building, but bringing that vision online could crash the system. Ponytails also made demands and asked for changes that had serious downstream consequences. Rendering a particular effect could mean weeks of programming—all of which cost money.

When the suits ran the show, investor relations and business models became the focus—to the detriment of content. American Cybercast executives low-browed the content of shows like *The Spot* and *Eon-4* to appeal to a broader audience, alienating its core fans in the process. The suits were correct in believing that the Net had to be a business first. But in their drive to shape it into a great advertising and commerce system, content became relegated to window dressing.

The cultural divide between the geeks and the ponytails in particular—Silicon Valley vs. Hollywood—seemed at times to be unbridgeable. Though the major studios opened interactive units, few of the people who ran Hollywood made a serious commitment to the Internet. David Wertheimer's Paramount Digital Entertainment was saddled by the need to show profits from year one, a standard to which no Internet start-up of the era was expected to hold. Compared to Paramount's other operations, Wertheimer's budget fell into the rounding-error range on the account books.

Hollywood was a private club, which became very clear as the Net pioneers tried to spin their Web shows into television series. *The Spot, GrapeJam, Madeleine's Mind*—none of these properties became television shows. The only online property that was adapted for television was AOL's *Santa's Home Page*. Even then, *Ozzie The Elf* was only a Christmas special, and it took the involvement of a player as big as Brandon Tartikoff to make it happen.

Technology companies like Microsoft exhibited a profound ignorance of the Hollywood culture with which they were locked into business. Both in its dealings with individual artists and in its relationship with Paramount, Microsoft showed no understanding of the industry's concerns about artistic ownership, intellectual property, or how things really worked on a creative level in Hollywood. Despite efforts to provide Bob Bejan and his group with the support they needed, Microsoft executives never quite knew what to do with the ponytails in their midst, and often undermined their efforts.

The large media and technology companies that created or acquired content teams like Lightspeed Media, Paramount Digital Entertainment, or MSN had trouble integrating those teams into their company cultures. Zakarin and his team were artistic entrepreneurs who were used to moving fast in a fast-moving industry. Working out of a house for over a year, they suddenly found themselves slowed by bureaucratic systems, corporate politics, and layers of accountability. For David Wertheimer, a major part of his job was conjuring the illusion that Paramount Digital Entertainment was a start-up company rather than a small unit in a mammoth media conglomerate.

Online Entertainment Didn't Fit Anyone's Models

As formidable as the technical and cultural problems were, online entertainment failed because it was so new and different that it didn't fit anyone's models or business practices.

Bill Gates never appreciated what every Hollywood studio executive knows from experience: most entertainment projects failed. Technology executives believed that most of their products would be successful—a presumption that grew out of the spectacular growth and success of the computer and software industries during the past twenty years.

But media is different from technology. Media is about creating experiences, not utility. Media is always a crap shoot—something the geeks at Microsoft found difficult to accept. Even if their online shows had been successful, the risk-return ratio for media was disappointing. The most successful film of all time, *Titanic*, cost $200 million to make and earned well over a billion dollars. Yet years from now *Titanic* will only be an item in a film library. The same $200 million could have been invested in the development of software products and technologies—a new operating system, video compression scheme, or wireless technology—that could bring much greater value for years to come. For Microsoft, content's value was limited to making its technology look good.

Unlike Microsoft, the major studios like Paramount understood that most of their products would fail. The media business was a numbers game that they understood well. Nine out of ten projects were flops, but it was the one hit in ten that paid for all the rest. One *Titanic* paid for a string of *Babe In the City*s. The problem with online interactive entertainment was that the infrastructure, business models, and install base (number of people online) didn't make it possible to have a financially successful online hit. The moguls of the entertainment industry saw the numbers, did the math, and subsequently gave the medium next to no attention. It didn't fit their models either.

Finally, AOL folded AOL Studios and cut back on Entertainment Asylum because it wanted to concentrate on the infrastructure of its online empire—making acquisitions and entering partnerships to build e-commerce systems, grow its membership base, and drive up advertising revenues. Content networks didn't fit its plans—at least at that moment.

The technology, entertainment, and online industries rushed into an embrace of entertainment and just as swiftly abandoned it. Time was what ultimately defeated the pioneers of the first wave of online entertainment—*Internet time.*

The Medium Was Prematurely Commercialized

A whole new array of companies have sprung up that never existed before—@Home, Yahoo, Amazon. As Jerry Seinfeld would say, "who are these people?"

—Lee Masters, former president of E! Entertainment Television, chairman, Liberty Digital

Internet time was the underlying theme of all the Net success stories and the story of Yahoo was the defining myth. Two Stanford graduate students named Jerry Yang and David Filo catalogued Web sites as an after-school dorm project. A year later AOL offered to buy Yahoo for $2 million. (Leonsis offered an amusing insight into how AOL arrived at the $2 million figure. The Webcrawler browser, which AOL had previously acquired for $1 million, was the creation of a single person. Since Yahoo was created by *two* persons, AOL offered *$2* million for it.) A couple of years after that, Yahoo went public and was transformed into a billion-dollar media company. Five years after its start, Yahoo is worth tens of billions of dollars.

Soon the great successes and failures—or as W3 Design CEO Nick Rothenberg put it, "the twenty-six-year-old who made $50 million in the IPO and the colossal error of American Cybercast"—defined the industry and shaped the psychology of the market. People expected rapid success—or failure—and lost patience with building companies in the territory in between.

Television had an experimental period of almost twenty years—1927 to 1948—in which its pioneers could begin to work out the kinks in the form before they put a single advertisement on the air. Cable television ran network television reruns for fifteen years before companies like HBO and Showtime began creating original content. The pioneers of online content had almost no time at all to learn the rules of their medium and found themselves forced to commercialize their earliest efforts. When the audiences remained relatively small, companies like AOL, Intel and Microsoft cut their losses and bolted.

The Coming of Broadband

By the time AOL folded AOL Studios and Microsoft disbanded its development division, M[3]P, content was anything but king. For the next couple of years, content would take a back seat while the ponytails ran for cover. Geeks and suits were in the ascendancy. Microsoft, AOL, and the whole online industry now concentrated their efforts on erecting the scaffolding of the future online world. Geeks were building and rolling out new broadband infrastructure and new platforms that expanded the Internet from the narrow confines of the desktop to the living room and everywhere else. Cable companies began installing millions of set-top boxes that would enable consumers to surf the Web from their televisions. Industry observers championed the "new digital TV paradigm: the seamless integration of traditional television with interactive computer technologies and networks" which promised to transform "TV into a two-way medium where the immediate consumer feedback [would] profoundly affect the industries at every level."[50]

Meanwhile, the suits were busy making e-commerce safe, friendly, and convenient for millions of new consumers. The 1998 Christmas season had been the best ever for online merchants, bringing total online sales for the year to $9 billion. New services, from grocery shopping to stock trading to wedding registries were no longer just novelties, but were becoming accepted parts of the consumer landscape. All this activity fueled a resurgent boom in Internet stocks and IPO's that surpassed the frenzy of the mid-'90s.

Broadband technologies—fatter "pipes" for delivering digital data to the home—had been talked about and anticipated for years. The speed and capacity of broadband networks would revolutionize the Internet, it was promised, and transform the medium. By 1999, cable modems, digital subscriber lines (DSL), wireless data broadcasting and other broadband systems of distribution were finally becoming available to a growing segment of the online audience. Broadband had always been something of a holy grail for content developers. It meant the end to glacial downloads—to Jane Fink's "stuck together pages." Better video. Great audio. Multimedia razzle-dazzle. A renaissance for online entertainment.

Reinventing Entertainment

"The Web is in fact not a mass medium, but a medium for the masses, who are already well along in the process of making it their own.

—Denise Caruso[51]

Online entertainment is coming back. There is reason for optimism this time. A survey by the market-research firm Cyber Dialogue reported the startling conclusion that 70 percent of the more than sixty million Internet users look for some form of entertainment content—shows, entertainment information, music, sports, and games—when they venture online. Unlike the mid-'90s, major Hollywood players are in the game. Two titans of the entertainment world, Michael Eisner and Barry Diller, embraced the Internet and made it a key element of their corporate strategies. Geraldine Laybourne, a former Disney Channel head and the creative executive who built up Nickelodeon during her days at Viacom, also embraced the Internet. Laybourne left Disney and formed a new company called Oxygen Media. "I want to get in on the ground floor," she said. "The Internet feels like the same environment I walked into in cable in 1979."[52] Laybourne subsequently made a deal with AOL to acquire three women-oriented sites from the company, Electra, Thrive, and Moms Online. Her deal with AOL in effect picked up Tartikoff's fallen torch. Shortly thereafter, Oxygen signed another deal with the television-production company Carsey-Werner and announced the intention to launch a "nonfiction cable network" for women by the year 2000.

1999 saw the proliferation of Internet portals such as Yahoo, Disney's Go Network, AOL.com, and others. From the vantage point of the average consumer, the portals all looked alike: search engine, e-mail, roughly the same content lineup. Eventually, portal managers will turn to entertainment as a means of differentiating themselves. Their direct marketing campaigns will increasingly incorporate contests, games, and story lines in order to get closer to consumers. (Seth Godin, vice-president of marketing at Yahoo, is a proponent of this approach, which he calls "permission marketing.")

The wide gulf between the technology, entertainment, and finance industries that existed in the mid-'90s was narrowing. A small but growing cadre of professionals was appearing on the scene who knew Hollywood, Silicon Valley, and Wall Street. The David Wertheimers, Steve Stanfords, Jeremy Verbas, and others of their ilk had the breadth of background needed to be bridge builders between those very different worlds.

Demographics were also building slowly in favor of the creators of interactive media. The Gen-Ners were getting older, and in a few years would start earning money of their own. Here was a generation that had experienced interactivity from the get-go and that was comfortable with technology. "The Internet is completely natural to children," Jake Winebaum once observed. "When a kid sees a door on a screen, she treats it like a door and opens it. When an adult sees the same door, he will hesitate and wonder what to do next." If there was any reason to take a long view of things, it was the children. There were even indications that the adult population might eventually come around.

Zakarin had once said of his *Spot* team that "no box can contain us." The box called "entertainment" was itself bursting at the seams. Millions of people were becoming content creators of their own, a phenomenon that was a throwback to the past. Brenda Laurel, a virtual-reality pioneer and one of the most original thinkers in the new-media space, wrote that in "earlier times entertainment was not the crisp little category we know it as today. In fact, it was not a category of activity at all, but rather an aspect of many kinds of experiences. Religious ceremonies and pilgrimages were occasions for revelry as well as high drama, all engaging the emotions and spirit."[53] Online entertainment, because of its active and social nature, harkened back to forms of amusement and diversion in the time before the advent of passive media like film, radio, and television. Before the twentieth century, people entertained themselves and each other. The Net seemed to restore that element of interpersonal interaction.

Skeptics still abound regarding the Net's appropriateness as a storytelling medium. "TV and film will continue to be the media that best deliver traditional three-act narrative storytelling," Charlie Fink told *Wired* magazine in 1997. "I don't think Steven Spielberg has anything to fear from the Internet."[54] Others, like Thomas Lakeman, believe that the desktop variety of the Internet is in fact an interactive storytelling medium in a way that television never could be. Lakeman referred to the desktop as the "ten-inch experience" as opposed to television, which was a "ten-foot" experience. The ten-inch distance between the user and the screen was approximately the same as the distance between an individual and an intimate friend. The desktop offered a level of intimacy and solitude necessary for interactivity that the television couldn't deliver—even with Web-browsing capability.

Laurel believed that the Internet could just possibly restore the storytelling traditions and narrative intelligence that had slowly withered away during the twentieth century. The Internet was "rediscovering that storytelling is about relationships," she said. "There's a kind of shamanic relationship between a teller and a hearer."

Whatever form entertainment finally takes—storytelling, online game shows, be-ins, immersive gaming environments, *whatever*—the creative energy needed to make it happen is all there. The only issue in doubt is the stick-to-it-ive-ness of the big players. Because the early pioneers had been cut loose or had dropped out, the industry is further behind the learning curve for original content than it had to be.

The dress rehearsal for entertainment's comeback will be in front of a live audience. At this writing, Time Warner is poised to launch a major online entertainment "hub" called Entertaindom, one of the most ambitious online entertainment plays to date. Former Disney Television president David Newman is one of the players behind the Digital Entertainment Network, an effort to bring television-style video programming to the Web. Santa Monica-based Intertainer promises to be a major broadband provider of entertainment content in the coming months and years. NBC, Disney and even AOL are factoring entertainment into their online strategies. Content is hot again.

Will the big players put up with low ratings, creative failures, and other missteps long enough for the medium to come into its own? Some feel that online entertainment is ultimately too big to fail, that Silicon Valley, Hollywood, and Wall Street will find some way to make it work. "The convergence of technology and entertainment has a quality of fate about it," Russ Collins said in 1996. "It's almost as if we have been led down this path, as if it were predetermined."

Legacy

You know what they say about pioneers. They're the ones with the arrows in their backs. What you want to be is a settler.

—Charlie Fink

The mecca of the online world had been Silicon Valley and its content satellite, San Francisco. The valley was where the geeks who created the enabling technology lived and worked, and where all the wealth associated with new technologies seemed to be generated.

The pioneers of online entertainment didn't live in the Bay area. Their base of operations was way south, in Hollywood, in spirit if not in fact. Their contribution to the evolution of the Internet was very much shaped by the town's spirit. "What a lot of us in Los Angeles did," Josh Greer noted, "was take a very geeky, technical, back-roots technology and for the first time give it a face. We gave it an interface that everyday people could use." As a group, the pioneers of online entertainment hacked the rules for the new medium and advanced the art of interactivity. Zakarin and the others were instrumental in getting the browser manufacturers to add new features. For many, *The Spot*, like *Myst* in the CD-ROM realm, gave people a reason to try out the new technology.

"What was different about us," Greer added, "is that we were literally like alchemists, slapping together these disparate tools just to see if the content would stick." These Hollywood wannabes were entrepreneurs who fused together the innovative spirit of the geeks with the love of media and storytelling. They stood outside Silicon Valley and Hollywood, straddling the two and belonging in neither world. They saw technology as a tool rather than an end in itself, which excluded them from geekdom. And they were not part of the very exclusive Hollywood club; they were too experimental, had too much of a penchant to improvise to fit into the media mainstream. The Internet was a medium that was still too geeky for the popular culture and too unstable to be commercialized. It was as if Picasso and Braque had been hired during their cubist period to paint greeting cards for the masses.

Today the Net is in the hands of the media, financial, and technology giants who will eventually make it work. But do these people really have the same understanding of the medium that the pioneers had? Where will the creative energy come from? The new ideas? Original concepts? Rebels are still needed. Until Ernie Kovacs came along, no one thought about using television for anything more than broadcasting stage plays.

"Ernie was fucking around with the camera and doing these new and innovative things," Greer said. He paused and smiled, perhaps reflecting on his peers' collective fate. "If you think about it long enough you realize . . . Where the hell is Ernie Kovacs?"

Coda

In December 1997 Matti Leshem settled in as editor in chief at Barry Diller's experimental station, WAMI-Channel 69 in Miami. WAMI was Diller's first go at creating a chain of local television stations focused on creating innovative local programming. "WAMI-Channel 69 is not a series of demographics, it's a sensibility, an irreverence and an attitude," Leshem told journalists. "It's Miami." The station featured such localized content as former *Miami Herald* reporter Edna Buchanan hosting a true-crime show, and a show adapted from the Latin magazine *Generation*.

Leshem went from managing twenty-five people at Cobalt Moon to almost three hundred at his new job. He was one of the first "Web people" to make the jump over to television, where he felt he was bringing a "Web sensibility" to television programming. One of Leshem's shows was *Traffic Jams*, which aired from 6:00 to 9:00 in the morning, providing viewers with continuous video feeds of Highway 95, the time, temperature, and "really cool music" in the background. *Traffic Jams* "looks like a Web page," Leshem said with a touch of pride. In the spring of 1999, Leshem's station launched a new online venture in collaboration with another Diller company, Ticketmaster Online/City Search. The Web sites would feature original content to complement the shows on WAMI. For Leshem, it was a chance to do some of the things he wanted to accomplish with Cobalt Moon.

David Wertheimer left Paramount Digital Entertainment in October 1998. He immediately began building a new entertainment-oriented Internet company, WireBreak Networks. He'd learned a lot from his entanglement with Microsoft. He felt the problem with MSN was that they needed a huge hit, something that was a clear breakthrough to justify their investment in content. Unfortunately, they invested "in singles, not home runs." Viewers weren't prepared to turn to the Net to watch singles.

He wanted WireBreak Networks to be different. Liberated from the bureaucracy and red tape of the studios, he wanted his company to grow and change with the industry. He believed wholeheartedly in the power of the creative home run. He was sure WireBreak Networks would deliver. "Someday people will wonder how anyone ever doubted it could be done," he said. As of this writing, WireBreak Networks is expected to launch in late summer 1999.

Josh Greer had been the COO of iXL's Los Angeles office for four months when he and his wife flew to Toronto for a family wedding and vacation (part of his deal) in the summer of 1998. When Josh got home, he learned that the company was two weeks away from hiring a new president for the Los Angeles office. He had the option of taking another role in the company or being bought out. Greer, who had been under the impression he was being prepared for the president's position, took the latter.

His first reaction was to call every headhunter in town to get another job. Then he started to think. Full broadband deployment was at least five years away. If he got a job at Web development companies like Razorfish or USWeb, it wasn't going to be about creating and innovating, it was going to be about selling and making money. Not that there was anything wrong with being profitable, but the thrill was gone.

Greer had enough money from his buyout that he didn't have to work for a few years if he didn't want to. He decided to take time off and have the luxury of taking some months to think about what he'd do next. He toyed with the idea of going back to college and getting a degree in biotechnology. Not the kind of person who was suited to sitting quietly on the beach, Greer flung himself into a series of flying lessons and earned a pilot's license. (He is now working on his commercial, aerobatic, and helicopter ratings.) He also began to play with animation programs. (Just for the fun of it, mind you, though he couldn't help but think the computer was exerting its inexorable pull on him again.) He'd spent four years in the whirlwind of the Internet business. While in it, everything seemed to move slowly. "Nothing ever happened fast enough." But once he stepped out of the business, "I realized that the whole time I'd been on a bullet train."

Thomas Lakeman became senior vice-president of Creative Services at iXL Los Angeles. He has no regrets about his days at Digital Planet.

The frustrations were many, he says, but "we had a lot of fun, and got to do things that never would have been allowed at Universal Pictures. Someday, when the broadband universe really happens, they may decide to take another look at our early efforts and appreciate them in the light of history. If so, that's reward enough for me."

Fattal-Collins merged with the advertising agency Houston Helm. Russ Collins is the vice-chairman of the combined agencies, which are due to get a name change. He is currently working on a book about human nature in the year 2999.

In the late Spring of '99, Jeremy Verba left E! Online to become Executive Vice President for Live Communties at Mpath Interactive, Inc.

For a while many wondered what happened to Bob Bejan. Some assumed that he had simply taken a long and indefinite vacation, enjoying the generous options he received when Laura Jennings enticed him into taking the job at MSN.

In fact, Bejan was still at Microsoft, though his duties had changed. He now headed up Microsoft's online advertising operation. He was part of the team involved in the $250 million acquisition of LineExchange, an online marketing outsourcer. Eternally enthusiastic and voluble, Bejan grew uncharacteristically laconic when talking about his new responsibilities.

Bejan's faith in online entertainment as a medium survived the collapse of Microsoft's entertainment initiatives. He believed that MSN had done some groundbreaking work, had nudged the medium several links down the evolutionary trail. He was particularly proud of having hashed out a methodology for producing online content. "Our production methodology and production methods," he said, "are now largely used in the content community today."

The cyclical nature of things played out for Bob Bejan. Legal hassles with Sony were finally resolved, and the interactive films he and his partner Bill Franzblau created through their company Interfilm began to "be ported to DVD." More than ever, he believed that interactivity would find its audience.

* * *

After the Entertainment Asylum reached one million hits per day, the numbers on the Web site began to drop considerably. The site had been scaled back and redesigned. Of the content sites that Greenhouse launched, Real Fans—the sports network—was eventually shut down. Electra—the women's network—became part of the women's channel that Oxygen Media acquired in the autumn of 1998. Love@AOL was folded back into AOL, where it continued to enjoy great popularity, being one of the company's most successful content ventures.

Ted Leonsis began reporting to Bob Pittman after the reorganization. He was put in charge of a content group with a dozen staffers, clinging to the name AOL Studios. After a period of being angry and depressed, he decided to stay at AOL despite the change in his fortunes. "This is the biggest stage," he told journalist Kara Swisher. "And, no matter how many times we change, I still have the best seat in the house."[55]

Danny Krifcher went to work for Leonsis as his aide-de-camp in the content group.

Charlie Fink left Leonsis's group to work for Barry Schuler as a vice-president and creative director. His responsibilities included managing AOL's various leisure-oriented content assets.

By the spring of 1999, Krifcher had been fully rehabilitated as a senior AOL executive. Rumor had it he was being groomed to head up AOL/UK. Leonsis also began to emerge publicly. AOL was making noise about getting back into the content business, and Leonsis was involved in those efforts. "We are this huge iceberg," Leonsis told a meeting of institutional investors at the BankBoston/Robertson Stephens conference in San Francisco in February. "What you're seeing is the media property above the waterline. What's going on below the waterline is even bigger."[56] In this case, Leonsis was talking about AOL's ability to use its databases to target specific audiences, but he might as well have been talking about his own dreams and ambitions. On May 12, 1999, it was announced that Ted Leonsis would spend more than $200 million to acquire a 100% stake in the National Hockey League's Washington Capitals, as well as large stakes in the Washington Mystics and Washington Wizards basketball teams. "I think I am probably the only team owner who reports to someone who reports to someone," Leonsis told the *Wall Street Journal*.

In early March, Charlie rejoined Leonsis and Krifcher, working on a cross-brand programming initiative targeting small businesses. Then on March 31, 1999, AOL laid off eight hundred and fifty employees. The layoff was a consequence of the company's headline-making acquisition of Netscape. One division president and six vice presidents were let go.

The division president was Monica Dodi. One of the departing veeps was Charlie Fink. The small business project he'd signed up to do had gone over to Netscape.

"Don't shed any tears for us tho," Charlie wrote in an AOL Instant Message the next day. "We were paid a king's ransom and would gladly submit to such mistreatment again."

Charlie had worked at AOL for more than three years. During the last twelve months AOL stock grew like a runaway computer virus. Charlie was almost instantly rich. He never had to work again if he chose. He wasn't sure what he was going to do next. "I've got a lot of ideas. And the resume to beat;)" he IM'ed. "I think I am going to take my time figuring it out."

Back in early 1996, shortly after joining AOL, Charlie began circulating a "quote of the week" to friends and AOL colleagues. The quotes were often pithy and offered bits of wisdom applicable to the challenges of working in a fast-changing industry (*The Art of War* was a favored source). What began as an office joke grew into a Web site (quoteoftheweek.com) and a listserver with more than eight thousand addresses. Charlie sent out a quote from *Winnie the Pooh* on his final day as an AOL employee:

"Never forget me, because if I thought you would, I'd never leave."

After the sacking, Scott, Troy, and Rich hatched plans to start a television-and-film-production company. Laurie went off on her own in pursuit of an acting career. Carl Genberg left the business entirely to take a position at Kroll Associates, the world's largest corporate investigations and intelligence firm. Carl heads up the firm's business-intelligence practice for the western United States Kroll has been described as a "private CIA" and conducts competitor intelligence and due diligence for investments, among other things.

Scott kept tabs on the new-media industry after he left Entertainment Asylum, but he was glad to be out of it. He was more than happy to let someone else be the pioneer for a while and looked forward to becoming better known for his work in film and television than for his earlier online innovations. He, Troy, and Rich launched Creative Light Entertainment in the spring of 1998, leasing a suite of offices in a bank building on Santa Monica Boulevard in Beverly Hills. Proving that old habits die hard, they quickly set up a Web site (www.crlight.com) and a message board. They described the company as "an innovative film and television entity with a unique slate of projects. . . .Creative Light is adept at establishing communities surrounding the projects they develop within both the business and consumer sectors."

Troy Bolotnick left the company shortly after the launch. After years of working without a break, he decided to take time off, to travel, and to manage his investments.

The company's first projects in development included *Rent-A-Family*, a comedy with a romantic edge that featured a bachelor who hires people to be members of his make-believe family in order to land his dream job. The team also wrote and taped several episodes of a sitcom called *Cindy: The Adventures of Cinderella's Daughter,* which they began to shop around to studios. Laurie Plaksin came back to star as Cindy in the series.

Scott and Rich also signed a development deal with Winddancer to write a television pilot for NBC called *Re-Wired*, a sitcom about a group of young people in a Web development house. The show would be reminiscent of their Lightspeed Media days. There was also talk about doing a movie based on Sid Caesar's life story.

By the spring of 1999, after a year of working exclusively in film and television production, Scott began to get the itch—to get back into the Web business. A former network top executive approached Scott about developing a "themed portal." Amazingly, there were hints that the rights to *The Spot* might become available to him. Scott and his partners began to develop a concept for a new webisodic, one built around a murder mystery. Through a variety of interactive platforms, the audience would become participants in the mystery. Eventually, the webisodic would be adapted as a motion picture. Scott hoped the project would be what *The Spot* should have become.

Back at the Asylum, Scott had brought a lot of film people on board and bragged that he could flip a switch and transform the operation into a film company. With this webisodic, he'd figured out a way to make it happen.

Acknowledgments

Digital Babylon is the story of a small group of Hollywood outsiders who tried to ignite an entertainment revolution by transforming the Internet into a major entertainment medium—and to gain some glory for themselves. We focused our narrative mainly on Scott Zakarin and others who took Hollywood as their inspiration. There were many notable and worthy individuals and companies developing other kinds of content for the Web during this period in San Francisco, New York, and other new media pockets that we did not have the space to write out: The Silicon Alley scene, online magazines like Salon and Feed, innovative Web shops in San Francisco like Organic and Construct and other entertainment plays like Warner Brothers Online in Burbank— all are stories worth telling.

This book is based primarily on interviews we conducted with the pioneers of online entertainment from July 1996 to March 1999. All the key figures in the book were interviewed at least once; most were interviewed several times, and a few on ten or more occasions. We exchanged e-mail with some subjects over a period of months, even years. Since many of our interviews were conducted during the course of the story we write about, we were able to record how people reacted to events as they unfolded.

This book is as much about the culture of the new-media business as it is a history of online entertainment. In order to better understand that hyper-driven culture we often interviewed far afield from online entertainment. We talked to entrepreneurs, computer programmers, writers, consultants, social scientists, artists, publicists, media executives and others. In total, more than eighty people provided in excess of three hundred hours of taped interviews. A small number of interviewees asked not to be identified.

We enjoyed near total access to the participants in this story until the spring of 1998, at which time America Online stopped making its employees available to us. By then the horse was already out of the barn; we'd completed the key interviews, and ex-employees remained available to us.

* * *

The creation of a book is much like the path of a winding river: It begins as a tiny brook and slowly swells into a powerful waterway as a myriad of streams feed into it along its course. Similarly, this book was fed by many people in the course of its research and writing.

First, we would like to gratefully acknowledge the people who cleared their calendars (often multiple times) to be interviewed. This book would have been an empty vessel without their recollections, stories, ideas and observations: Ellen Baker, Ph.D., Eli Barkat, David Baron, John Bates, Bob Bejan, Eric Benhamou, Suzanne Biegel, Troy Bolotnick, Corey Bridges, Layne Leslie Britton, Cat Chapman, Russell Collins, Mihaly Csikszentmihalyi, Jeff Dachis, Monica Dodi, David Dorman, Richard Doyon, Charlie Fink, Phil Flora, Tod Foley, Rebecca Fuson, Carl Genberg, Lisa Goldman, Adam Gould, Joshua Greer, Bill Gross, Richard Hoefer, Donna Hoffman, John Hughes, K. Charles Janac, Mark Jeffrey, Steven Johnson, Stacy Jolna, Jim Jonassen, Craig Kanarick, Steven Koltai, Joe Kraus, Scott Lahman, Thomas Lakeman, Brenda Laurel, Ted Leonsis, Matti Leshem, Richard Lindheim, J. Russell Maney, Michael Mascha, Lee Masters, Mark Meadows, Tim Miller, Halsey Minor, Miguel Monteverde, Jr., Michael Naimark, Rebecca Odes, Jeannine Parker, Meryl Perutz, Tony Perutz, Mark Pesce, Laurie Plaksin, Kim Polese, Fran Pomerantz, Josh Quittner, Louis Rossetto, Nick Rothenberg, Kyle Shannon, Rohit Shukla, Steve Stanford, Carl Steadman, Kevin Stein, Howard Stringer, Stephanie Syman, Richard Tackenberg, the late Brandon Tartikoff, Allison Thomas, Annie Van Bebber, Jeremy Verba, Watts Wacker, Karl E. Weick, David Wertheimer, Seema Williams, Jake Winebaum, Ann Winblad, Debra Zakarin, Scott Zakarin, and Harry Zink.

We also send thanks to the small number of interviewees who wished to remain anonymous and to the many others who spoke to us informally, sharing the benefits of their experiences in the maelstrom of the new media industry.

We have gone to great lengths to fact check the manuscript. Several of the people we write about were shown portions of the manuscript in order to identify and correct errors of fact. It goes without saying that the interpretations of those facts are our own—as are any residual errors that may still lurk in the text.

* * *

This book would not have been written if our agent, Daniel Mandel of the Sanford J. Greenburger Agency, hadn't befriended us and encouraged us to make a go at it. He stuck with us during an often stormy journey, represented us well, put up with our neurotic ravings while patiently explained the intricacies of the New York publishing world.

We were lucky to be in the hands of two wonderful editors at Arcade Publishing. As our first editor, Sean McDonald was instrumental in setting the course for the book and suggesting its main structure. His enthusiasm and support were much appreciated at a point in the project when we badly needed it. Coates Bateman carried the project through to completion, giving us a level of support, critical thinking, and attention that far exceeded our hopes and expectations. We fed off his energy and élan, enjoyed his e-mails, and benefited greatly from his blue pencil.

The manuscript greatly profited from Sarah Richards Doerries's copyediting. (Coates told us that copy editors "are better than you or I." He is right.) Thanks also to Janet Coleman who, while working at another publishing house, thought we had the germ for a good Internet book.

A million thanks to Allison Thomas for reading an earlier draft of the book and contributing her insights into the new-media entertainment industry, a business few know as well as she.

Another million thanks to producer Alan Sacks, who also read an early draft of the book. His unflagging support, intimate knowledge of the television and film industries, and insight into cultural trends inspired and informed us.

Robert Tercek of the Columbia Tristar Television Group treated us to a number of illuminating lunchtime conversations about the future of digital media.

John Geirland: Writing this book would have been both impossible and a lot less fun without the support and prodding of my wife Juliana Carnessale. Her knowledge of the economics of the entertainment business gave us important insights into the new-media industry. More important, her love sustained and inspired me. This book is for our three children—our oldest, Nicholas, and our twins Michael and Antonia, who were born midway through its writing.

Eva Sonesh-Kedar: To my husband, partner and friend Ofir Kedar, whose own contribution the Silicon Valley story brought experience to my words and depth to my voice; and to my sons Ori and Tom who light my days with brightness and joy.

John Geirland
Studio City, California
June 1999

Eva Sonesh-Kedar
Los Altos Hills, California
June 1999

Bibliography

Periodicals and online sources that were helpful in rounding out the story were the *New York Times, Wall Street Journal, Los Angeles Times, Wired, Wired News, CNET, Variety, the Hollywood Reporter, Salon* and others—many of which are cited in the text.

Books used in the writing of this narrative are cited in the text. We especially liked the following books and found them helpful in providing context or ideas:

Auletta, Ken. *Three Blind Mice: How the TV Networks Lost Their Way*. New York: Vintage Books, 1992.

Brockman, John. *Digerati: Encounters with the Cyber Elite*. San Francisco: Hardwired, 1996.

Csikszentmihalyi, Mihaly. *The Evolving Self: A Psychology for the Third Millennium*. New York: Harper Collins, 1993.

———. *Flow: The Psychology of Optimal Experience*. New York: Harper & Row, 1990.

Eyman, Scott. *The Speed of Sound: Hollywood and the Talkie Revolution, 1926–1930*. New York: Simon & Schuster, 1997.

Hall, Edward T. *The Silent Language*. New York: Doubleday, 1959.

Johnson, Steven. *Interface Culture: How New Technology Transforms the Way We Create and Communicate*. San Francisco: HarperEdge, 1997.

Kidder, Tracy. *Soul of a New Machine*. New York: Avon Books, reprint, 1995.

McCloud, Scott. *Understanding Comics*. New York: Harper Perennial (Paperback), 1994.

Reid, Robert H. *Architects of the Web: 1,000 Days that Built the Future of Business*. New York: John Wiley & Co., 1997.

Rushkoff, Douglas. *Playing the Future: How Kids' Culture Can Teach Us to Thrive in an Age of Chaos*. New York: HarperCollins, 1996.

Schrage, Michael. *No More Teams: Mastering the Dynamics of Creative Collaboration*. New York: Currency Doubleday, 1995.

Swisher, Kara. *AOL.com: How Steve Case Beat Bill Gates, Nailed the Netheads, and Made Millions in the War for the Web*. New York: Times Business, 1998.

Tartikoff, Brandon, & Charles Leerhsen. *The Last Great Ride*. New York: Random House, 1992.

Weick, Karl. *The Social Psychology of Organizing*. Reading, Mass: Addison-Wesley Publishing, 1979.

Notes

[1] John Brockman, *Digerati: Encounters with the Cyber Elite, Hardwired*, San Francisco, 1996, p. 11

[2] Douglas Rushkoff, *Playing The Future: How Kids' Culture Can Teach Us to Thrive in an Age of Chaos*, (New York: Harper Collins, 1996), p. 225

[3] Dan Gray, "Hit the Spot!" *WWWiz Magazine* 2, 1995 (wwwiz.com)

[4] Michael Lynch, "The Spot Hits Silicon Reef," *New Media*, March 11, 1996 (www.newmedia.com)

[5] Russ Mitchell, "Fill My Bandwidth, Baby," *Wired*, July 1996.

[6] John McCoy (ed.), *Mastering Web Design* (Berkeley, CA: Sybex, 1996)

[7] Robert Reid, *Architects of the Web: 1,000 Days That Built the Future of Business*, (New York: John Wiley & Sons, 1997.)

[8] Patrick E. Cole, *Los Angeles Times Magazine*, May 12, 1996

[9] "Q&A: *Madeleine's Mind* and Beyond....", n.a., *Wideguide*, November 1996 (www.wideguide.com)

[10] Edstrom and Eller, *Barbarians Led by Bell Gates: Microsoft from the Inside*, (New York: Henry Holt, 1998), p. 201

[11] Don Clark, "Microsoft New Creative Czar Goes From Turtles to Teddies," *Wall Street Journal*, March 20, 1997.

[12] Ibid.

[13] Brandon Tartikoff, "The Second Golden Era: How and Why I Joined Up with Greenhouse," August 25, 1997. (Posted to the Entertainment Asylum's prelaunch Web site.)

[14] Esther Dyson first referred to Leonsis as the cyber equivalent of a bartender.

[15] Kara Swisher, *Aol.com: How Steve Case Beat Bill Gates, Nailed the Netheads, and Made Millions in the War for the Web*, (New York: Times Business, 1998), p. 107.

[16] Brandon Tartikoff and Charles Leershen, *The Last Great Ride*, (New York: Random House, Inc., 1992), p. 209.

[17] The Palace was (and is) a company that produces server software that allows companies and communities to create "palaces," i.e., sites where people can engage each other in 2-D chat. Visitors who have downloaded Palace-user software are able to visit 2-D palace environments around the world (there are thousands), and to customize their own personal avatars.

[18] Jared Sandberg, "On-Line: Inside AOL's Bid to Develop Its Own Sites," *Wall Street Journal*, November 21, 1997.

[19] John Geirland, "Making AOL a Media Company," *Wired*, November 1997.

[20] Ibid.

[21] "Honey, What's on Microsoft?" *Business Week*, October 21, 1996.

[22] Nick Winfield, "MS Revamps Network for Launch," CNET, September 30, 1996 (www.news.com)

[23] Richard Tedesco, "Cobalt Moon Profile Rising on MSN: Second City Brings Attitude to Internet," *Broadcasting & Cable's Telemedia Week*, December 2, 1996.

[24] Gillian Newson, "Cobalt Moon Puts TV on the Web," *New Media*, February 10, 1997.

[25] Geirland, "Making AOL a Media Company."

[26] Karen Kaplan, "Ex Marks 'The Spot' for Upset Devotees," *Los Angeles Times*, December 9, 1996.

[27] Janelle Brown, "Financial Trauma Spurs Drama of AMCY Plea," *Wired News*, January 7, 1997.

[28] Geirland, "Making AOL a Media Company."

[29] The source for much of the backstory on *MrShowBiz* came from the January 13, 1997 broadcast of "Hollywood Wrap," a radio program hosted by Nikki Finke on KCRW in Santa Monica, California. Finke interviewed Susan Mulcahy as part of a show about Hollywood on the Internet.

[30] "America Online's Triumvirate in Cyberspace," *New York Times*, February 16, 1998.

[31] "Microsoft to Slash Internet Workers, Web Sites," *Los Angeles Times*, February 27, 1997.

[32] Leslie Helm, "Not Ready When You Are, B. G. Microsoft and Bill Gates Discover That on the Web Show Business is Slow Business," *Los Angeles Times*, April 7, 1997.

[33] Ibid.

[34] Bruce Haring, "Launching Entertainment Vehicles in Cyberspace," *USA Today*, March 10, 1997

[35] Geirland, "Making AOL a Media Company."

[36] Amy Harmon, "At Microsoft, the Hip Gives Way to the Useful," *New York Times*, October 13, 1997.

[37] Geirland, "Dana Beth Ardi," *Business 2.0*, September 1998.

[38] Haring, "AOL Tries Hand at Entertainment News," *USA Today*, October 27, 1997.

[39] Alex Gove, "Stone Cold Diller," *Red Herring Magazine*, February 1997.

[40] Haring, "AOL Tries Hand at Entertainment News."

[41] Thomas Lakeman's recollection differs from Josh's. According to Lakeman, only two full-time employees were laid off out of a staff of thirty-five. Both employees received severance pay, and only one of the two had been employed at Digital Planet for more than a year. One of the two ex-staffers was rehired when things picked up.

[42] "MSN moves from Content to Access," *Wired News*, February 26, 1998.

[43] Harmon, "At Microsoft, the Hip Gives Way to the Useful." Higgins took leave of absence from Microsoft in the fall of 1998. As of this writing, the company is searching for a new executive to head the interactive group.

[44] Ibid.

[45] Ibid.

[46] Swisher, *AOL.com*, 316.

[47] "Jobs to Broadcasters: I Got Your Technology," *Wired News*, April 6, 1998.

[48] Caruso, panel discussion at Networked Entertainment World, February 13, 1998, Beverly Hills, California.

[49] Geirland, "The New Mouseketeers," *Wired*, June 1998.

[50] PricewaterhouseCooper position paper, "Digital Television '99: Navigating the Transition in the U.S., Steven M. Abraham et al., 1998.

[51] Denise Caruso, "Digital Commerce: Rethinking the Portal Concept," *New York Times*, March 15, 1999.

[52] Sallie Hofmeister, "Disney's Cable TV Chief Will Leave to Form New Venture," *Los Angeles Times*, May 29, 1998.

[53] Brenda Laurel, "The L Is for Location," paper presented at Digital World, Beverly Hills, 1992.

[54] Geirland, "Making AOL a Media Company."

[55] Swisher, AOL.com.

[56] Craig Bicknell, "AOL: We Want Your Credit Card," *Wired News*, February 22, 1999. (www.wired.com)